ACCOUNTABILITY AND RESPONSIVENESS
AT THE MUNICIPAL LEVEL

1 *Local Self-Government
   and the Right to the City*
   Warren Magnusson

2 *City-Regions in Prospect?
   Exploring Points between
   Place and Practice*
   Edited by Kevin Edson Jones,
   Alex Lord, and Rob Shields

3 *On Their Own
   Women and the Right
   to the City in South Africa*
   Allison Goebel

4 *The Boundary Bargain
   Growth, Development, and the
   Future of City–County Separation*
   Zachary Spicer

5 *Welcome to Greater Edendale
   Histories of Environment, Health,
   and Gender in an African City*
   Marc Epprecht

6 *Still Renovating
   A History of Canadian Social
   Housing Policy*
   Greg Suttor

7 *Order and Disorder
   Urban Governance and the Making
   of Middle Eastern Cities*
   Edited by Luna Khirfan

8 *Toward Equity and Inclusion
   in Canadian Cities Lessons from
   Critical Praxis-Oriented Research*
   Edited by Fran Klodawsky, Janet
   Siltanen, and Caroline Andrew

9 *Accountability and Responsiveness
   at the Municipal Level
   Views from Canada*
   Edited by Sandra Breux and
   Jérôme Couture

Accountability and Responsiveness at the Municipal Level

Views from Canada

Edited by

SANDRA BREUX and JÉRÔME COUTURE

McGill-Queen's University Press
Montreal & Kingston • London • Chicago

© McGill-Queen's University Press 2018

ISBN 978-0-7735-5328-6 (cloth)
ISBN 978-0-7735-5329-3 (paper)
ISBN 978-0-7735-5374-3 (ePDF)
ISBN 978-0-7735-5375-0 (ePUB)

Legal deposit second quarter 2018
Bibliothèque nationale du Québec

Printed in Canada on acid-free paper that is 100% ancient forest free
(100% post-consumer recycled), processed chlorine free

Funded by the Government of Canada | Financé par le gouvernement du Canada | Canada | Canada Council for the Arts | Conseil des arts du Canada

We acknowledge the support of the Canada Council for the Arts, which
last year invested $153 million to bring the arts to Canadians throughout
the country.

Nous remercions le Conseil des arts du Canada de son soutien. L'an dernier,
le Conseil a investi 153 millions de dollars pour mettre de l'art dans la vie
des Canadiennes et des Canadiens de tout le pays.

Library and Archives Canada Cataloguing in Publication

Accountability and responsiveness at the municipal level:
views from Canada / edited by Sandra Breux and Jérôme Couture.

(McGill-Queen's studies in urban governance; 9)
Includes bibliographical references and index.
Issued in print and electronic formats.
ISBN 978-0-7735-5328-6 (hardcover). – ISBN 978-0-7735-5329-3 (softcover). –
ISBN 978-0-7735-5374-3 (ePDF). – ISBN 978-0-7735-5375-0 (ePUB)

1. Municipal government – Canada. 2. Local elections – Canada. I. Breux,
Sandra, editor II. Couture, Jérôme, 1980–, editor III. Series: McGill-Queen's
studies in urban governance; 9

JS1710.A23 2018   320.80971   C2018-901203-X
                                            C2018-901204-8

This book was typeset by Marquis Interscript in 10.5/13 Sabon.

Contents

Tables and Figures   vii

Acknowledgments   xi

Introduction   3
Sandra Breux and Jérôme Couture

PART ONE DISCUSSING POLITICAL PARTIES

1 Sins of the Brother: Partisanship and Accountability in Toronto, 2014   23
Laura B. Stephenson, R. Michael McGregor, and Aaron A. Moore

2 Accountability without Parties? Political Business Cycle and the Re-election of Incumbents   49
Jérôme Couture and Sandra Breux

3 Political Accountability and Responsiveness: What Is the Role of Municipal Political Parties?   76
Jérôme Couture, Sandra Breux, and Laurence Bherer

PART TWO DISCUSSING THE CAREER AND FUNCTION OF ELECTED OFFICIALS

4 Responsiveness, Accountability, and the Long-Term Development of Local Political Careers in Calgary and Edmonton   107
Jack Lucas and Anthony Sayers

5 What Happened to Incumbent Councillors in Greater Sudbury and
London, Ontario, in 2014? The Role of the Ontario Ombudsman's
Reports on Alleged Secret Meetings   132
Andrew Sancton

6 Accountability and Local Politics: Contextual Barriers and
Cognitive Variety   153
Anne Mévellec

PART THREE ISSUES REGARDING SERVICES AND GOVERNANCE
IN MULTILEVEL GOVERNMENTS

7 Accountability and Local Collaborative Governance   177
Joseph Lyons and Zachary Spicer

8 The Responsiveness Issue and the Blurry Lines of Accountability
in Regional Transportation Planning, Governance, and Finance:
The Case of Metrolinx   200
Fanny R. Tremblay-Racicot

9 Mirror Image: The Fight against Homelessness in Calgary
and Montreal   223
Alison Smith

CONCLUSIONS

Accountability and Responsiveness at the Municipal Level:
Limitations and Opportunities   249
Ruth Dassonneville

Do Responsiveness and Accountability Matter
at the Municipal Level?   266
Jérôme Couture and Sandra Breux

Contributors   281

Index   285

Tables and Figures

TABLES

I.1   2004–2014 voter turnout in the last three mayoral
elections   4

I.2   Percentage of voter turnout in provincial elections in
Quebec, Ontario, and British Columbia between 2005
and 2014   4

I.3   Percentage of voter turnout in federal elections in
Quebec, Ontario, and British Columbia between 2006
and 2015   4

1.1   Perceived candidate party ties   33

1.2   The determinants of satisfaction with mayoral
performance   35

1.3   Satisfaction with Rob Ford and voting for Doug Ford   38

2.1   Descriptive analysis   61

2.2   Logistic regression with RCVE   63

2.3   Operationalization and data source   67

2.4   Robustness test logistic regression with RCVE   68

2.5   Pearson correlation matrix   69

3.1   Elements of the British Columbia (2014) and Quebec (2013)
party systems   87

3.2   Competition systems in the ten biggest cities in British
Columbia and Quebec   89

3.3   Political competition system typology   91

3.4   Municipal non-partisan system typology   93

3.5   Municipal political party typology   96

3.6   Accountability and responsiveness according to municipal
       political party type   97
3.7   Parties in each city   97
4.1   Four responsiveness/accountability regimes   109
4.2   Municipal politicians with provincial/federal careers   118
4.3   Direction of political careers   118
4.4   Impact of shared gender, city, and time period on sequence
       distance   123
4.5   Summary of career types in Calgary and Edmonton   124
5.1   Election results for 2014 incumbent councillors in Greater
       Sudbury, 2010 and 2014 elections   142
5.2   Election results for 2014 incumbent candidates for London
       council condemned by ombudsman in 2013, elections of
       2010 and 2014   147
5.3   Election results for 2014 incumbent candidates for London
       council not condemned by ombudsman in 2013, elections
       of 2010 and 2014   147
7.1   London, Ontario, special-purpose bodies   187
7.2   London, Ontario, inter-local agreements   190
7.3   Website URLs of London's special-purpose bodies   193
8.1   Impact of institutional design on accountability, democracy,
       and effectiveness   219

FIGURES

1.1   Satisfaction by partisan compatibility   37
1.2   Probability of voting for Doug Ford by satisfaction
       and perceived similarities between the Ford brothers   40
2.1   The citizen-candidate model   54
2.2   The new citizen-candidate model and a change
       in the tax rate   56
2.3   Predictive margins of parties by change in the tax rate   64
3.1   Hierarchy of responsiveness and accountability according
       to the partisan competition system   90
3.2   Hierarchy of clarity of responsibility according to the
       political competition system   92
3.3   Hierarchy of clarity of responsibility according to
       non-partisan systems   95
4.1   Average career lengths in Calgary and Edmonton   112
4.2   Calgary and Edmonton careers by length and first year   113

4.3 Incumbent candidate success in Calgary and
Edmonton 114

4.4 Year-by-year stability rates, Calgary and Edmonton 115

4.5 Term-by-term stability rates, Calgary and Edmonton 116

4.6 Proportion of councillors elected provincially, by
decade 119

4.7 Career types in Calgary and Edmonton, 1885–2015 125

10.1 Public opinion and policy at different levels of
government 253

Acknowledgments

This publication was made possible through the financial support of the Fonds de recherche Société et Culture and the support of the réseau Villes Régions Monde (VRM). We would also like to thank Cathleen Poehler for revising and editing the first draft of the book.

ACCOUNTABILITY AND RESPONSIVENESS
AT THE MUNICIPAL LEVEL

Introduction

Sandra Breux and Jérôme Couture

WHY LOOK AT ACCOUNTABILITY AND RESPONSIVENESS AT THE CANADIAN MUNICIPAL LEVEL?

In Canada, the quality of municipal democracy is called into question by three facts, or phenomena. First, voter turnout in Canada is generally lower at the municipal level than it is at the other levels of government. In fact, in the hundred largest cities of Canada, the average voter turnout over the last three elections[1] was 36.42 per cent (see table I.1).

Table I.1 shows that voter turnout at municipal elections is often 13 to 30 per cent lower than it is at other levels of government. This applies to both provincial elections (see table I.2) and federal elections (see table I.3) for all four provinces where the hundred largest cities are concentrated.

Second, the re-election rate of incumbent candidates is relatively high (Breux, Couture, and Koop 2017). Third, in recent years corruption and other scandals have deeply tarnished the image of representative democracy at the municipal level (Taylor 2011; Breux and Bherer 2011). Together, these findings could lead us to believe that democracy at the municipal level suffers from a deficit of representation, which begs for a closer analysis of the nature of representation at this level of government.

In theory, two concepts serve to uphold the principle of democratic representation: 1) accountability and 2) the responsiveness of elected officials to the preferences of citizens (Gerstlé 2003). These concepts shape and inform public decision-making processes as well as the quality of democracy. However, what do accountability and

Table I.1

2004–14 voter turnout in the last three mayoral elections

	% of voter turnout
Election 1[1]	35.80
Election 2	35.97
Election 3	37.49
Average voter turnout	36.42

[1] When municipal elections are not held at the same time in different provinces, Election 1 represents the earliest election year between 2004 and 2014 and Election 3 represents the most recent election year between 2004 and 2014. For additional information, see Breux, Couture, and Koop 2017.

Source: Breux, Couture, and Koop 2017.

Table I.2

Percentage of voter turnout in provincial elections in Quebec, Ontario, and British Columbia between 2005 and 2014

Results of provincial elections in Quebec		*Results of provincial elections in Ontario*		*Results of provincial elections in British Columbia*		*Results of provincial elections in Alberta*	
2007	71.23	2007	52.1	2005	58.19	2008	40.59
2008	57.43	2011	48.2	2009	50.99	2012	54.37
2012	74.60	2014	51.3	2013	55.32	2015	57.02

Sources: Elections Ontario, "Official Election Results," http://www.elections.on.ca/en/resource-centre/elections-results/official-past-elections-results.html; Elections BC, "Voter Turnout in British Columbia," http://elections.bc.ca/docs/stats/voter-turnout-1983-2017.pdf; Directeur général des élections du Québec, "Élections générales au Québec, 1867–2014," http://www.electionsquebec.qc.ca/documents/pdf/tableau_synthese_1867_2014.pdf; "Overall Summary of Ballots Cast and Voter Turnout 1975–2015," http://www.elections.ab.ca/news-reports/reports/statistics/overall-summary-of-ballots-cast-and-voter-turnout.

Table I.3

Percentage of voter turnout in federal elections in Quebec, Ontario, and British Columbia between 2006 and 2015

Results of federal elections in Quebec		*Results of federal elections in Ontario*	*Results of federal elections in British Columbia*	*Results of federal elections in Alberta*	*Canada overall*
2006	63.9	66.6	63.7	61.9	64.7
2008	61.7	58.6	60.1	52.4	58.8
2011	62.9	61.5	60.4	55.8	61.1
2015	67.3	67.8	70.0	68.2	68.3

Source: Elections Canada, "Quarante-deuxième élection générale 2015," http://www.elections.ca/res/rep/off/ovr2015app/41/table4F.html.

responsiveness really mean? According to Fearon, "person A is accountable to another, B, if two conditions are met. First, there is an understanding that A is obliged to act in some way on behalf of B. Second, B is empowered by some formal institutional or perhaps informal rules to sanction or reward A for her activities or performance in this capacity" (Fearon 1999, 55). The term "responsiveness," for its part, denotes that the "government 'responds' to changes in citizens' views by moving policy in the direction of those views" (Tausanovitch and Warshaw 2014, 606). It is in this way, democratic theory suggests, that elected representatives are tasked and incentivized to implement the preferred policies of voters. The role of voters in this interplay is to reward or punish elected representatives based on how government performance corresponds with citizens' expectations. In that context, elections present an ideal, if not the only, opportunity for such an evaluation. By analyzing municipal democracy in Canada on the basis of these two concepts, then, we seek to capture the quality of the democratic processes taking place in this country.

However, while the definitions of these two terms are relatively clear and enjoy broad consensus among political scientists, they have several limitations. To begin, the idea of accountability within representative democracies is based on the so-called principal–agent theory, which "tends to assume a bilateral relationship between P (the people) and A (their agents), where A is to serve P's interest" (Philip 2009, 30). The first limitation is that these agents can serve interests other than those of P, especially when there is an imbalance in the amount of information held by A regarding the responsibilities of P. Additionally, strictly speaking it is only the elected officials who are held accountable, whereas a substantial amount of the work and decision-making is carried out by public service workers, who are not directly elected by the electorate. The second major limitation is that with a principal–agent approach to accountability, the latter is defined as requiring contingent conditions as necessary conditions. For example, "Fearon assumes that whether or not A is accountable is a function of P's capacity to reward or sanction, but sanctioning is not essential to accountability per se" (Philip 2009, 30).

Moreover, because elections are held in regular intervals of, usually, several years, it is difficult to make generalizations about the numerous and diverse evaluations that the electorate take into consideration when casting a ballot (Ackerman 2004). According to Ackerman, "even if the accountability signals were somehow clearly discernible, the fact that most politicians are elected by only a small portion of the population often forces politicians to favour patronage, 'pork' or corruption over initiatives that would bring long-term benefit to the public as a whole" (2004, 449).

The concept of responsiveness can be analyzed along the same lines. First, the importance of responsiveness is fundamentally based on the importance of a given issue. Additionally, the issue may be of a large enough scale for there to be a preference adjustment in the public regarding the representatives. If the issue is important enough, the responsiveness will lead to a certain form of manipulation of the public attention and its resulting interpretation (Gerstlé 2003). In other words, "information is the principal means of controlling the public attention, and it is one that is also a concurrent path to the formation of a political agenda" (Gerstlé 2003, 884). Other researchers have likewise observed that policy congruence is only one part of the definition: "It is also important that political parties listen to their voters with regard to the policy issues they emphasize in democratic societies" (Spoon and Klüver 2014, 48). This means that responsiveness also induces the idea of choice, responding to the needs of citizens, among the range of issues available, and the idea of a prioritization developed by the elected officials or political parties, even if, as Spoon and Klüver emphasize, "we recognize that there may be a reciprocal relationship between voters and parties, that is that parties are not only responding to voters' preferences, but that voters might also respond to parties' issue emphasis" (2014, 54).

Finally, these two concepts also have in common that their applicability is strongly dependent on the context. Choquette and Godbout, for example, consider that "in addition to a marked deficit in the political knowledge of the electors, the institutional complexity of federations seems to impair the responsibility of elected officials. In other words, it makes it more likely that incumbents will be punished (by not being re-elected) for reasons that they are not politically responsible for or that they will not be punished (re-elected) despite political failings for which they are indeed responsible" (2015). The adaptability of the concept of accountability therefore depends on the context (Veselý 2013, 326), as does responsiveness. Indeed, Spoon and Klüver demonstrate that "the issue responsiveness of political parties is not constant across all elections, but that it varies with the electoral context" (2014, 57). These authors have shown that in Europe political parties tend to listen to voters more at national-level elections than at so-called second-order elections (Spoon and Klüver 2014).

Thus, while accountability/responsiveness is central to the notion of representation in democratic systems, and while there is consensus regarding their definitions, the context, and specifically the institutional context, seems to have a non-negligible impact on how these two concepts are likely to manifest. It is therefore relevant to look at how accountability/responsiveness is seen at the municipal level, particularly in view of the above-mentioned electoral data.

A MATTER OF CONTEXT?
WHAT DO WE KNOW ABOUT ACCOUNTABILITY
AND RESPONSIVENESS AT THE MUNICIPAL LEVEL?

Considerable research has already been invested in examining political accountability and responsiveness. Yet these studies focus mainly on the national level, and of the few studies that examine the municipal level, most document primarily the US context. It is therefore necessary, first, to adopt a more differentiated understanding of the concepts of accountability and responsiveness – especially since these two concepts seem to translate differently at the municipal and national levels – and, second, to address the Canadian context.

More specifically, while national-level studies have shown a distinct relationship between accountability and responsiveness, including how the principle of democratic representation is carried out (Pétry 1999; Stimson, MacKuen, and Erickson 1995; Erickson, Wright, and McIver 1993; Lax and Philips 2012), the opposite was observed for the municipal level. The local context presents many economic, political, and legislative constraints to the responsiveness of elected officials. In addition, the local level has a limited flow of political information (Elmendorf and Schleicher 2012), making it difficult to focus on or highlight important issues and rendering the relevance of political parties at this level of government somewhat questionable (Peterson 1981). These constraints are also a roadblock to finding a balance between citizens' preferences and government policy (Gerber and Hopkins 2011; Peterson 1981; Leigh 2008; Nivola 2002; Self 2003). Many feel that such a balance, if and when attained, results more from fiscal federalism (Tiebout 1956) and path dependency (Collin and Hamel 1993). However, these conclusions are merely speculative, since they are based solely on theory (Trounstine 2010). Tausanovitch and Warshaw (2014), for example, demonstrated that the responsiveness of local-level elected officials is undermined because municipal voters are considered especially sensitive to budgetary investments and to changes made during the mandate of the elected official.

A similar debate exists on the topic of accountability at the municipal level. Elmendorf and Schleicher (2012), for example, observe that voters take little account of the performance of local officials and attribute this to the fact that municipal politics is often characterized by a lack of readily available information. In this "low-information context," voters then tend to support those candidates whom they know best, i.e., the incumbents (Oliver and Ha 2007). This, in turn, accounts for the low turnover rate of representatives (Trounstine 2008), questioning both the imputability of elected officials and the notion that voters effectively reward (or punish) these representatives. However, analyses of citizens' evaluations of municipal performance show that incumbents who perform well do not necessarily have an advantage (Boyne et al. 2009). That being said, the probability that a politician will be re-elected is greatly reduced if her or his performance is considered weak and practically drops to zero when it is judged to be poor. Researchers have also identified a link between public spending, the electoral cycle, and the re-election of local governments. Specifically, increased spending ahead of elections favours the re-election of the sitting municipal government (Sakurai and Menezes-Filho 2008; Drazen and Eslava 2010; Aidt, Veiga, and Veiga 2011; Sedmihradska, Kubik, and Haas 2011; Balaguer-Coll et al. 2014).

These examples show that "there remain outstanding questions about the quality of democratic representation in local government" (Levine and Kogan 2016, 4; Trounstine 2010). While this finding applies to the United States, similar observations could well be made of the Canadian municipal context. There, aside from the above-mentioned electoral data, three additional characteristics warrant a broadening of the concept of accountability and responsiveness: the virtual absence of political parties; the high rate of re-election of incumbents; and multilevel governance and its consequences.

While these characteristics (or at least the latter two) are not specific to the Canadian municipal scene and could just as well take place in the United States, analyzing accountability/responsiveness from these three angles can serve to advance research on this topic while improving our knowledge of the Canadian municipal level. Thus, while research on the North American municipal scene, in general, has experienced a boom in recent years, various aspects concerning the Canadian context remain understudied.

MUNICIPAL-LEVEL GOVERNMENT IN CANADA

At the North American level, several observers have suggested that one of the main differences between national-level and municipal-level governments is the fact that "unlike national offices, the politics of local governments are rarely fought along ideological lines" (Oliver, Ha, and Callen 2012, 7). In fact, one of the distinguishing features of municipal government in Canada is the near absence of political parties – this is referred to only as "near" absence, since certain parties and political groups do indeed exist in certain provinces, such as British Columbia and Quebec. Overall, this near absence of political parties is what sets Canada apart from its American neighbour. However, even in those provinces where a party system is present, the ideologies behind political platforms are often similar, underdeveloped, or overall difficult to pinpoint. Additionally, these systems see themselves as being "non-partisan" compared to the political entities operating at higher levels of government. Add to this the fact that, in Quebec for example, "it is not uncommon to see a candidate elected as part of one political party change to another during the course of his or her mandate or as the elections approach" (Bherer and Breux 2012, 173). Thus, in light of such a pronounced political neutrality, the agenda of municipal politics is often hard to grasp, even more so because it does not necessarily represent a lack of political ideology (Bherer and Breux 2012). It is also worth noting that the average lifespan of a political party is six years (DGEQ 2013).

In addition to this, there are also institutional factors to consider. The municipal system is quasi-presidential in nature (Quesnel 1986), since the mayor is elected by direct universal suffrage. Mayoral candidates, whether they claim to be part of a certain political party or not, focus on issues that tend to concern the municipality overall. This can, however, be different for municipal council candidates who, depending on the context, are elected either at the district level or the city level. The issues focused on by those at the district level may not necessarily be the same (Mévellec and Tremblay 2016; Koop and Kraemer 2016) and, in fact, can be significantly contrary to the issues put forth by political parties at the city level.

This context is specific to local governments in Canada, since elections elsewhere can generally be studied using a party-based political model inspired by the work of Downs (1957). In the party-based system, political parties compete for power and develop a political platform in accordance with the distribution of voter preferences. When it is time for elections, voters must then choose between the different options available to them. However, this means of understanding political representation creates a strange paradox. The existence of political parties encourages responsiveness, and the party that is able to give voters what they want is generally the one that ends up winning. This also reinforces the mechanisms of accountability, since voters are able to judge the government based on the implementation of electoral promises (Klingemann, Hobberfert, and Budge 1994). By contrast, the Michigan School has shown that individuals' electoral behaviour is significantly driven by their affiliation with a political party (Campbell et al. 1960), meaning that voters are likely to vote for their preferred party at all costs. The presence of any such loyal partisanship would then invalidate the notion that accountability/ responsiveness are effective constructs. But what happens when there are no parties or when the parties are non-partisan or too short-lived to boast any real membership? How can such formations, when they do exist, be responsive in any way? And how exactly do voters make their choice in the absence of political parties?

By examining these questions, and looking at how accountability works within this context, we hope to better understand the role that political parties and partisan affiliation play. Ideally, this will also allow us to overcome the traditional dichotomy found in studies that examine how political parties affect voter turnout (Alford and Lee 1968) by using the theme of responsiveness in order to better understand the role that political party affiliations play at a "non-partisan" level of government.

The second focus of this book concerns the high turnover rate of incumbents, which is often said to account for the "political monopoly" observed at this level of government (Bherer 2011; Trounstine 2008). Some researchers see the municipal government as strictly reactive, with voters considered to be acting as a function of the political parties that best serve their interests. Other researchers, by contrast, maintain that local governments have little leeway for action because of their reliance on higher levels of government (Levine and Kogan 2016). Indeed, according to the economic vote theory, voters are inclined to use the current economic situation as a political short-cut to sanction or reward (via re-election) the incumbent official. Moore, McGregor, and Stephenson (2017) showed that, in the case of Toronto, the economy served as a "proxy" by which voters judged the performance of elected officials. The authors put forth several hypotheses to explain this finding: 1) the absence of political parties leads voters to look for political shortcuts to judge the performance of elected officials; 2) voters make erroneous connections between the economic situation and the mayor, especially in cases where mayors themselves claim recognition for economic successes. These hypotheses highlight just how important disclosure of information truly is (Moore, McGregor, and Stephenson 2017). Additionally, Achen and Bartels (2016) theorize that voters punish politicians for events that do not fall under their jurisdiction. This idea aligns perfectly well with the rational choice theory, which assumes the presence of a "rational voter." According to this theory, if voters arbitrarily punish the incumbent, it is not because they are incapable of assessing their own level of well-being but rather because they are not able to draw a connection between their well-being and the actions of the government. Consequently, a shark attack – the analogy used in the book – would threaten the well-being of the voter. In other words, blinkered voters punish the incumbent for threatening their well-being even when the event is unrelated to his or her performance.

There is a need to examine how performance affects accountability as well as the issue of ethics and elected officials, because these may be determining factors in voter decision-making. We will also look at the career trajectories of elected officials at the municipal level and the increasing professionalization of elected officials, which, by its very nature, affects responsiveness and accountability. As part of this analysis, we will focus on answering the following questions: What meaning do elected officials give to these two concepts in the daily exercise of their mandate? Do elected officials take accountability and responsiveness into account when representing citizens? Are they responsive? Are voters more likely to punish or reward incumbents for their performance?

Focusing on these types of questions constitutes a relatively novel and interesting approach to understanding how politics works at the municipal level in Canada. As mentioned earlier, while there are many European studies on elected officials and their careers (Guérin-Lavignotte and Kerrouche 2006; Steyvers and Reynaert 2006), there is very little Canadian research on this issue (Simard 2005; Mévellec and Tremblay 2016; Lucas 2015; Breux and Jacquet 2015). Moreover, to our knowledge no studies to date have established a connection between accountability/responsiveness and the careers or everyday work life of elected officials.

A final characteristic to consider is the multilevel nature of governance at the Canadian municipal level, which makes it more difficult to understand the scope of power. In fact, because there are so many levels of government, citizens are mostly unaware what is under their local government's jurisdiction. And the fact that the provincial government is responsible for overseeing municipalities makes it even more confusing to distinguish between the various powers. Moreover, the above-mentioned lack of citizen awareness, or understanding, is exacerbated by an information deficit about this level of government. Indeed, several authors have already noted the presence of an information deficit in municipal politics (Cutler and Matthews 2005). Bherer and Breux (2011) attribute this deficit to a weaker flow of information and the lower quality of information at the municipal level compared to other levels of government. The latter is essentially explained by the small size of many municipalities, the huge number of municipalities, and a lack of journalists dedicated to local news. Additionally, citizens generally tend to misunderstand the jurisdictions of the different political levels (Cutler 2008). This element is important because the public services or issues that concern a municipality often concern several institutions and even several levels of government. Although municipal services are delivered by municipalities, it is important to remember that there are often two levels of municipal government and that certain services may also be delivered by specialized organizations. In other words, if citizens are not in a position to identify the responsibilities and competencies of those running for office, then both responsiveness/accountability and the quality of representation need to be called into question.

OBJECTIVES, STRUCTURE, AND RELEVANCY OF THIS BOOK

The aim of this book is to engage in a new reflection on local Canadian democracy using two key concepts of democratic theory: responsiveness and accountability. This work primarily targets the question of whether accountability and responsiveness matter at the municipal level. To answer this question, we will address the concepts of account-ability and responsiveness through the three characteristics of the Canadian municipal scene detailed above. The book is divided into three parts, each comprised of three chapters.

In part 1, we discuss the importance of the partisan or non-partisan context of the municipal level for accountability/responsiveness in a non-partisan environment on the one hand and in a partisan context on the other. More specifically, this first part aims to identify how the voter makes his or her choice and the role that accountabil-ity/responsiveness eventually plays in this decision. In the first chapter of part 1, Laura Stephenson, Michael McGregor, and Aaron Moore question the role of partisanship in a so-called non-partisan election and the influence thereof on accountability, namely with reference to the case of the 2014 municipal election in Toronto. In the second chapter of part 1, Jérôme Couture and Sandra Breux pursue similar reflections, in their case about the 2009 and 2013 municipal elections in the province of Quebec. More specifically, they ask whether voters respond more to the performance of elected officials in a non-partisan context and how this manifests. To conclude part 1, Jérôme Couture, Sandra Breux, and Laurence Bherer offer a more theoretical reflec-tion on the definition of a municipal political party and develop a typology of them in connection with the concepts of accountability and responsiveness.

Part 2 of the book is devoted to municipal officials, their careers, and their daily work. The aim here is to understand the career paths of elected officials and their everyday practice and to see how such trajectories are related to notions of accountability and responsive-ness. In the first chapter of part 2, Jack Lucas and Anthony Sayers present a comparative analysis of the political careers of local elected officials in Edmonton and Calgary and discuss the impact of such trajectories on accountability/responsiveness. The subsequent chapter, by Andrew Sancton, analyzes how in London (Ontario) and in Sudbury (Ontario) voters were influenced by a highly publicized decision of the Ontario ombudsman that punished incumbents. Apart from offer-ing a reflection on voter behaviour, this chapter also questions the position of the ombudsman in that context. The third chapter of part 2 engages in our research from a broader angle by demonstrating how the concepts of accountability and responsiveness are central to the discourse and practices of politicians. Based on the analysis of several medium- and large-sized cities in the province of Quebec,

Anne Mévellec shows that the accountability and responsiveness concepts define how elected officials, regardless of their respective governance styles, present themselves.

The last part of this book, part 3, returns to the context of Canadian multilevel governance, examining how certain public policies are implemented. In the first chapter of this part, Joseph Lyons and Zachary Spicer measure the accountability of special-purpose bodies and inter-local agreements based on the case of London, starting from the idea that accountability is inevitably distorted when a government does not have full responsibility for the delivery of a specific public service. In the subsequent chapter, Fanny Tremblay-Racicot pursues a similar question with reference to Toronto regional planning institutions, stressing that responsiveness/accountability can vary significantly depending on the geopolitical actors in place. In the last chapter of part 3, Alison Smith looks at how the homelessness crisis questions political effectiveness and responsiveness in Calgary and Montreal while also showing the impact of multilevel governance.

The book ends with two concluding texts. The first one, by Ruth Dassonneville, offers a broader reflection on the Canadian municipal scene while highlighting the contributions of each contributing author and questioning the so-called specificity of the municipal level. In the second and last conclusion, Jérôme Couture and Sandra Breux reflect on each chapter with regard to our initial question by examining their respective theoretical, empirical, and normative contributions. They conclude the book by returning to the role of information policy at the municipal level and its impact on the quality of the representation that may take place at this level of government.

Besides questioning the ways in which accountability and responsiveness manifest, this book also aims to contribute to the collection and dissemination of municipal-level data. Several years ago, Jessica Trounstine (2009) observed that in the United States, the lack of centralized municipal electoral data impeded the work of researchers insofar as they had to find such information on their own. Indeed, this restriction has been seen to account for the scarcity of sociological studies (Hajnal and Lewis 2003) and longitudinal analyses of municipal elections (Hajnal and Trounstine 2014). However, whereas in the United States this situation has changed over the past dozen years – namely, as a result of initiatives to create more robust databases (Marschall, Shah, and Ruhil 2011) – the same cannot be said of the Canadian context, at least not for the time being. For example, municipalities increasingly tend to announce election results online, yet unfortunately they do not do so in any uniform or coordinated manner. As a result, currently there is no centralized system for capturing and organizing the municipal electoral data of all Canadian provinces. Nor is there, apart from electoral data, any centralized data about elected officials and their careers. We therefore consider this book a first step in the effort to build a database on municipal elections in Canada – an effort that is, admittedly, a veritable challenge.

From a theoretical standpoint, the difficulty of accessing electoral data is translated into a misunderstanding of Canadian municipal elections. Recently, Taylor and Eidelman (2010) as well as Breux and Bherer (2011) highlighted the lack of research on municipal democracy and the dearth of written works dedicated to this topic in political science. Moreover, as mentioned earlier, despite a boom in work on municipal politics in recent years, most of this research is centred on governance and participative democracy, as a result of which the topic of representative democracy tends to be overlooked. In all fairness, several publications and projects have recently contributed to breaking ground in the field, such as the Toronto Election Study (see torontoelectionstudy.com), the Internet Voting Project (see internet votingproject.com), and the Laboratory on Local Elections (http:// www.labelectionslocales.ca/en). Last but not least, another motivation behind this book is to promote networking among researchers from all Canadian provinces who are interested in the municipal level. It is our hope that this book can serve as the beginning of a large body of research on Canadian municipal elections.

NOTE

1 Between 2004 and 2014. The one hundred largest municipalities are concentrated in four provinces: Ontario, Quebec, British Columbia, and Alberta. For additional information, see Breux, Couture, and Koop (2017).

REFERENCES

Achen, Christopher H., and Larry M. Bartels. 2016. *Democracy for Realists: Why Elections Do Not Produce Responsive Government.* Princeton, NJ: Princeton University Press.

Ackerman, John. 2004. "Co-governance for Accountability: Beyond 'Exit' and 'Voice.'" *World Development* 32(3): 447–63.

Aidt, Toke S., Francisco J. Veiga, and Linda G. Veiga. 2011."Election Results and Opportunistic Policies: A New Test of the Rational Political Business Cycle Model." *Public Choice* 148: 21–44.

Alford, Robert, and Eugene Lee. 1968. "Voting Turnout in American Cities." *The American Political Science Review* 62(3): 796–813.

Balaguer-Coll, Maria Teresa, Maria Isabel Brun-Martos, Anabel Forte, and Emili Tortosa-Ausina. 2014. "Determinant of Local Government's Reelection: New Evidence Based on a Bayesian Approach." *Universität Jaume I Economics Department Working Papers*: 1–24.

Bherer, Laurence. 2011. "Pourquoi un sixième mandat pour le maire de Laval en 2009? Les sources d'un monopole politique." In *Les élections municipales au Québec en 2011: enjeux et perspectives*, edited by Sandra Breux and Laurence Bherer, 233–65. Quebec: Presses de l'Université Laval.

Bherer, Laurence, and Sandra Breux. 2011. "Démocratie locale et élections: prémices d'une comparaison." In *Les élections municipales au Québec en 2011: enjeux et perspectives*, edited by Sandra Breux and Laurence Bherer, 1–29. Quebec: Presses de l'Université Laval.

– 2012. "L'apolitisme municipal." *Bulletin d'Histoire politique* 21(1): 170–84.

Boyne, George A., Oliver James, Peter John, and Nicolai Petrovsky. 2009. "Democracy and Government Performance: Holding Incumbents Accountable in English Local Governments." *The Journal of Politics* 71(4): 1273–84. doi:10.1017/S0022381609990089.

Breux, Sandra, and Laurence Bherer. 2011. *Les élections municipales au Québec: enjeux et perspectives*. Quebec: Presses de l'Université Laval.

Breux, Sandra, Jérôme Couture, and Royce Koop. 2017. "Turnout in the 100 Biggest Canadian Cities (2004–2014)." *Canadian Journal of Political Science*. Published online before print 3 July 2017. doi:https:// doi.org/10.1017/S0008423917000018X.

Breux, Sandra, and Vincent Jacquet. 2015. "Local Politics in Quebec and Wallonia: Local Political Dynamics as Seen through the Mayoral Career." In *Minority Nations in Multinational Federations. A comparative study of Quebec and Wallonia*, edited by Min Reuchamps, 104–23. London/New York: Routledge.

Campbell, Angus, Philip E. Converse, Warren Miller, and Donald E. Stokes. 1960. *The American Voter*. Chicago: University of Chicago Press.

Choquette, Éléna, and Jean-François Godbout. 2015. "Fédéralisme et responsaibilité électorale des élus: l'un exclut-il l'autre?" *Observatoire des fédérations*. Accessed 8 August 2017. https://papyrus.bib.umontreal.

ca/xmlui/bitstream/handle/1866/12646/20150117_editorial_ODF.
pdf?sequence=1&isAllowed=y.

Collin, Jean-Pierre, and Pierre J. Hamel. 1993. "Les contraintes structurelles
des finances publiques locales: les budgets municipaux dans la région de
Montréal en 1991." *Recherches sociographiques* 34(3): 439–67.

Cutler, Fred. 2008. "Whodunnit? Voters and Responsibility in Canadian
Federalism." *Canadian Journal of Political Science* 38(2): 359–82.

Cutler, Fred, and J. Scott Matthews. 2005. "The Challenge of Municipal
Voting: Vancouver 2002." *Canadian Journal of Political Science* 38(2):
359–82.

DGEQ (Directeur Général des élections du Québec). 2013. "Candidatures
aux élections municipales du 3 novembre – Le DGE présente un bilan
des candidatures dans les municipalités où résident 5 000 personnes
et plus.» Accessed 27 July 2017. http://www.electionsquebec.qc.ca/
francais/actualite-detail.php?id=5523,

Downs, Anthony. 1957. *An Economic Theory of Democracy*. New York:
Harper and Row.

Drazen, Allan, and Marcela Eslava. 2010. "Electoral Manipulation via
Voter-Friendly Spending: Theory and Evidence." *Journal of
Development Economics* 92: 39–52.

Elmendorf, Christopher, and David Schleicher. 2012. "Districting for a
Low-Information Electorate." *Yale Law Journal* 121(7): 1846–86.

Erickson, Robert S., Gerald C. Wright, and John P. McIver. 1993.
*Statehouse Democracy: Public Opinion and Policy in the American
States*. Cambridge: Cambridge University Press.

Fearon, James D. 1999. "Electoral Accountability and the Control of
Politicians: Selecting Good Types versus Sanctionning Poor
Performance." In *Democracy, Accountability, Representation*, edited by
Adam Przeworski, Susan E. Stokes, and Bernard Manin, 55–98. New
York: Cambridge University Press.

Gerber, Elisabeth, and Daniel J. Hopkins. 2011. "When Mayors Matter:
Estimating the Impact of Mayoral Partisanship on City Policy."
American Journal of Political Science 55(2): 326–39.

Gerstlé, Jacques. 2003. "La réactivité aux préférences collectives et
l'imputabilité de l'action publique." *Revue française de science politique*
53(6): 859–85.

Guérin-Lavignotte, Élodie, and Eric Kerrouche. 2006. *Les élus locaux en
Europe*. Paris: La documentation française.

Hajnal, Zoltan L., and Paul G. Lewis. 2003. "Municipal Institutions and
Voter Turnout in Local Elections." *Urban Affairs Review* 38(5): 645–68.

Hajnal, Zoltan L., and Jessica Trounstine. 2014. "What Underlies Urban Politics? Race, Class, Ideology, Partisanship and the Urban Vote." *Urban Affairs Review* 50(1): 63–99.

Klingemann, Hans-Dieter, Richard I. Hobberfert, and Ian Budge. 1994. *Parties, Policies and Democracy*. Boulder, CO: Westview Press.

Koop, Royce, and John Kraemer. 2016. "Wards, At-Large Systems and the Focus of Representation in Canadian Cities." *Canadian Journal of Political Science* 49(3): 433–48.

Lax, Jeffrey R., and Justin H. Philips. 2012. "The Democratic Deficit in the States." *American Journal of Political Science* 56(1): 107–21.

Leigh, Andrew. 2008. "Estimating the Impact of Gubernatorial Partisanship on Policy Settings and Economic Outcomes." *American Journal of Political Science* 56(1): 256–68.

Levine, Katherine Einstein, and Vladimir Kogan. 2016. "Pushing the City Limits: Policy Responsiveness in Municipal Government." *Urban Affairs Review* 52(1): 3–32.

Lucas, Jack. 2015. "Local Governance and the Local Political Career in Canada: A Sample Dataset." *Canadian Public Administration* 58: 605–17.

Marschall, Mélissa., Paru Shah, and Anirudh Ruhil. 2011. "The Study of Local Elections." *Political Science and Politics* 44(1): 97–100.

Mévellec, Anne, and Manon Tremblay. 2016. *Genre et professionnalisation de la politique municipale*. Montreal: Presses universitaires du Québec.

Moore, Aaron A., Michael R. McGregor, and Laura B. Stephenson. 2017. "Paying Attention and the Incumbency Effect: Voting Behavior in the 2014 Toronto Municipal Election." *International Political Science Review*: 85–98.

Nivola, Pietro S. 2002. *Tense Commandments: Federal Prescriptions and City Problems*. Washington: Brooking Institution Press.

Oliver, J. Eric, and Shang E. Ha. 2007. "Vote Choice in Suburban Elections." *American Political Science Review* 101(3): 393–408. doi:10.1017/S0003055407070323.

Oliver, J. Eric, Shang E. Ha, and Zachary Callen. 2012. *Local Elections and the Politics of Small-Scale Democracy*. Princeton, NJ: Princeton University Press.

Peterson, Paul E. 1981. *City Limits*. Chicago, London: University of Chicago Press.

Pétry, François. 1999. "The Opinion Policy Relationship in Canada." *The Journal of Politics* 61(2): 540–50.

Philip, Mark. 2009. "Delimiting Democratic Accountability." *Political Studies* 57: 28–53.

Quesnel, Louise. 1986. La démocratie municipale au Québec. *Politique* 9: 61–97. doi:https://doi.org/10.1017/S000842391700018X.

Sakurai, Sergio N., and Naercio A. Menezes-Filho. 2008. "Fiscal Policy and Reelection in Brazilian Municipalities." *Public Choice* 137: 301–14.

Sedmihradska, Lucie, Rudolf Kubik, and Jakub Haas. 2011. "Political Business Cycle in Czech Municipalities." *Prague Economics Papers* 1: 59–70.

Self, Robert O. 2003. *American Babylon: Race and Struggle for Postwar Oakland*. Princeton, NJ: Princeton University Press.

Simard, Carolle. 2005. "Qui nous gouverne au municipal: reproduction ou renouvellement?" In *La ville autrement*, edited by Pierre Delorme, 97–119. Sainte-Foy: Presses de l'Université du Québec.

Spoon, Jae-Jae, and Heike Klüver. 2014. "Do Parties Respond? How Electoral Context Influences Party Responsiveness." *Electoral Studies* 35: 48–60.

Steyvers, Kristof, and Herwig Reynaert. 2006. "'From the Few Are Chosen the Few …' On the Social Background of European Mayors." In *The European Mayor. Political Leaders in the Changing Context of Local Democracy*, edited by Henry Bäck, Hubert Heinelt, and Annick Magnier, 43–73. Wiesbaden: VS Verlag für Sozialwissenschaften.

Stimson, James A., Michael B. MacKuen, and Robert S. Erickson. 1995. "Dynamics Representation." *American Political Science Review* 89(3): 543–65.

Tausanovitch, Chris, and Christopher Warshaw. 2014. "Representation in Municipal Government." *American Political Science Review* 108(3): 605–41.

Taylor, Zack. 2011. "Who Elected Rob Ford, and Why? An Ecological Analysis of the 2010 Toronto Election." Conference paper, Canadian Political Science Association, Waterloo.

Taylor, Zack, and Gabriel Eidelman. 2010. "Canadian Political Science and the City: A Limited Engagement." *Canadian Journal of Political Science* 43(4): 961–81.

Tiebout, Charles M. 1956. "A Pure Theory of Local Expenditures." *The Journal of Political Economy* 64(5): 416–24.

Trounstine, Jessica. 2008. *Political Monopolies in American Cities: The Rise and Fall of Bosses and Reformers*. Chicago: University of Chicago Press.

– 2010. "Representation and Accountability in Cities." *Annual Review of Political Science* 13: 407–23. doi:10.1146/annurev.polisci.032808. 150414.

Veselý, Arnošt. 2013. "L'imputabilité en Europe centrale et orientale: entre concept et réalité." *Revue internationale des sciences administratives* 79(2): 325–43.

PART ONE

Discussing Political Parties

1

Sins of the Brother: Partisanship and Accountability in Toronto, 2014

Laura B. Stephenson, R. Michael McGregor, and Aaron A. Moore

INTRODUCTION

Regular, competitive, and fair elections are tools that allow voters to reward or punish politicians on the basis of past performance. In other words, through elections voters can hold their representatives accountable for their actions. In that context, re-election, and the potential wrath of voters, has become the main incentive for politicians to be responsive to the will of the electorate and to constrain their behaviour. In this chapter, we focus on voters and therefore the accountability side of the relationship.

Retrospective evaluations influence many voters' decisions in the sense that voters ask themselves whether they like what the government has done or whether they want change. Whereas candidates with no record in office have a relatively blank slate with voters, the presence of political parties introduces a new layer of complexity. As Dalton (2002, 125, 126) notes, parties "define the choices available to voters" and "shape the content of election campaigns," and they also provide important links across elections. Even in races with no incumbents, party labels tie candidates to previous contests and governments, making it difficult for them to be viewed independently of the failures or successes of predecessors. Party ties can also colour the retrospective evaluations of voters regarding government performance (Duch, Palmer, and Anderson 2000; Anderson and McGregor

2014) such that governments of one's preferred party may be evaluated more generously and those of opposing parties more harshly. If such evaluations factor into future vote choices, then partisanship can be considered to have a complex relationship with accountability. On the one hand, partisanship can bias perceptions and weaken accountability; on the other, it can ensure that "fresh starts" are not granted to politicians unduly.

Although party systems are well established at the federal and provincial levels in Canada, most municipal elections in the country are non-partisan in nature.[1] At first glance, one might expect such non-partisan contests to be just that – untouched by partisan sentiment. One might also expect that voters would put more weight on evaluating incumbents on their actual performance, since party cues are not available. Such evaluations would then enhance accountability because voters would be responding to actual behaviour and politicians would be more mindful of re-election. However, if such evaluations are biased, then the accountability function of non-partisan elections is questionable. Accordingly, the purpose of this chapter is to investigate whether, and the extent to which, partisan bias affects accountability in non-partisan contests.

We focus on two types of bias. The first concerns cross-level partisanship and examines whether party ties developed in the federal political arena shape retrospective evaluations of candidates running in non-partisan municipal elections. Specifically, we focus on the 2014 Toronto mayoral race. McGregor, Moore, and Stephenson (2016) have shown that most voters associated the candidates in that race with political parties despite the official lack of such labels. The question we ask here is: Do those perceptions, and voters' own partisan biases, affect evaluations of the incumbent's performance? The second type of partisan ties we consider are cross-candidate ties in the form of an unofficial "quasi-party" link between candidates. This leads to our second research question: Are evaluations and support affected when voters perceive links between previous politicians and new candidates?

The 2014 Toronto mayoral election is particularly well-suited to providing insight into these questions and therefore evaluating the influence of partisan/quasi-partisan ties on accountability in a non-partisan setting. While the election was ostensibly non-partisan in nature, the candidates had varying degrees of partisan links. By differentiating the voters who did from those who did not attribute partisan ties to candidates, we are able to improve our understanding of how partisan attitudes formed at one level of government can affect accountability in a non-partisan race at another. In addition, the incumbent mayor (the late Rob Ford) withdrew his candidacy at the last moment, only to be replaced by his brother (Doug Ford). However, as Rob's term in office had been saturated with media spectacle and scandal, it is unclear whether and to what extent Doug was held accountable for the actions of his brother. Therefore, as a dynasty of sorts, the Fords also created a quasi-partisan scenario in which voter attitudes toward the new candidate may have been shaped by their attitudes toward the outgoing mayor in a manner similar to how party labels might influence attitudes. This election thus provides us with an opportunity to study two ways in which a non-partisan election may be influenced by evaluations of parties or individuals outside of the specific race itself.

Analyses conducted with Toronto Election Study data reveal that cross-level partisanship and quasi-party bias did factor into vote choice in two ways. First, evaluations of the previous mayor's performance were significantly biased by the partisan leanings of electors. Second, support for Doug Ford in the 2014 contest was shaped heavily by evaluations of his brother's performance, independently of evaluations of Doug himself. In other words, support for Doug Ford reflected the actions of his brother and were tainted by attitudes toward political parties at another level of government.

PARTIES, PARTISANSHIP, AND ACCOUNTABILITY

To properly evaluate partisan bias in non-partisan elections, we first need to understand the role that parties play in elections. From the perspective of voters, the importance of parties in elections is threefold. First, party affiliations provide issue position information for those who need to choose among candidates. Knowing which party a candidate is associated with provides some indication of ideology and the policy stances he or she is likely to support. Voters can use this information to make an informed estimate of which candidate is most closely aligned with their preferences. Indeed, partisan cues have been shown to help electors vote "correctly" or to accurately identify the candidate they should support, based in part on a comparison of voter policy preferences with the positions of candidates (see Lau and Redlawsk 1997).

The second reason parties are useful to voters is that their reputations provide information about issue performance over time, across multiple elections. In addition to knowing what policies candidates support in a particular contest, knowing how, or if, others from that party have delivered on policy promises in the past may inform estimates of what is likely to occur in the future. If a voter really cares about a specific issue, past experience with the party can provide an indication of whether promises are likely to be delivered. This aligns with the logic underlying the valence model of electoral choice because if voters care about choosing representatives that are "a safe pair of hands" (Clarke, Kornberg, and Scotto 2009, 23) for guiding the actions of government, then party affiliation (and past party performance) is key information.

Finally, and emerging directly from the second reason, party reputations facilitate the accountability function of elections. Fiorina's (1981) discussion of Downsian retrospective voting makes clear that party connections across elections are important. As Fiorina interprets Downs, "a good guide to what a party will do in the future is what it has done in the past" (1981, 12). Politicians will therefore be mindful of their behaviour in office because they know that judgments about their performance will factor into decisions during the next election. Even if incumbent candidates do not seek re-election, their party can benefit from or be disadvantaged by their past performance.

Party labels therefore provide a straightforward heuristic that voters can draw upon in low-information contexts, allowing them to hold parties and politicians accountable. Even when voters know little about the candidates or the issues of an election, they can draw upon their experience with the incumbent government party to form a judgment about whether they wish to "throw the rascals out" (vote for an opposition party) or stay with "the devil they know" (the incumbent party). This type of reasoning can be very useful for voters when making their judgments and help to promote democratic accountability (Key 1966).

Although the above-mentioned reasons point to the benefits of partisan contests for the accountability function of elections, the presence of parties and partisanship also poses a potential problem. Partisan attitudes may bias evaluations of past performance. The "perceptual screen" discussed by Campbell et al. (1960, 133) may lead co-partisans (people who identify with the same party) to evaluate governments more positively than warranted and partisans of other parties to evaluate them more negatively. Accountability may therefore be diminished in partisan contests if incumbent performance is misperceived.

Now consider accountability in non-partisan elections. If there truly are no party cues available to voters, then retrospective evaluations and attitudes toward candidates will not be biased by partisan attitudes.[2] Unbiased evaluations would be based upon issue stances, policy promises, and performance. Furthermore, previous activities would only be a factor if the incumbent is running, in which case he or she could be held accountable for his or her own actions because there would be no party ties across candidates. Non-partisan contests should therefore allow for greater accountability than partisan contests, but *only* if no partisan information is available. In the case that it is available, the degree of bias and accountability is uncertain. It is therefore important to understand what party cues, ties, and links may exist, or be perceived, in non-partisan elections.

CROSS-LEVEL AND CROSS-CANDIDATE TIES

Little is known about whether evaluations of non-partisan municipal politicians are affected by perceptions of parties at other levels of government. However, cross-level influence has been shown in other contexts. Canadian researchers have suggested that partisan ties at one level can shape attitudes toward parties at another (Clarke and Stewart 1987; Stewart and Clarke 1998),[3] and research from countries where local and national party systems align suggests that national-level considerations can affect municipal election results (Heath et al. 1999; Martins and Veiga 2013; Cassette, Farvaque, and Héricourt 2013). Finally, partisan links at one level of government have been shown to correlate to municipal vote choice in Canada (Cutler and Matthews 2005; McGregor, Moore, and Stephenson 2016).

It is possible that non-partisan municipal elections may be "quasi-partisan" in nature if candidates hold ties to parties at other levels of government. First, politicians may have partisan histories. There are many instances of Canadian politicians "jumping" between the federal, provincial, and municipal levels, and in such instances party relationships are readily available cues for voters.[4] Second, the ideological leanings of the candidates or endorsements may imply that ties exist to parties at other levels of government. Research done in the US has shown that in "low-information" elections, such as at the municipal level, partisan cues can be particularly important for voters (Squire and Smith 1988; Schaffner and Streb 2002; Bonneau and Cann 2015). Voters can use party cues and their own partisanship at other levels of government to inform their vote choices, so the extent to which elections provide true accountability may depend more on the extent to which candidates are *perceived* to be non-partisan than on the actual absence of party involvement or ties.

Non-partisan accountability may also be threatened by quasi-party or "dynastic" ties between former and current candidates. Even when there is no incumbent, outgoing politicians may have "anointed" successors. While the potential benefits for doing so are obvious (at least if the outgoing politician is popular), such an arrangement can tie the new candidate to the record of the incumbent, in essence making the candidate accountable for actions he or she did not take. In most cases, perceiving these quasi-party ties would depend on the knowledge levels of individual voters but less so if the link was obvious because of a shared last name. "Dynastic politicians," defined as those whose family members have served in the same position in the past (Asako et al. 2015) are very common in many parts of the world (e.g., see Bohlken and Chandra 2012 on India; Taniguchi 2008 on Japan; Camp 1995 on Mexico; Mendoza et al. 2012 on the Philippines; and Feinstein 2010 on the United States). They enjoy "brand name advantage" and higher electoral success than their non-dynastic competitors (Asako et al. 2015; Feinstein 2010). Such politicians are less common in party-based systems (Doyle et al. 2015) but are not altogether unheard of in Canada, especially not in Toronto.[5] If candidates are punished for the sins committed by fellow "party" members, then this represents another form of (quasi-) partisan bias in non-partisan elections, with obvious implications for electoral accountability.

THE 2014 TORONTO MAYORAL RACE

The Toronto mayoral election, held on 27 October 2014, undoubtedly received the most media coverage of all the municipal elections held across the province of Ontario that day. This was due not only to the size and national prominence of the City of Toronto but also to the infamy of its incumbent mayor, Rob Ford. The latter attracted local, national, and international media attention for reasons ranging from a conflict-of-interest trial to his substance abuse scandal to his refusal to resign from office. Initially, Rob Ford registered to run for re-election but withdrew from the mayoral race for health reasons just an hour before the candidate registration deadline – whereupon his brother Doug quickly registered to take his place on the ballot. Thus, the election was not a typical low-information municipal contest.

There were three noteworthy contenders in the mayoral race. Aside from Doug Ford, the other two were high-profile politicians at the provincial and federal levels, respectively. John Tory is a past mayoral candidate, provincial politician, leader of the right-wing Ontario Progressive Conservative Party, corporate CEO, and radio talk show host. Olivia Chow had resigned her seat as an NDP member of Parliament to run in the race. She is a former Toronto city councillor, served as the chair of the Community Services Committee and vice-chair of the Toronto Transit Commission, and is the widow of Jack Layton, the former leader of the federal NDP. Although neither of the Ford brothers had official partisan ties, the two had fairly prominent links to Conservative prime minister Stephen Harper – Rob and the prime minister were self-described "fishing partners" and attended political events in support of one another (Wallace 2011). This made for a contest in which even moderately informed electors were able to grasp the candidates' party leanings.

As noted above, strictly speaking there was no incumbent in the race. However, the connection between Doug Ford and his brother may well have created a "Ford" party or dynastic link for voters. The brothers had a strong, highly publicized association, and they shared more than a last name (or label). Their voting records on the city council were very similar, Doug was a high-profile advisor to Rob, the two brothers co-hosted a radio show, and even their respective campaign websites were nearly identical. Both brothers ran under the banner of "Ford Nation," and Doug appeared to keep many of the same advisors and volunteers. For example, the spokesperson who withdrew Rob Ford from candidacy was the same person who later filed the registration papers for Doug (Hui, Church, and Lum 2014). Finally, by all accounts Doug Ford ran on the same platform as his brother. In short, this situation is the closest to a party that one is likely to find in an officially non-partisan setting: the familial ties, branding, and organization of the two brothers suggest the existence of a quasi-party. It is thus quite possible that voters held Doug accountable for the actions of Rob.

To summarize, the focus of this chapter is on understanding whether two types of partisan bias affected voting in an officially non-partisan election. The specifics of the Toronto election create an interesting set of circumstances in which to probe accountability in municipal elections without parties. Obvious party ties existed for some candidates, and there was a quasi-party dynastic link between the previous mayor and one of the candidates. Officially, however, it was a non-partisan election with no incumbent. In the analysis that follows, we investigate accountability in the 2014 Toronto mayoral election by answering the following research questions:

1 Did partisan ties, when recognized, influence retrospective evaluations of Rob Ford's performance as mayor?
2 Did retrospective evaluations have an independent effect on vote choice in the 2014 election, even in the absence of an incumbent candidate?

DATA AND METHODOLOGY

This chapter draws on data from the Toronto Election Study (TES), a two-wave Internet survey of Torontonians conducted around the time of the 2014 Toronto municipal election. Three thousand respondents were interviewed in the weeks before election day, nearly 75 per cent of whom also completed a post-election questionnaire. The questionnaire includes a variety of questions about attitudes and behaviour, similar to those contained in many national election studies, and is the first dataset of its kind to allow for a thorough consideration of voting behaviour in a non-partisan Canadian municipality.[6] Note that in order to maximize the generalizability of our findings, all results discussed below are weighted for age, gender, and education.

To address our research questions, we present several pieces of empirical evidence. First, we establish the extent to which Torontonians associated the three major candidates with parties. In a previous work, we (McGregor, Moore, and Stephenson 2016) conducted an analysis of a question from the pre-election wave of the TES, which asked respondents which party, if any, they associated with the candidates.[7] This simple question allowed us to determine what share of the population linked the candidates with parties and which parties. Such an indicator is vital to understanding the effect of party cues on accountability in a non-partisan election.

After presenting data on if and how candidates are associated with parties, we examine the effect of partisanship on retrospective evaluations of Rob Ford's performance as mayor. We consider two measures of partisanship. The first indicates the partisan ties of the individual electors: respondents are either classified as supporters of the Liberals, Conservatives, NDP, or Greens or as non-partisans. Based on those findings, supporters of parties other than the one associated with the outgoing mayor are shown to have rated his past performance less positively than supporters of the former mayor's party. The second measure of partisanship is an indicator of compatibility. In a non-partisan contest, partisan links must be inferred by voters, and these assessments are, by definition, going to be less consistent than is the case with officially partisan races (where party labels are ubiquitous, including on ballots themselves). As such, we consider a measure of partisan compatibility, based on a comparison of the partisan attachments of respondents with the parties that individual respondents associate with the candidates.[8] We expected that partisan (in)compatibility should colour evaluations of the incumbent's performance (in this case, Doug Ford as a quasi-incumbent through his ties to his brother). Specifically, we expect Doug Ford co-partisans to be most satisfied with the performance of Rob Ford and anti-partisans to be least satisfied (with other voters somewhere between these extremes).[9]

The indicator of satisfaction with Rob Ford's performance is measured with a question in the pre-election survey ("How satisfied are you with the performance of the current mayor?"). If we observe a relationship between either measure of partisanship and the evaluations of Rob Ford's performance, such an effect would arguably diminish the accountability function of the 2014 mayoral election, since this would indicate that attitudes toward Ford were shaped by attitudes forged on the basis of partisan politics at the federal level rather than on the basis of Ford's performance itself. Note that a series of controls are included in our analysis to ensure that we have properly isolated the effect of partisanship upon our outcome variable.

We then turn to our second research question and evaluate the extent to which voters held Doug Ford accountable for the performance of Rob. Recall that we conceptualize accountability as voting in accordance with one's evaluation of the performance of the incumbent. Presumably, if a respondent is unsatisfied with the mayor's performance, *ceteris paribus*, he or she should be less likely to vote for the incumbent than a respondent who is relatively satisfied. Of course, in theory retrospective evaluations and electoral accountability are only relevant if an incumbent candidate or party is present.

Accordingly, this portion of our analysis evaluates the extent to which voters held Doug Ford accountable for the actions of his brother. Through a series of logistic regression vote choice models, where vote choice is the outcome variable, we consider the relationship between satisfaction with Rob Ford and support for Doug Ford and examine whether this relationship is moderated by the extent to which voters viewed the policies of the two brothers as dissimilar (or the perception of Doug as a pseudo-incumbent). If Doug is held accountable for Rob's performance, our analysis should reveal that those who viewed the two brothers as similar to one another were more likely to vote in accordance with their evaluation of Rob's record (high levels of satisfaction should be correlated with support for Doug). Again, we include a series of controls in this analysis.

RESULTS

Party Links and Partisan Compatibility

Table 1.1 reveals which party, if any, each of the three mayoral candidates was linked to according to the electors. This table is reproduced in full from McGregor, Moore, and Stephenson (2016). For the purposes of this study, the most important trend shown in the table is that even in the ostensibly non-partisan Toronto election, most voters associated candidates with established political parties. Ford was associated with a party by 62 per cent of respondents, while the analogous figures for Chow and Tory are 79.5 per cent and 75 per cent, respectively. The modal response for both Ford and Tory was "Conservative," and Chow was most commonly associated with the NDP, although we should note that each of the candidates was also associated with other parties by many respondents.[10]

Analyzing our partisan compatibility variable reveals that 20.7 per cent of TES respondents were Doug Ford co-partisans and 34.6 per cent were anti-partisans (the remaining respondents either were non-partisans or did not associate Ford with a party). The corresponding values for Tory are 21.6 per cent co-partisan and 45.6 per cent anti-partisan. A total of 12.0 per cent and 59.0 per cent of respondents were Chow co- and anti-partisans, respectively. Thus, Ford had the second highest rate of co-partisanship (a mere 1 per cent less than Tory) but by far the lowest level of anti-partisanship. In our sample, 82.8 per cent of respondents reported federal partisan ties, of whom

Table 1.1
Perceived candidate party ties (%)

	Olivia Chow	Doug Ford	John Tory
None	5.6	14.7	6.8
Conservative	2.4	46.2	55.8
Liberal	4.8	10.1	15.5
NDP	68.5	2.0	1.2
Green	3.2	1.8	1.7
Other	0.6	1.9	0.9
Don't know	14.9	23.3	18.2

N = 2850

Entries report column percentages.

the Liberal Party claimed the most (39.2 per cent), followed by the Conservative (25.0 per cent), New Democratic (13.0 per cent), and Green parties (4.6 per cent).[11]

Our analysis does not hinge on whether respondents were able to "accurately" associate candidates with parties; rather, we focus on how perceived party associations combine with partisan preferences to shape evaluations of Rob Ford's performance and, in turn, vote choice in the 2014 election. Nevertheless, to ensure that our results are not driven by political sophisticates (who may be better able to recognize party leanings), we control in the analysis below for political knowledge, attentiveness, education, and age.[12]

Cross-Level Party Bias

Our two research questions relate to the accountability process: Did federal partisanship affect satisfaction with mayoral incumbent performance? And did this measure of satisfaction affect vote choice more among those who perceived close ties between the Ford brothers in the 2014 Toronto election? We begin by considering the first question, evaluating whether and to what extent partisanship biased evaluations of the incumbent's performance. Partisans might view a politician whom they associate with their preferred party more favourably than they would in the true absence of partisan ties. Conversely, those who identify with an incompatible party might evaluate that person's performance more harshly than they would otherwise.

We consider this matter by regressing satisfaction with the mayor's performance onto the two types of partisanship variables described above (those based on the partisan ties of voters alone as well as the Ford co-partisan and anti-partisan variables). The results of this analysis are found in table 1.2. Ideally, we would like to have a measure of Rob Ford's partisan ties, but since such data are unavailable, we use a question about Doug. We consider this substitution to be justified because, when asked how similar they believed Doug's policies to be to those of Rob, 86.2 per cent of TES respondents stated that the brothers' policies were all or mostly the same. Only 10.4 per cent of respondents stated that they did not know whether the two brothers' platforms were similar, and only 3.4 per cent were of the opinion that the platforms were either mostly or entirely different. Additionally, the Pearson correlation between the 101-point feeling thermometers of the two brothers is an impressive 0.90, and perceptions of the ideology of the two brothers were nearly identical.[13] We therefore believe that Doug Ford partisan compatibility is an acceptable proxy.

Our measure of satisfaction with Rob Ford's performance is the dependent variable, coded to range from 0 to 1, with five categories. Table 1.2 presents the results of four ordered logit models – two with only the partisanship variables and another two with controls added. We include controls for economic and social conservatism (which may predispose an individual to be satisfied with the outcome of Ford's conservative agenda) as well as the measures of sophistication discussed above. Note that with the exception of age, which is coded in years, all variables are coded from 0 to 1.

Table 1.2 provides compelling evidence of the biasing effect of partisanship on satisfaction. The models that contain only elector partisanship variables (2A and 2B) reveal strong evidence that Liberal, Conservative, and NDP partisanship is related to satisfaction with Rob Ford's performance. Model 2B, which includes a series of ideological and sophistication measures as controls, is particularly compelling. Liberal and NDP partisans were relatively unsatisfied with Ford's performance while Conservatives were satisfied (non-partisans were in the middle). Models 2C and 2D reveal that voters whose party affiliation is compatible with their perception of Doug Ford's partisanship had an increased likelihood of being satisfied with the performance of Rob Ford while those who saw Doug Ford as a partisan foe had an increased likelihood of being dissatisfied. Again, this pattern

Table 1.2
The determinants of satisfaction with mayoral performance

	Model 2A	Model 2B	Model 2C	Model 2D
Liberal Partisan	–0.74 (0.15)***	–0.32 (0.16)**		
Conservative Partisan	0.56 (0.15)***	0.78 (0.17)***		
NDP Partisan	–1.02 (0.20)***	–0.77 (0.21)***		
Green Partisan	–0.32 (0.26)	0.37 (0.27)		
Ford Anti-partisan			–0.76 (0.12)***	–0.43 (0.12)***
Ford Co-partisan			1.30 (0.14)***	1.42 (0.15)***
Economic conservatism		1.06 (0.28)***		1.02 (0.27)***
Social conservatism		1.32 (0.21)***		1.27 (0.22)***
Knowledge		–1.20 (0.17)***		–1.18 (0.17)***
Attentiveness		0.59 (0.26)**		0.53 (0.26)**
University education		–0.48 (0.10)***		–0.44 (0.10)***
Age		–0.02 (0.00)***		–0.02 (0.00)***
Cut 1	–0.79 (0.13)	–1.40 (0.28)	–0.53 (0.08)	–1.17 (0.25)
Cut 2	–0.19 (0.13)	–0.72 (0.27)	0.10 (0.08)	–0.47 (0.25)
Cut 3	0.42 (0.13)	–0.04 (0.27)	0.73 (0.08)	0.23 (0.25)
Cut 4	1.79 (0.15)	1.42 (0.27)	2.16 (0.11)	1.77 (0.25)
Pseudo R^2	0.0348	0.0838	0.0545	0.1013
N	1805	1805	1805	1805

Entries report regression coefficients and standard errors (in parentheses).

*: $p < 0.10$, **: $p < 0.05$, ***: $p < 0.01$

holds even after the addition of several controls that might influence either evaluations of candidates or perceptions of partisanship.[14]

Table 1.2 also suggests that the partisan compatibility variables better explain satisfaction levels than do the voter-only variables. The Pseudo R^2 values are higher in the partisan compatibility models – this value jumps from 0.0838 in Model 2B to 0.1013 in Model 2D. Additionally, the co-partisan variable in Model 2D has the greatest magnitude of any variable in all models in table 1.2. Such a finding indicates that sharing partisanship with Ford had a particularly large effect on retrospective evaluations. Thus, in non-partisan elections it is partisan compatibility, rather than simply the partisan ties of voters themselves, that matters most.[15]

To better understand the results of table 1.2 we present figure 1.1, which shows the predicted probability that anti-partisans and co-partisans will fall into each category of the satisfaction variable as well as the results for the whole sample. Note that the results are based on Model 2D and were calculated by manipulating values for the partisanship variables while leaving values for the control variables unchanged.

Figure 1.1 reveals substantially different patterns of satisfaction between Ford co- and anti-partisans and demonstrates that both of these groups differ from the sample as a whole. Voters who see Ford as a co-partisan have a probability of 0.62 of being either fairly or very satisfied, while the probability of being dissatisfied is a mere 0.24. Conversely, Ford anti-partisans are much more likely to view his performance negatively (probability = 0.65) than positively (0.22). The results of table 1.2 and figure 1.1 thus show an undeniable pattern: even in a non-partisan election, partisanship can bias retrospective evaluations.

Cross-Candidate Accountability

We next turn to consider whether these biased evaluations affected support for Doug Ford, even independently of attitudes toward the 2014 candidates themselves. We theorized above that cross-partisan ties could bias perceptions, but we also questioned whether cross-candidate ties had implications for accountability. Did voters hold Doug responsible for Rob's performance? Table 1.3 reports the results of a series of logistic regression vote choice models in which the dependent variable is a vote for Doug Ford (1) compared to any other

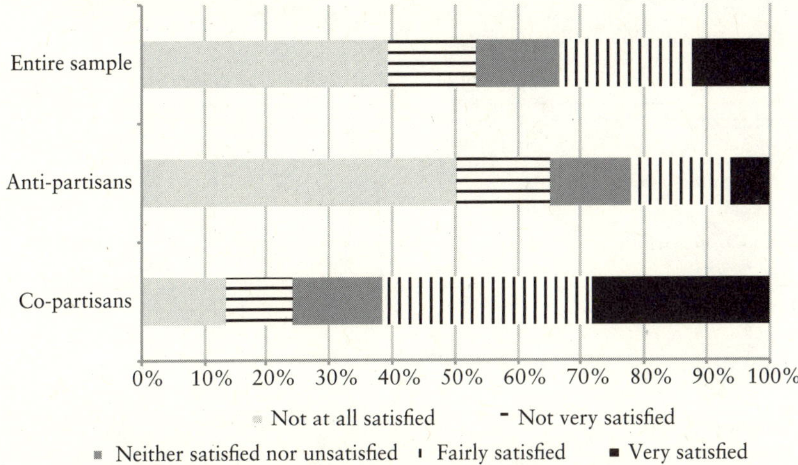

Figure 1.1   Satisfaction by partisan compatibility

candidate (0) and in which our primary independent variable of interest is satisfaction with Rob Ford's performance. To properly model the relationships that we expect to see, we interact the satisfaction variable with a "similarity" variable. This interaction allows us to determine whether the extent to which respondents saw the brothers as similar had an effect on whether they held Doug accountable for Rob's performance.[16] In other words, were those who considered Doug and Rob to belong to the same "party" more likely to vote on the basis of their evaluation of the incumbent? Note that the similarity variable is coded as a dummy for ease of interpretation – those who saw the brothers as very similar or mostly similar are compared to all other respondents.[17]

We also include in table 1.3 models without interactions to provide a baseline indication of the relationship between satisfaction with Rob and support for Doug. Furthermore, we specify models with and without controls to evaluate the robustness of any observed effects. In addition to the controls used in table 1.2, we also include candidate evaluations (this allows us to account for the possibility that candidate ratings may have complicated retrospective evaluations or attitudes about the similarity of the Ford brothers).

Put plainly, table 1.3 suggests that the relationship between satisfaction with Rob Ford and voting for Doug Ford does indeed depend on whether voters viewed the two brothers as sharing similar policy

Table 1.3
Satisfaction with Rob Ford and voting for Doug Ford

	Model 3A	Model 3B	Model 3C	Model 3D
Satisfaction with Rob Ford	5.98 (0.38)***	1.32 (0.99)	3.26 (0.67)***	−1.29 (1.64)
Ford brothers similar	0.77 (0.51)	−2.70 (0.75)***	0.29 (0.57)	−3.01 (1.02)***
Satisfaction X similar		5.14 (1.07)***		5.17 (1.64)***
Rating of Doug Ford			4.27 (0.72)***	4.24 (0.72)***
Rating of John Tory			−3.28 (0.56)***	−3.36 (0.58)***
Rating of Olivia Chow			−1.01 (0.48)**	−0.91 (0.47)*
Economic conservatism			−0.55 (0.59)	−0.60 (0.58)
Social conservatism			0.26 (0.51)	0.34 (0.53)
Knowledge			0.51 (0.41)	0.61 (0.39)
Attentiveness			−1.67 (0.66)**	−1.79 (0.71)**
University education			0.00 (0.24)	0.01 (0.24)
Age			0.01 (0.01)	0.14 (0.01)
Constant	−5.06 (0.61)***	−1.92 (0.69)***	−2.67 (0.97)***	0.21 (1.21)
Pseudo R^2	0.4524	0.4669	0.5893	0.5999
N	1469			

Entries report regression coefficients and standard errors (in parentheses).

*: $p < 0.10$, **: $p < 0.05$, ***: $p < 0.01$

ideas. This finding is robust to the addition of several control variables. In the models without the interaction, satisfaction with Rob is positively related to support for Doug (the "similarity" variable is insignificant on its own, but this is unsurprising, since we have no theoretical reason to expect this variable to drive vote choice on its own). The introduction of the interaction term shows, however, just how important the "similarity" variable is to the relationship between satisfaction and vote choice. The positive and significant interaction effects in Models 3B and 3D reveal that voters who were satisfied with Rob's performance were more likely to vote for Doug if they believed the policies of the brothers were similar. In other words, if voters thought the two brothers belonged to the same political "party," the likelihood of voting for Doug was positively correlated with retrospective evaluations of Rob. This is what one would expect if this were a partisan election – the virtues of the previous administration would be reflected in support for a future administration of the same political stripe.

As with table 1.2, the raw logistic regression results in table 1.3 reveal little more than direction and statistical significance, so we present figure 1.2, which displays the vote choice/satisfaction/similarity relationship graphically. Values in the figure represent the predicted probability of voting for Doug Ford for each value of the satisfaction variable (values are determined through post-estimation, based on Model 3D, where the variables of interest are manipulated and controls are left unchanged). Each line represents a value for the *similarity* variable. Such a figure provides some context to the interactive relationship observed in table 1.3. Note that the predicted probability of supporting Ford for the sample as a whole is 0.23.

Figure 1.2 confirms that among voters who viewed the policies of the brothers as similar, satisfaction with Rob was positively associated with support for Doug. It also reveals the magnitude of this effect: very satisfied voters have a predicted probability of 0.40 of voting for Ford, while this value is only 0.07 for the "not at all satisfied" category. Note that while the slope of the "not similar" line is negative, it is not significantly different from zero, suggesting that satisfaction is not related to vote choice among voters who do not see the Ford brothers as similar to one another. This is what we would expect if candidates were not tied to one another, since there is no reason for a voter to consider the performance of the previous administration if they perceive no ties with current candidates.

The key takeaway message from figure 1.2 is that there is a statistically significant difference between the two lines. For those voters who viewed Doug Ford as a pseudo-incumbent, satisfaction works very much as one would expect in a partisan election – it is positively associated with incumbent support. In this technically non-partisan election, therefore, many voters held Doug accountable for the actions of his brother.

DISCUSSION AND CONCLUSION

In theory, politicians can only be held accountable for their actions if they have previously held power. We have shown here, however,

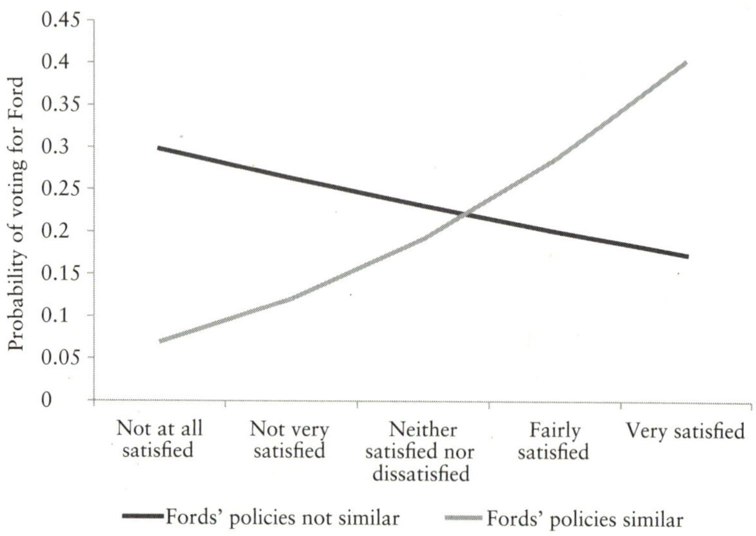

Figure 1.2 Probability of voting for Doug Ford by satisfaction and perceived similarities between the Ford brothers

that this is not always the case in practice. Partisanship and party cues can play an important role in officially non-partisan contests, depending on the perception of partisan ties by voters. Cross-party and cross-candidate ties can exist in officially non-partisan settings that lack an incumbent. When voters associate candidates with parties, perceptions can bias evaluations of the performance of politicians. These evaluations can, in turn, influence vote choice if links are perceived between candidates. Partisan ties, while adding a degree of accountability to non-partisan elections, can also distort it by introducing (potentially undeserved) bias.

This chapter has addressed the two stages of electoral accountability. First, voters must make an assessment of the incumbent's past performance. Second, voters must decide whether or not to factor this information into their vote choice. Toronto Election Study data reveal that even in a non-partisan election, partisanship can play a role in both of these components of electoral accountability. Partisan perceptions coloured evaluations of Rob Ford's performance, and quasi-partisan, or dynastic, links between Rob and Doug Ford moderated the relationship between evaluations of satisfaction and vote choice.

In terms of non-partisan elections more generally, the electorate's seeming desire to use party ties (even quasi-party ones) to structure their choices calls into question whether any election can be truly non-partisan. Our findings indicate clearly that many voters have a tendency to employ shortcuts when formulating decisions in non-partisan municipal contests, even if such shortcuts provide little benefit in terms of accountability. Partisanship and familial associations are two such shortcuts, although gender and ethnic affinity voting has also been observed in the 2014 Toronto mayoral contest, suggesting that many voters fall back on socio-demographic cues when making their decisions (Bird et al. 2016). Furthermore, despite the fact that Canadian mayors have little to no influence over a city's economy, voters have nevertheless been found to hold incumbents accountable for economic performance (Cutler and Matthews 2005; Anderson et al. 2017). To be clear, we do not seek to pass judgment about the normative implications of the reliance on such cues. However, we can conclude that in the absence of an incumbent candidate, none of these shortcuts advance the accountability function of elections. Indeed, our findings suggest that incumbents who decide not to seek re-election are given the choice of either remaining responsive to voters in order to create positive retrospective evaluations or of "poisoning the well" for associated politicians that succeed them. Politicians should therefore be mindful of the fact that non-partisanship does not insulate future candidates from punishment for previous behaviours. After all, be it right or wrong, Doug Ford was not judged solely on the basis of his own merits or lack thereof.

APPENDIX:
TORONTO ELECTION STUDY SURVEY QUESTIONS

SURVEY QUALITY CONTROL QUESTION: To ensure that your browser is downloading the content of this survey, please select the number four below: *One, Two, Three, Four, Five, Don't know.*

FEELING THERMOMETERS: How do you feel about (Doug Ford, Olivia Chow, John Tory, Rob Ford)? Use a scale from 0 to 100, where zero means you really dislike the candidate and one hundred means you really like the candidate. *0–100.*

IDEOLOGICAL PLACEMENT OF CANDIDATES: On a scale from 0 to 10, where 0 means left and 10 means right, where would you place (Doug Ford, Olivia Chow, John Tory, Rob Ford)?

SIMILARITY OF DOUG AND ROB FORD: In your opinion, how similar are Doug Ford's politics to those of his brother Rob? *All the same, Mostly the same, Mostly different, All different, Don't know.*

SATISFACTION WITH INCUMBENT: How satisfied are you with the performance of the current mayor? *Not at all satisfied, Not very satisfied, Neither satisfied nor unsatisfied, Fairly satisfied, Very satisfied, Don't know.*

CANDIDATE PARTY ASSOCIATION: Which political party, if any, would you associate with (Doug Ford/Olivia Chow/John Tory)? *None, Conservative Party of Canada, Green Party of Canada, Liberal Party of Canada, New Democratic Party of Canada, Other federal party, Green Party of Ontario, Ontario Liberal Party, New Democratic Party of Ontario, Progressive Conservative Party of Ontario, Other provincial party, Don't know.*

PARTISANSHIP: In federal politics, do you usually think of yourself as a: *Liberal, Conservative, NDP, Green, Other, None of the above, Don't know.* How strongly do you associate with [answer to question above] party? *Very strongly, Fairly strongly, Not very strongly, Don't know.*

ECONOMIC CONSERVATISM INDEX: Government should leave it entirely up to the private sector to create jobs (*Strongly agree, Agree, Disagree, Strongly disagree, Don't know*). Government should see to it that everyone has a decent standard of living (*Strongly agree, Agree, Disagree, Strongly disagree, Don't know*).

SOCIAL CONSERVATISM INDEX: How do you feel about each of the following groups? Please use the sliders to indicate your feelings on a scale from 0 to 100, where zero means you REALLY DISLIKE the group and one hundred means you REALLY LIKE the group. Racial minorities *(0–100)*, Feminists *(0–100)*, Gays and lesbians *(0–100)*.

KNOWLEDGE: Do you know the name of the mayor of Toronto prior to Rob Ford? Do you know the name of the Governor General of Canada? Do you know the name of the Finance Minister of Canada? Do you know the name of the leader of the New Democratic Party of Ontario?

ATTENTIVENESS: How much attention did you pay to the mayoral election campaign? *0–100.*

UNIVERSITY EDUCATION: What is the highest level of education that you have completed?

AGE: In what year were you born?

NOTES

1 There are some notable exceptions. In Vancouver, well-established municipal parties exist, but they differ from those at the provincial and federal levels. In many cities in Quebec, elections are contested by a mixture of independent candidates and parties, as well as "équipes" (slates of candidates that form around specific mayoral candidates).

2 Our focus in this chapter is on partisan biases, but ideology may also function as a related shortcut for voters. If someone identifies as left-wing and a candidate is perceived to be right-wing, then evaluations of that candidate may be coloured by a general preference for policies on the other side of the ideological spectrum. However, evaluating a candidate on the basis of their ideology is distinct from partisan perceptions. Partisan ties may indicate ideology, but the reverse is not necessarily true. In addition, sharing an ideology may not create the same sort of tie between candidates and governments as a party does. We do not consider ideological biases here, but it is a subject worthy of future consideration.

3 This situation is most likely in Ontario, where the federal and provincial party systems correspond with one another. Not only are the competitive parties the same at both levels, but they are currently ranked in the same order in both legislatures. As of the 2015 election, at the federal level the Liberals have 80 seats in Ontario, compared to 33 for the Conservative Party and 8 for the NDP. In the provincial legislature (reflecting the outcome of the 2014 election), the Liberals hold 58 seats, the PC Party 28, and the NDP 21. Furthermore, the parties themselves are also linked. The NDP is "fully integrated" in that joining the provincial NDP automatically makes one a member of the federal wing of the party. Although the Liberal and (Progressive) Conservative parties lack this formal link, they do engage in extensive resource- and expertise-sharing during election time (Esselment 2010).

4 For example, Jean Charest left the federal Progressive Conservatives to lead the Liberal Party of Quebec, and former NDP premier of Ontario Bob Rae joined the federal Liberal Party. There are also many instances of politicians shifting to the municipal level from partisan politics at the federal or provincial level. For example, the current mayor of Brampton (Linda Jeffrey) is a former Ontario member of provincial Parliament, and the mayor of Mississauga (Bonnie Crombie) served in both the provincial and federal legislatures before taking municipal office.

5 At the federal level, the country's current prime minister, Justin Trudeau, is the son of one of the country's longest-serving prime ministers, Pierre Trudeau. In Toronto in 2014, in addition to Doug Ford replacing Rob

Ford on the mayoral ticket, Michael Ford (a nephew of the Ford brothers) was going to run for Toronto City Council in Ward 2, Doug's old seat, only to be replaced by Rob Ford after he dropped out of the mayoral race. Mike Layton, son of former councillor and former leader of the federal NDP, Jack Layton, is also a high-profile councillor from Ward 19.

6 As a quality control measure, the TES included a question to ensure that respondents were answering questions seriously (respondents were reimbursed for their participation in the TES). The 3.1 per cent of respondents who "failed" this question are excluded from our analysis.

7 Appendix 1 contains the wording of all survey questions used in this chapter's analysis.

8 Note that we use the perceptions of individual respondents rather than an aggregate sample estimate of candidate partisanship. Furthermore, while the TES contains measures of respondent partisanship from both the federal and provincial levels, the analyses in this chapter make use of federal-level responses. The party systems are the same at the two levels of government and, unsurprisingly, federal and provincial partisanship are closely correlated. The substantive conclusions of all analyses below remain unchanged if provincial partisanship is used instead.

9 For this analysis we are aided by the non-partisan nature of the election. In a partisan contest, evaluations of the incumbent's performance might conceivably influence the partisan leanings of respondents, meaning that an analysis of this nature would be subject to concerns over endogeneity and that causal conclusions would be difficult to make. In this case, however, since the mayor of Toronto is not technically associated with a party (regardless of voter perception), we expect no such effect to be present; in other words, we cannot reasonably expect Rob Ford's performance to influence federal-level partisanship. However, Conservative voters may see his ties to the party as a cue that he is most like them and deserves their support. Thus, in the case of the 2014 Toronto election, we can be confident that the causal relationship between partisanship and satisfaction with the mayor is unidirectional.

10 Both Tory and Ford were viewed as "Conservatives" by many electors. If perceived partisan ties affect vote choice, the fact that there were two Conservatives in the contest may complicate voter calculus. Such a contention lies, however, outside the purview of this study. Rather than determining the direct effect of Conservative partisanship upon vote choice, we focus upon how such partisan attitudes affect retrospective evaluations of Rob Ford.

11 A total of 1.3 per cent of respondents reported being partisans of an "other" party. These individuals were dropped from subsequent analyses because

they can neither be included in the partisan compatibility measure (since we do not know which party they are referring to) nor be grouped together as supporters of a single party. The respondents who associated Ford with an "other" party were dropped for similar reasons.

12 An analysis not shown (but available from the authors) reveals that these four factors are positively associated with linking Chow and Tory to the NDP and Conservatives, respectively. The relationships are all significant at $p < 0.05$ in both bivariate and multivariate comparisons.

13 TES respondents were also asked to place the brothers on a left–right (0–10) ideological scale. Average values for Doug and Rob were 7.46 and 7.45, respectively. In contrast, Chow was assigned a score of 2.9 and Tory a value of 7.5.

14 As table 1.1 reveals, many TES respondents associated both Ford and Tory with the Conservative Party (there were also some respondents who associated Ford and Chow with the same party). To test for the possibility that grouping such respondents together as Ford co- or anti-partisans may have caused us to underestimate the effects of the partisanship variables in Models 2C and 2D, we ran another model (results not shown but available from the authors) that included dummy variables for respondents who were co-partisans with multiple candidates. The model revealed no significant effects for the new variables, and the effects observed for the co- and anti-partisanship variables were the same as those in Model 2D.

15 TES data provide further evidence of the importance of partisan compatibility in this non-partisan race. Among NDP partisans, 55.9 per cent of those who identified Chow with the NDP supported her. Only 33.3 per cent of NDP partisans who did not recognize her as an NDP member voted for her. Similarly, 66.2 per cent of Conservative partisans who recognized Tory as a Conservative supported him compared to only 34.2 per cent of those who did not. These numbers can be compared to values for Ford – 46.7 per cent of Conservative partisans who considered Ford to be a Conservative voted for him, while only 27.9 per cent of those who did not see him as a Conservative did the same. Party ties were more evident for Chow and Tory, and they provided a clear advantage among those who perceived them as co-partisans. Among those who did not perceive them that way, however, vote support was much lower. This additional piece of evidence confirms that it is important to understand non-partisan elections as they are really perceived by voters.

16 It is conceivable that, given the controversial nature of his brother, some voters who liked Doug may have dissociated the two brothers in their

minds in order to justify supporting Doug. If such an effect is present, it could introduce noise into the analysis below (though we doubt that it would bias the observed relationship between satisfaction and support for Doug). In fact, however, we find no evidence of such an effect. We find that attitudes toward Doug Ford (as measured through a 101-point feeling thermometer) are statistically the same among TES respondents who see the brothers as the same and those who see them as different (N = 2,680).

17 In this dummy, the "don't know" category is grouped with those individuals who saw the brothers as very or mostly different. This is due to reasons pertaining to sample size (given that so few respondents saw the brothers as different) as well as to theoretical issues. Neither group can be expected to hold Doug responsible for the actions of Rob and, if anything, they are less likely to hold him accountable than those individuals who view the brothers similarly. Note that the substantive conclusions of this analysis remain unchanged if an ordinal "similarity" variable is used instead of a dummy.

REFERENCES

Anderson, Cameron D., and R. Michael McGregor. 2014. "Economic Attitudes and Political Identities Evidence from Canada." *International Journal of Public Opinion Research* 27(3): 361–82.

Anderson, Cameron D., R. Michael McGregor, Aaron A. Moore, and Laura B. Stephenson. 2017. "Economic Voting and Multilevel Governance: The Case of Toronto." *Urban Affairs Review* 53(1): 71–101.

Asako, Yasushi, Takeshi Iida, Tetsuya Matsubayashi, and Michiko Ueda. 2015. "Dynastic Politicians: Theory and Evidence from Japan." *Japanese Journal of Political Science* 16(1): 5–32.

Bird, Karen, Samantha Jackson, R. Michael McGregor, Aaron A. Moore, and Laura B. Stephenson. 2016. "Sex (and Ethnicity) in the City: Affinity Voting in the 2014 Toronto Mayoral Election." *Canadian Journal of Political Science* 49(2): 359–83.

Bohlken, Anjali, and Kanchan Chandra. 2012. "Dynastic Politics and Party Organizations: Why Family Ties Improve Electoral Performance in India." Unpublished manuscript.

Bonneau, Chris W., and Damon M. Cann. 2015. "Party Identification and Vote Choice in Partisan and Nonpartisan Elections." *Political Behavior* 37(1): 43–66.

Camp, Roderic A. 1995. *Political Recruitment across Two Centuries: Mexico, 1884–1991.* Austin: University of Texas Press.

Campbell, Angus, Philip E. Converse, Warren E. Miller, and Donald E. Stokes. 1960. *The American Voter.* New York: John Wiley & Sons.

Cassette, Aurélie, Etienne Farvaque, and Jérôme Hericourt. 2013. "Two-Round Elections, One Round Determinants? Evidence from the French Municipal Elections." *Public Choice* 156(3): 563–91.

Clarke, Harold D., Allan Kornberg, and Thomas J. Scotto. 2009. *Making Political Choices: Canada and the United States*. Toronto: University of Toronto Press.

Clarke, Harold D., and Marianne C. Stewart. 1987. "Partisan Inconsistency and Partisan Change in Federal States: The Case of Canada." *American Journal of Political Science* 31(2): 383–407.

Cutler, Fred, and J. Scott Matthews. 2005. "The Challenge of Municipal Voting: Vancouver 2002." *Canadian Journal of Political Science* 38(2): 359–82.

Dalton, Russell J. 2002. *Citizen Politics*. 3rd ed. New York: Chatham House Publishers of Seven Bridges Press, LLC.

Doyle, David Thomas, Eoin O'Malley, Gemma McNulty, and Akisato Suzuki. 2015. "Democratic Dynasties: Explaining Their Prevalence in Modern Democracies." Available at *Social Science Research Network*: http://dx.doi.org/10.2139/ssrn.2556830.

Duch, Raymond M., Harvey D. Palmer, and Christopher J. Anderson. 2000. "Heterogeneity in Perceptions of National Economic Conditions." *American Journal of Political Science* 44(4): 635–52.

Esselment, Anna L. 2010. "Fighting Elections: Cross-Level Political Party Integration in Ontario." *Canadian Journal of Political Science* 43(4): 871–92.

Feinstein, Brian D. 2010. "The Dynasty Advantage: Family Ties in Congressional Elections." *Legislative Studies Quarterly* 35(4): 571–98.

Fiorina, Morris P. 1981. *Retrospective Voting in American National Elections*. New Haven, CT: Yale University Press.

Heath, Anthony, Iain McLean, Bridget Taylor, and John Curtice. 1999. "Between First and Second Order: A Comparison of Voting Behaviour in European and Local Elections in Britain." *European Journal of Political Research* 35(3): 389–414.

Hui, Ann, Elizabeth Church, and Fred Lum. 2014. "Rob Ford Drops out of Mayoral Race, Doug Ford Running in His Place." *The Globe and Mail*, 12 September.

Key, V.O., Jr. 1966. *The Responsible Electorate: Rationality in Presidential Voting, 1936–1960*. Cambridge, MA: The Belknap Press of Harvard University Press.

Lau, Richard R., and David P. Redlawsk. 1997. "Voting Correctly." *The American Political Science Review* 91(3): 585–98.

McGregor, R. Michael, Aaron A. Moore, and Laura B. Stephenson. 2016. "Political Attitudes and Behaviour in a Non-partisan Environment: Toronto 2014." *Canadian Journal of Political Science* 49(2): 311–33.

Martins, Rodrigo, and Francisco José Veiga. 2013. "Economic Voting in Portuguese Municipal Elections." *Public Choice* 155(3): 317–34.

Mendoza, Ronald U., Edsel L. Beja, Jr., Victor S. Venida, and David B. Yap. 2012. "Inequality in Democracy: Insights from an Empirical Analysis of Political Dynasties in the 15th Philippine Congress." *Philippine Political Science Journal* 33(2): 132–45.

Schaffner, Brian F., and Matthew J. Streb. 2002. "The Partisan Heuristic in Low-Information Elections." *Public Opinion Quarterly* 66(4): 559–81.

Sproule-Jones, Mark. 2011. "Political Parties at the Local Level of Government." In *Canadian Parties in Transition*, edited by Alain-G. Gagnon and A. Brian Tanguay, 3rd ed., 241–54. Toronto: University of Toronto Press.

Squire, Peverill, and Eric R.A.N. Smith. 1988. "The Effect of Partisan Information on Voters in Nonpartisan Elections." *The Journal of Politics* 50(1): 169–79.

Stewart, Marianne C., and Harold D. Clarke. 1998. "The Dynamics of Party Identification in Federal Systems: The Canadian Case." *American Journal of Political Science* 42(1): 97–116.

Taniguchi, Naoko. 2008. "Diet Members and Seat Inheritance." In *Democratic Reform in Japan: Assessing the Impact*, edited by Sherry Martin and Gill Steel, 65–80. Boulder, CO: Lynne Reinner.

Wallace, Kenyon. 2011. "Rob Ford Barbecue Has Surprise Guest: 'Fishing Partner' Stephen Harper." *Toronto Star*, 3 August 2011.

2

Accountability without Parties?
Political Business Cycle
and the Re-election of Incumbents

Jérôme Couture and Sandra Breux

INTRODUCTION

According to the traditional democratic theory, responsiveness and political accountability are the two main criteria for examining the implementation of voter preferences by elected officials (Gerstlé 2003). For example, at election time voters either reward or punish elected officials on the basis of accountability understood as the degree to which their performance has met their expectations. In that sense, elections figure as the main mechanism for negotiating or expressing accountability. The partisan model of political competition inspired by the work of Downs (1957) is commonly regarded as useful for understanding this mechanism. In this context, the electoral supply depends on the presence of political parties. Candidates for elected office are representatives of a party and are selected through procedures such as open primaries and nominations from party members or by being put on lists that are submitted directly to the voters.

For the partisan model to work at the local level, elections taking place there should be in line with those of the other levels of government. This leads to a so-called "nationalization" of local elections whereby the national parties present candidates for municipal elections (Parodi 2004). This type of election then features parties or coalitions whose positions on the left–right spectrum are relatively well known to the voters. Yet such a direct link between the electoral supply at the municipal level and those of other levels of government does not exist in Canada.

Indeed, the Canadian municipal electoral supply consists mainly of independent candidates. Thus, although municipal political parties do exist, their weight and presence is negligible. Moreover, those parties do not have an affiliation with the parties from other levels of government. Instead, they express a certain apolitical attitude with regard to the political divisions at higher levels (Bherer and Breux 2012). Consequently, it is not possible for voters at such municipal elections to "punish" the higher levels of government through their vote, as is suggested, for example, by the referendum voting model (Remmer and Gélineau 2003). "[E]ven in the absence of parties, there is evidence of variation in policies in areas that could be important sources of partisan division, including immigration and multicultural-ism and environmental policies. Furthermore, significant variation in municipal responsiveness to immigrants also exists within a city region. This variation suggests that partisanship (and, more funda-mentally, politics) might not be irrelevant in all policy area and politi-cal context" (Good 2017, 441). Canadian municipal elections therefore serve more as an opportunity for voters to punish or reward the elected officials directly, whether these officials are representatives of a local political party or not. In that sense, the municipal electoral supply in Canada is tailored to each single municipality more than to national political parties. Moreover, the municipal electoral supply is tailored to each province. For example, the situation in the province of Quebec differs from that in the other Canadian provinces in that it is the only one to have an electoral law that governs the formation of political parties (Act Respecting Elections and Referendums in Municipalities, 1978). In Quebec, which has 1,096 municipalities, there were only 292 registered political parties in the 2009 municipal elections.[1] Moreover, only 97 cities have a real partisan system – in other words, elections with at least two contesting parties, including the one of the incumbent mayor. During the municipal elections of 2013, there were only 307 political parties registered and 116 munici-palities with a true party-based system. These political parties have no ideological ties with their associates at higher levels of government. They are often named after the leader or the municipality, making it difficult to discern their position on the political spectrum.

Thus, the electoral supply in most Quebec cities was not based on a partisan system, although the number of political parties is higher in bigger cities. Still, there was no partisan system in the 2009 elections of five out of the ten biggest cities and three in the 2013 election.[2] Thus, the partisan model is largely inconsistent with the electoral supply in Quebec's municipalities. Further, a substantial number of elections in Quebec are determined by acclamation.[3] Indeed, in the 2009 elections, half of the mayors were elected without opposition and 47 per cent in 2013. Of those mayors, 80 per cent were incumbents in 2009 and 78 per cent in 2013. Only 24 per cent of incumbent mayors did not seek re-election in 2009 and 2013.

Moreover, in Canada mayoral elections are held by universal suffrage, meaning that municipal politics is governed by a presidential type of system yet without a limit on the mandate commonly found in this type of regime. In Quebec municipalities, the large majority of elections for the office of mayor include incumbents in the running.[4] Voters can then directly punish or reward their head of government, which amounts to a personalization of politics. In such a context, when there are political parties, candidates are less able to ride on the popularity of their political team. Accountability is individual, not collective, unlike the parliamentary system in which voters are more likely to punish the ruling party (Ferejohn 1999).

INCUMBENT ADVANTAGE

Elmendorf and Schleicher (2012) point to the repercussions that the absence of purely local political parties in the United States has on the electoral dynamics there. For one, in such a context the performance of local elected officials is little taken into consideration by voters. Moreover, the incumbents have a distinct advantage over the challengers, which is then seen to result in the formation of political monopolies (Trounstine 2008). A similar finding has been made for Canada, where incumbents have considerable leverage. There, this uneven playing field is in fact one of the main drivers for the creation of municipal political parties, which are seen as a means of counterbalancing the power of the incumbent mayors (Mévellec 2011).

Incumbents enjoy greater recognition by the public, have more sophisticated campaigns, and can gain access to more funding for their election campaigns (Breux, Couture, and Bherer 2014). All this gives them an advantage in elections. However, Trounstine (2011) observes that these benefits of the incumbent carry less weight at the local level, where media visibility is not as critical and election campaigns not as professionalized. Still, incumbents at the municipal level do stand to gain from their status of being incumbent (Krebs 1998), albeit for reasons that lie elsewhere.

Some researchers attribute this to a political selection effect (Jacobson and Kernell 1981) whereby the winning candidate is seen to win an election, or subsequent elections, because of qualities he or she had already demonstrated prior to his or her first election (Erikson and Wright 1980). Yet other researchers view the mere fact of being in office as the main determinant of the maintenance of superiority. According to Oliver and Ha (2007), when voters are less informed about their options, they tend to vote for the incumbent. It could be argued that familiarity with the name of the incumbent, although this hardly qualifies as information as such, plays in favour of the incumbent being re-elected.

Another explanation of the advantages enjoyed by incumbents is related to their performance. Using an indicator of the performance of municipalities as assessed by the citizens of 139 British municipalities during local elections in 2001 and 2007, Boyne et al. (2009) show that incumbents with a good performance do not necessarily benefit from it. However, the probability of being re-elected is greatly reduced when the performance is considered weak and becomes practically zero when considered poor.

Here, a retrospective evaluation of government performance is considered as reducing the need for voters to be politically informed (Key 1966; Fiorina 1981). This idea has been promulgated in particular with the notion of the so-called economic vote (Kramer 1971; Lewis-Beck 1990) whereby voters are seen to reward governments when the economy is doing well and to punish them when it is on a downward slide. However, empirical results tend to invalidate this proposition, given that there are limits to the degree to which governments can manipulate the economy in favour of their re-election (Alesina, Roubini, and Cohen 1999). Moreover, economic voting is hardly relevant for local elections, since municipal governments do not have the instruments to influence macroeconomic indicators (Foucault and François 2005).

Instead, for this level of government the theory of the political business cycle (Nordhaus 1975; Tufte 1978; Rogoff and Sibert 1988; Rogoff 1990), which posits that a link exists between changes in spending or taxation and the re-election of an incumbent, is more appropriate (Mouritzen 1989; Lago-Peñas and Lago-Peñas 2008;

Foremny and Riedel 2014). A number of studies on the municipal level have shown a link between the political business cycle and the re-election of local governments. More specifically, a change in spending before elections was shown to positively correlate with the re-election of the incumbent municipal government (Franco et al. 2014; Sakurai and Menezes-Filho 2008; Drazen and Eslava 2010; Aidt, Veiga, and Veiga 2011; Sedmihradskà, Kubik, and Hass 2011; Balaguer-Coll et al. 2015).

Furthermore, Persson and Tabelini (2003) hold that a decrease in taxes is an effective tool for achieving a quick and direct impact on a large portion of the electorate. In fact, examining the public accounts of sixty democracies over a period of nearly forty years, they show that this type of behaviour by incumbents is a universal phenomenon. Moreover, Sakurai and Menezes-Filho (2008) show that a change in taxes before elections was negatively correlated with the re-election of incumbents in Brazilian municipalities. However, all of these results linking the performance of local governments with their re-election concern partisan municipal contexts in which national parties present candidates for local elections.

For the electoral dynamics in Quebec municipalities, the issue is that of arriving at a theoretical understanding of accountability in the absence of political parties. In this regard, another model – the citizen-candidate model (Osborne and Slivinski 1996; Besley and Coate 1997) – allows us to identify the effect of the absence of political parties on the responsiveness of elected officials to citizens' preferences. The model suggests that this political dynamic is not as dysfunctional as one might think and that it instead merely differs from the logic of partisan politics.

THE CITIZEN-CANDIDATE MODEL

To examine this context in which the electoral supply does not depend on the presence of political parties, Osborne and Slivinski (1996) propose a theoretical model of the citizen-candidate. In this model, every citizen is a potential candidate. The number of candidates running for an election in such a context is thus endogenous to the electorate rather than being determined by the need for political parties to develop a political platform oriented toward the preferences of the median voter. These electoral dynamics are played out in two phases. First, each individual citizen-candidate must decide whether

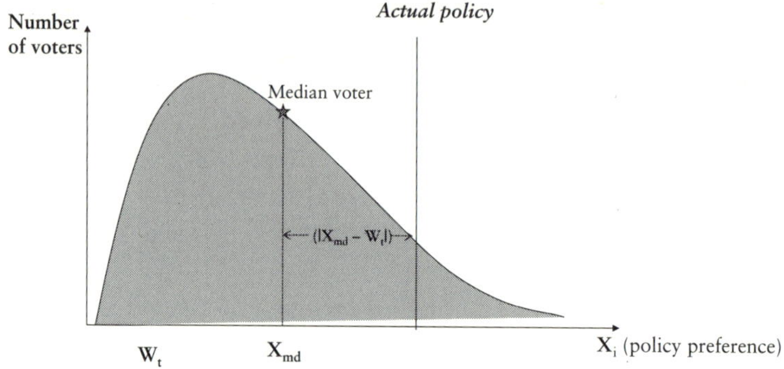

Figure 2.1 The citizen-candidate model

they wish to run for election. Then, following a race among candidates, a "winner takes all" takes office. A citizen can be expected to run for election if the benefits outweigh these costs.

Figure 2.1 illustrates this model by focusing on the preferences of the median citizen (X_{md}). First, every citizen-candidate has a preference (X_i) on a unidimensional axis. The position of each citizen-candidate is known by all the others; it is public information. The benefits to be drawn by each citizen-candidate are based on the distance between his or her position on the axis (X_i) and the policy currently implemented on that axis (W_t). Consequently, the benefits for each citizen-candidate is measured as the absolute value of the difference between his or her position and the position of the current political agenda ($| X_i - W_t |$).

The winner of the election implements his or her preferences and receives the benefits in return ($| Xi - Wt |$). In addition, citizens who decide to run for an election must pay an entry cost (C) whereby the model distinguishes between low entry costs and high entry costs. Thus, each citizen-candidate calculates the probability (p) of winning the election by assessing his or her position on the axis relative to those of other citizen-candidates. He or she will run for election if the expected benefits outweigh the costs of entry into the electoral game ($p * B > C$).

Based on these factors, Osborne and Slivinski (1996) predict the number of candidates for an election. The model predicts that in the presence of high entry costs, there will be only one candidate in the running. As entry costs fall, the model predicts an equilibrium between two candidates. Using an experimental research design, Cadigan (2005) confirms the predictions of the model of Osborne and Slivinski (1996). Other versions of the citizen-candidate model have also been proposed. Of these, the most often cited version is the one by Besley and Coate (1997), which predicts the exact same equilibria as Osborne and Slivinski, although starting from a space of multidimensional preferences. The citizen-candidate model aligns quite well with the municipal electoral dynamics in Quebec and is particularly relevant when studying non-partisan politics. Moreover, although widely cited in the literature, the citizen-candidate model has never been the object of an empirical test in a natural environment.

The only existing empirical studies are based on experimental designs. The reasons for this research gap are simple. One, few electoral contexts exhibit an electoral supply that is endogenous to the electorate. This aspect becomes irrelevant here, since such a theoretical context does in fact exist in Quebec municipalities, where political parties are virtually absent from the electoral process and do not fully determine the electoral supply. In addition, in Quebec the rules on the eligibility of candidates are similar to those concerning the endogeneity of the electorate.[5] A further reason is that in order to test the model, we must know the distribution of the preferences of citizens on the axis (X_i). This is difficult to ascertain outside the laboratory setting.[6] However, we propose two changes to the citizen-candidate model that will allow us to get around this last problem.

Our new version of the citizen-candidate model is illustrated in figure 2.2. The first modification consists of assuming that the incumbent is not an ordinary citizen. It is he or she who implements the actual policy (W_t). According to the original model, the utility the incumbent can draw from running for an election is always zero. Indeed, his or her preferences (X_i) are exactly aligned with the policy. As a result, incumbents are not expected to run for election if the calculation is based on a marginal utility measured between citizen preferences and the actual policy. By definition, this utility is always equal to zero for the incumbent $(\mid X_i - W_t \mid = 0)$. Yet such a prediction is wholly inconsistent with reality, since many incumbents run for re-election (Clingermayer and Feiock 1993; Trounstine 2008; 2011). As in the moral hazard models of elections, originating with Barro (1973) and Ferejohn (1986), the desire to be re-elected in the future motivates politicians to exert effort while in office. As a result, the

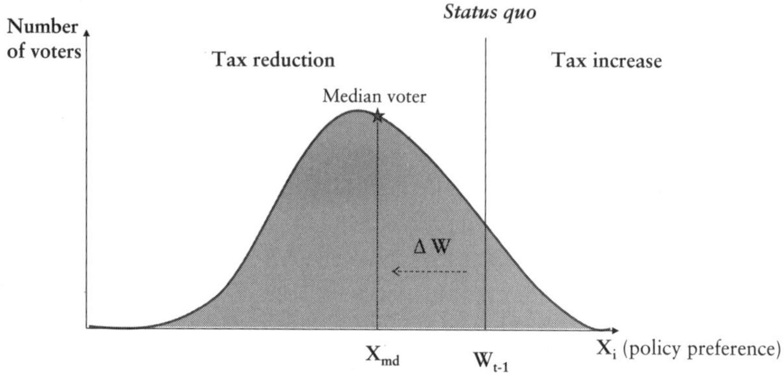

Figure 2.2 The new citizen-candidate model and a change in the tax rate

benefits that incumbents draw come more from their re-election than from the implemented policy.

The second modification is the assumption that the policy (W) is a variable that the incumbent controls. In a first phase, the incumbent can use the policy to decrease the benefits that other citizen-candidates could derive from running for election. Specifically, by changing the actual policy (ΔW or ($W_t - W_{t-1}$)), the incumbent provides benefits to citizens and at the same time decreases the utility he or she might have from running for election. To achieve the withdrawal of the most threatening candidates for re-election, he or she must approximate the position of the largest number of voters on the axis of preferences (X_i). For example, the incumbent may vary spending or the tax rate with the nearing of an election and in this way align with the preferences of the median citizen. The incumbent will thus promote the withdrawal of the greatest number of potential candidates from the race (if $|\Delta W| > |X_i - W_t|$).

In a second phase, the incumbent, still facing political competition, can also draw electoral benefits from a change in the actual policy (ΔW). To obtain the benefit, this change must accommodate the median voter ($X_{md} \approx W_t$). As a result, the position of the political opponent on the axis of preferences (X_i) is equal to or farther away from the median voter than that of the incumbent (W_t). Similar to a retrospective vote, the median voter supports the incumbent who implemented the preferred policy rather than a challenger whose ability to lead is unknown. Despite its apparent complexity, our model is actually quite intuitive. It is often argued that weak competition during local elections stems from the level of satisfaction that citizens feel toward incumbents. In fact, this is the underlying principle of our model. Our model is also consistent with the literature regarding factors that explain why an individual decides to run as a candidate during an election. With the theory of nascent political ambition, Fox and Lawless (2004) established a model that allows for a better understanding of the process leading to an individual's decision to become a candidate. Based on this theoretical framework, certain researchers have shown that the decision to run stems from the desire to implement changes with regard to specific policies (Crowder-Meyer, Kushner Gadarian, and Trounstine 2015). By comparing the gap between a citizen's position regarding a given policy and the policy itself, the citizen-candidate model allows for a precise formulation of the desire for change. This theoretical proposition of the citizen-candidate model is therefore compatible with the theory of the political business cycle (Rogoff and Sibert 1988; Rogoff 1990), which predicts the same type of responsiveness to voter preferences by politicians, albeit in a context of an electoral supply that depends on the presence of political parties.

THEORETICAL FRAMEWORK

The option to vote for the political opponent is not directly formalized in the citizen-candidate model. Instead, the presence of an opponent is a consequence of the performance of the elected official. Indeed, every citizen must first decide if he or she wishes to participate in the electoral game. Consequently, the act of punishing the incumbent in the citizen-candidate model means running for election rather than voting for the political opponent. Voters who do not go on the ballot implicitly give their support to the incumbent government. The latter is thus rewarded for having implemented the policy preferred by the largest number of voters. By contrast, the partisan model directly formalizes the alternative of voting for the political opponent in the choices available to the voter. As a result, these voters will tend to vote for the incumbent government unless a poor performance encourages them to opt for the opponent instead.

In fact, there are two important differences between the Downsian model and the citizen-candidate model. One concerns the mechanism for ensuring the responsiveness of elected officials to the preferences of the population, and the other concerns the mechanism leading to political accountability. These differences were identified by Lee et al. (2004) in their article "Do Voters Affect or Elect Policies? Evidence from the U.S. House." In concrete terms, this means that one model highlights the presence of a voter who contributes to changing the position of the policy implemented by the government and the other the presence of a citizen-candidate who decides whether to support or oppose that same position.

In a bipartisan Downsian model, the utility derived by the voter from voting for the party of the incumbent government is expressed with the following equation:

EQUATION 1: $R = p * ((|X_i - \text{party B}|) - (|X_i - \text{party A}|)) - C$
Where
R = utility of voting for the incumbent
p = probability that the vote is decisive on the outcome of the election
X_i = position of the voter on the axis of preferences
party A = position currently implemented on the axis of preferences by the party of the incumbent government
party B = proposed position on the axis of preferences of the other party
C = cost of voting

The citizen-candidate model, for its part, exposes the utility derived by the voter from running in an election against the incumbent. This utility is expressed with the following equation.

EQUATION 2: $R = p * (|X_i - W_t|) - C$
Where
R = utility of voting for the incumbent
p = probability of being elected
X_i = position of the citizen on the axis of preferences
W_t = position currently implemented on the axis of preferences
C = cost of entry in the electoral game

A comparison of the two equations shows that the Downsian model considers responsiveness to the population's preferences to be exogenous to the position of voters. In this model, political parties define a position on the axis of preferences. The proximity of this position to that of the median voter is, then, what determines the winner of the election. The presence of an election encourages responsiveness to the preferences of the public among different parties. It is therefore the votes of voters that allows for, or engenders, this responsiveness. Voters do not decide on the position of the government but can contribute to change it. In terms of political accountability, the Downsian model defines an electoral reward as a vote for the party in power and electoral punishment as a vote for the opposition party.

The citizen-candidate model, for its part, presents responsiveness to the preferences of the population as being endogenous to the electorate. Citizens present themselves with the goal of implementing their own position along the axis of preferences. The presence of an election encourages only one citizen, the incumbent, to adopt the position preferred by a majority of citizens, with the specific objective of eliminating electoral competition. Thus, the vote is not necessary for ensuring responsiveness to the preferences of the population. Rather, it is the nomination process that ensures that the position of the current policy corresponds with the preferences of the majority of citizens. In this context, it is the citizens who decide on the position of the policy. From the point of view of the mechanism leading to political accountability, the model defines electoral reward as not running for an election and electoral punishment as running as a candidate in an election.

A deeper comparison of the two models would seem worthwhile. However, there is one further intuition regarding the nature of accountability in party and non-party contexts. We expected that electors would show a tendency to punish incumbent mayors for their performance in a party-based system. However, we found instead that electors tended to reward outgoing mayors in a non-party context.

Applying these theoretical models, we posit three hypotheses for explaining the re-election of incumbent mayors in Quebec municipalities in the 2009 and 2013 elections. These hypotheses are formalized by Equation 3.

EQUATION 3: Incumbent result
= a + b1 (ΔTax rate) + b2 (Parties) + b3 (ΔTax rate ∗ Parties) + Zi + v
Where
Incumbent result: dummy variable (1 if incumbent wins; 0 if incumbent loses)
a: constant

b1: change in tax rate (Tax rate $_{\text{election year}}$ – Tax rate $_{\text{pre-election year}}$)
b2: dummy variable (1 if there are party systems; 0 if there are no party systems)
b3: interaction variables (ΔTax rate * Parties)
Zi: control variables
v: error term

Specifically, our first hypotheses are the following. Incumbent mayors who reduce taxes in an election year are more likely to be re-elected than others. This means that they will be rewarded by the voters. In the same way, incumbent mayors who increase taxes in an election year are more likely to be defeated than others. This means that they will be punished by voters. This is the standard hypothesis for the political business cycle, which has proved its relevance once again in both party and non-party contexts. Our second hypothesis is that incumbent mayors are more likely to be defeated in the presence of a political party system. Our third hypothesis looks into whether there is an interactive effect between the presence of a party system and a change in the taxation rate. More precisely, we hypothesized that a negative correlation between the taxation rate and the probability of re-election for an incumbent mayor was more significant in municipalities with a partisan system than in municipalities without a partisan system.

METHODOLOGY AND DATA

Our dependent variable is dichotomous, since it refers to either the victory (1) or the defeat (0) of the incumbent mayor in the Quebec municipal elections of 2009 and 2013. In those elections, an incumbent mayor faced political opposition in a total of 399 municipalities in 2009 and 430 municipalities in 2013. We have complete data for 806 of these municipalities.[7] We presented two specifications for analysis using logistical regression.[8]

Model 1 was estimated without the interaction terms specifying contingent effects for a change in the tax rate and the presence of a party system. This model provides estimates of the direct effects on incumbent re-election of these two measures, which are the subject of conditional hypothesis 3.[9]

Taxes are the top policy priority of local politicians in Canada (Goodman and Lucas 2015). The property tax is the main tax base

Table 2.1
Descriptive analysis

Without party	Mean	Minimum	Maximum	S.D.
Incumbent victory	0.59	0	1	–
Δ tax rate	–0.03	–0.62	0.50	0.13
Party system	0.26	0	1	–
Log number of electors	3.12	2.15	5.26	0.51
Log density	1.37	–1.52	3.65	0.83
Unemployment rate	8.82	0.00	54.40	6.97
Ownership rate (%)	80.79	34.39	100.00	10.09
Median income	57,246	24,540	104,550	1,682
Only one opponent	0.71	0	1	–
Turnout (%)	58.73	26.87	91.40	12.41

of Canadian municipalities (Slack and Bird 2015). The tax rate is measured as a municipality's share of own-source revenues in the value of its total property value. This is the indicator used by Quebec's Ministry of Municipal Affairs (MAMOT) to compare municipalities with each other and is readily available, being indicated on voters' tax bills. We were thus able to calculate the change in tax rates between election year and pre-election year.[10]

We controlled for the economic situation using the unemployment rate for each of the municipalities. The unemployment rate is the only means available to measure the economic situation within each of the municipalities. We also took into account the most significant contextual elements at the municipal level (Cancela and Geys 2016; McGregor and Spicer 2016; Carr and Tavares 2014; Goodman and Leland 2013), including the number of electors, density, ownership, and income as a control for the environmental context. Additionally, we controlled for the political situation by using the turnout rate and number of candidates. This variable was measured using a dummy variable: only one opponent versus more than one opponent.

We also tested the effect of a change in the tax rate for other years of the political cycle, but the results did not prove to be statistically significant. We also made similar analyses for spending, budget balance, and debt, which likewise did not yield statistically significant results. These variables are therefore not found in the regression table.

The data come from three different sources. All variables are measured at the municipal level. One, the financial data are derived from the financial profiles and the management indicators available online at the MAMOT website. Two, the socio-demographic data were obtained from Statistics Canada's 2006 and 2011 Community Profiles. And three, the electoral data were obtained from the database of the 2009 and 2013 municipal elections. The operationalization of each variable and the sources used in their construction are presented in the appendix, which also shows the distribution of each in table 2.1 and a correlation matrix in the appendix. The results of the logistic regression analysis are given in table 2.2.

RESULTS

Model 1 confirms our first hypothesis. *Ceteris paribus*, the change in taxation rate is negatively correlated with the re-election of incumbent mayors. Therefore, an increase in the tax rate reduces the probability of re-election for the incumbent mayor. In the same vein, a reduction in the tax rate favours their re-election. This relationship is significant with a threshold of 1 per 1,000. The second hypothesis, however, is not confirmed by Model 1. Consequently, the presence of a party system does not directly hinder the re-election of an incumbent mayor.

Regarding the control variables that were found to be statistically significant in the first model, only one is related to the environmental context – the ownership rate. The higher the ownership rate across the municipality, the weaker the incumbent mayor's chance of re-election. This relationship is significant with a threshold of 5 per cent. The variables, including number of electors, density, unemployment rate, and median income, were not found to be statistically significant.

As for political context, both variables were significant. Additionally, and all things being equal, the larger the voter turnout, the slimmer the chances of the incumbent mayor being re-elected. This relationship is significant with a threshold of 1 per 1,000. Additionally, in the presence of a single opponent to an incumbent mayor, the probability of re-election is larger than when there are two opponents or more. This relationship is significant with a threshold of 1 per 1,000.

Model 2 confirms our third hypothesis. Both the interaction and its constituent terms are statistically significant in this model. However, as noted in an earlier section, the interpretation permitted by these coefficients is limited because the interaction's constituent terms indicate the marginal effect of the one variable on re-election when the

Table 2.2
Logistic regression with RCVE

Dependent variable	Model 1		Model 2	
Incumbent victory (1)/ Incumbent defeat (0)	β	(S.E.)	β	(S.E.)
Independent variables				
Constant	3.58*	(1.46)	3.88*	(1.53)
1) Δ tax rate	−2.26***	(0.61)	−1.71**	(0.64)
2) Party system	0.28	(0.20)	−0.83**	(0.26)
3) Parties * Δ tax rate			−1.05***	(0.22)
4) Log number of electors	−0.20	(0.24)	−0.29	(0.25)
5) Log density	0.20	(0.16)	0.17	(0.16)
6) Unemployment rate	0.01	(0.01)	0.01	(0.01)
7) Ownership rate	−0.02*	(0.01)	−0.02*	(0.01)
8) Median income	0.92	(6.29)	3.01	(6.37)
9) Only one opponent	0.76***	(0.07)	0.73***	(0.17)
19) Turnout	−0.03***	(0.03)	−0.03***	(0.08)
11) Election 2009	−0.04	(0.15)	−0.13	(0.16)
(n)	(806)		(806)	
Number of clusters	605		605	
Log likelihood	−506.93		−490.27	
Wald chi^2	40.69***		68.52***	
Correctly classified (%)	64.6		67.1	
Pseudo R^2	0.07		0.10	

*p< 0.05; ** p<0.01; *** p < 0.001 (statistical significance of the regression coefficient)

Party system. Only one opponent and election 2009 are dummy variables with the following reference categories: no party system, more than one opponent, and election 2013.

other is zero (Brambor, Clark, and Golder 2006). Note that all the significant variables in Model 1 remained significant in Model 2 as well. As shown by the coefficient of interaction, a change in the taxation rate has a more negative impact on the re-election of the incumbent mayor in the presence of a party system. Additionally, hypothesis 2 is confirmed under this condition. The presence of a party system therefore has an indirectly negative effect on the re-election of incumbent mayors. Figure 2.3 illustrates the effect produced using Model 2.

Figure 2.3 represents the marginal effects of a change in the tax rate by comparing municipalities that have a party system to those that do not. Marginal effects indicate the change in probability of re-election occurring for a one-unit change (from its mean) in the

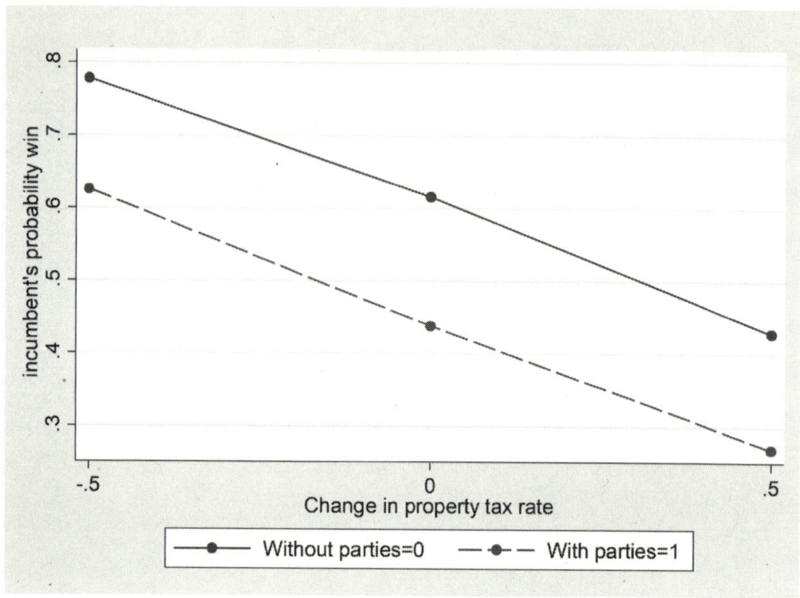

Figure 2.3 Predictive margins of parties by change in the tax rate

independent variable while the other independent variables are set at their means. As indicated by the estimates, an incumbent mayor who reduces the tax rate by 0.5 per cent has a 78 per cent probability of re-election in the absence of a party system, whereas this likelihood is lowered to 62 per cent under a party system. This is a 16 per cent difference. Additionally, an incumbent mayor who increases the tax rate by 0.5 per cent has a 44 per cent probability of re-election in the absence of a party system, whereas this likelihood is lowered to 26 per cent in the presence of a party system – a difference of 18 per cent. The effect of a party system can therefore be evaluated when there is no change the in tax rate. In this context, the probability of re-election is 61 per cent in a non-party system and 44 per cent in a party system – a difference of 17 per cent. This is in line with the theory posited in hypothesis 2. The figure allows for an evaluation of the effect of a one-point change in the tax rate, which is the 1 per cent change between a reduction of 0.5 per cent and an increase of 0.5 per cent. In the context of a party system, the probability of re-election goes from 62 per cent to 26 per cent, a 36 per cent difference. In the context of a non-party system, the probability of re-election goes from 78 per cent to 44 per cent, a 34 per cent difference. This is in line with the theory posited in hypothesis 1.

DISCUSSION

These results raise two main questions. The first question concerns the need for political parties to ensure the political accountability of elected officials. Indeed, the citizen-candidate model provides a mechanism by which elected officials can meet the preferences of citizens and by which citizens can make elected officials accountable for their actions without the need for political parties. However, this alone would not justify proclaiming an end to political parties. In fact, responsiveness and accountability in this model can only be envisioned if there is an incumbent. Conversely, another version of the citizen-candidate model suggests that political parties are a bulwark that is essential in the presence of an extreme candidate in elections, particularly elections where there are no incumbents.

The anti-median voter theorem developed by Großer and Palfrey (2014) modifies one of the central assumptions of the original citizen-candidate model. The authors show very convincingly that there is an information asymmetry among citizen-candidates about the position of each and every one on the axis of preference (X_i). This is due mainly to the fact that this information is considered private. In such a context, the model predicts the citizen-candidate who wins the election to be an extreme candidate. Indeed, if no one knows the position of the others, extreme candidates have as much chance of being elected as moderate candidates. Conversely, the utility of running for election, measured by the distance between the actual policy (W_t) and the position of the citizen-candidate, is greater for those who have an extreme position.

For Großer and Palfrey (2014), the presence of an incumbent candidate, the investitures of political parties, and political parties themselves constitute efficient institutions for limiting the presence of extreme candidates during a poll. It would thus be interesting to apply an empirical test of the anti-median voter theory to the case of Quebec municipalities. These municipalities constitute an institutional environment where one can find elections without an incumbent elected official in the race, without political parties, and where there is little information available on the position of the various candidates.

The last question concerns the nature of the link between the political business cycle and the re-election of the incumbent government. The results show that a re-election is linked to the performance of the elected official, which aligns perfectly with the concept of accountability. However, is this really a manifestation of the responsiveness of the elected official to voter preferences? Or is it not, instead, a deliberate manipulation on the part of the elected official, with the result of harming the voter in the future? Both of these interpretations of the link between the political business cycle and re-election can be found in the literature.

One interpretation presents elected officials as opportunistic and voters as "myopic." Voters are also portrayed as suffering from a condition called "fiscal illusion," meaning that they tend to overestimate the benefits they currently draw from public action and to underestimate their future tax burden. The fiscal illusion then pushes voters to vote for an elected official who will provide immediate gains, even if this comes at the expense of their anticipated well-being (Imbeau and Couture 2010). The politicians, motivated by their re-election, will then benefit from this misconception to reduce taxes just before elections (Nordhaus 1975; Tufte 1978).

The other interpretation presents a voter who anticipates the approach of the election and is aware of the annoying tendency of politicians to seek re-election. Voters assess politicians prospectively and prefer to vote for the candidate who can maximize their anticipated well-being. In this case, there is no possible political business cycle that can be inferred by a fiscal illusion. Elected officials who threaten voters' anticipated well-being will not be rewarded for having reduced taxes before elections. Such a behaviour may nevertheless reappear in the presence of two conditions. One, the voter does not know the competence of the politician or that of his political opponent. Two, control over public resources can be regarded as the means elected officials use to signalize their competence to the voter. Voters will prefer to vote for the incumbent politician who adopted good policies, in line with those that maximize their anticipated well-being, rather than for the opponent on whom they have only limited information. As a result, the incumbent politician would do well to "signalize" his or her competence by reducing taxes with the nearing of elections (Rogoff and Sibert 1988; Rogoff 1990). However, this reduction in taxes should not be done at the expense of the anticipated well-being of the voter.

APPENDIX

Table 2.3
Operationalization and data source

Dependent variable	Operationalization	Source
Incumbent victory	1 = incumbent win 0 = incumbent loss	
Independent variables		
Only one opponent	1 = one challenger 0 = more than one challenger	MAMOT 2009, 2013 election data
Turnout (%)	(Valid votes/voters registered) * 100	
Log number of electors	Log (registered voters)	
Δ Tax rate	(Tax rate $_{ey}$ – Tax rate $_{preey}$)[1]	MAMOT 2008/2013 financial data
Ownership rate (%)	(Owned housing/total housing) X 100	Community profile 2006–2011 *Statistics Canada*
Median income	Median income ($)	
Log density	Log (inhabitants/km^2)	
Unemployment rate	Unemployed/labour force * 100	

1 Tax rate = (independent municipal income/property value) X 100

ey = election year; preey = pre-election year

Table 2.4
Robustness test logistic regression with RCVE

Dependent variable	Model 3 (Δ tax rate)		Model 4 (Δ tax rate + environmental context)		Model 5 (Δ tax rate + political context)		Model 6 (Δ tax rate + parties + interaction)	
Incumbent victory (1)/ Incumbent defeat (0)	b	(S.E.)	b	(S.E.)	B	(S.E.)	b	(S.E.)
Independent variables								
Constant	0.30**	(0.10)	1.78	(1.06)	1.86***	(0.42)	0.39**	(0.11)
1) Δ tax rate	−2.52***	(0.60)	−2.27***	(0.60)	−2.32***	(1.15)	−1.95**	(0.64)
2) Parties					−0.28	(0.18)	0.77**	(0.23)
3) Log number of electors			−0.03	(0.20)				
4) Log density			0.18	(0.15)				
5) Unemployment rate			0.01	(0.01)				
6) Ownership rate			−0.02*	(0.01)				
7) Median income			1.47	(5.92)				
8) Only one opponent					0.73***	(0.16)		
9) Turnout (per 10% points)					−0.03***	(0.01)		
10) Election 2009	−0.02	(0.15)	−0.02	(0.15)	−0.05	(0.15)	−0.13	(0.16)
11) Parties * Δ tax rate							−1.13***	(0.23)
(n)	(806)		(806)		(806)		(806)	
Number of clusters	605		605		605		605	
Log likelihood	−536.38		−527.55		512.80		−515.40	
Wald chi^2	17.58***		32.05***		56.20***		32.11***	
Correctly classified (%)	59.7		60.4		66.0		62.8	
Pseudo R^2	0.02		0.03		0.06		0.06	

* p < 0.05 ; ** p < 0.01; *** p < 0.001

Table 2.5
Pearson correlation matrix

Variables	Incumbent victory	Δ tax rate	Parties	Log electors	Log density	Unemployment	Ownership rate	Median income	One opponent	Turnout
Incumbent victory	–	–0.15	–0.01	0.12	0.12	–0.02	–0.14	0.07	0.15	0.19
Δ tax rate	***	–	–0.08	–0.13	–0.11	0.06	–0.15	–0.13	0.02	0.13
Parties	n.s.	*	–	0.42	0.40	–0.20	–.05	0.29	–0.11	–0.25
Log electors	***	***	***	–	0.73	–0.27	–0.49	0.54	–0.21	–0.66
Log density	***	***	***	***	–	–0.39	–0.42	0.58	–0.12	–0.51
Unemployment	n.s.	n.s.	***	***	***	–	0.04	–0.32	–0.01	0.29
Ownership rate	***	***	n.s.	***	***	n.s.	–	–0.10	0.08	0.27
Median income	*	***	***	***	***	***	**	–	–0.09	–0.41
One opponent	***	n.s.	**	***	***	n.s.	*	**	–	0.04
Turnout	***	***	***	***	**	***	***	***	n.s.	–

NOTES

1 The exact number of parties is ascertainable in Quebec, which, unlike other Canadian provinces, has a law requiring municipal political parties to be registered for census purposes.

2 In 2009, these cities were Saguenay, Trois-Rivières, Sherbrooke, Terrebonne, and Gatineau. In addition, there was a single party in the city of Lévis, where the elected mayor ran unopposed. Moreover, the mayor of Quebec City – the second largest city in the province of Quebec – won his first term through by-elections in 2007 running as an independent candidate and later started a political party for the 2009 elections. He took over from the former mayor who had passed away in office after she had been elected through contested elections. She had run under no political party, with no political agenda, no banner, and no organized election campaign. In 2013, Gatineau, Saguenay, and Trois-Rivières had only one party in the race.

3 Of the 1,096 municipalities, 548 (50 per cent) had a mayor elected by acclamation in 2009. Some 80 per cent of them (or 438) were incumbent mayors (MAMOT 2009). In 2013, 517 of the 1,096 municipalities (47 per cent) had a mayor elected by acclamation. Some 78 per cent of them (or 404) were incumbent mayors (MAMOT 2013).

4 Seventy-six per cent or 837 of the 1,096 municipalities (MAMOT 2009)

5 To be eligible for office at the municipal level in Quebec, the candidate must have been registered on the electoral roll of the municipality and have been domiciled in the territory of the municipality for at least one year. To become registered on the electoral roll, the candidate must be a Canadian citizen and have been domiciled on the territory of the municipality for at least six months. Domicile is defined as the main residence. A Canadian citizen may also be a voter in a municipality if he or she has been the owner of a building located in the municipality for at least one year.

6 Besley and Coate themselves might not even support the idea of testing their model. The reason for this is that they find multiple equilibria, which renders empirics tests extremely difficult (see their 1997 piece on page 98: "For those who would like a clean empirical prediction, our multiple equilibria will raise a sense of dissatisfaction").

7 A total of 227 incumbent mayors won the election, and 157 incumbents lost the election in 2009. A total of 250 incumbent mayors won the election, and 175 incumbents lost the election in 2013.

8 Our research design consists of a time-series-cross-section, since our data is organized based on a cross-section and a longitudinal section. To correct

our estimates, we instead used the method with an RCVE (robust cluster variance estimator), which is a procedure recommended, among others, by Wooldridge (2010) for correcting panel issues. In addition, we added a dummy variable that allowed us to control the effect of the year of the election.

9 Because the interaction terms are omitted from this first model, the coefficients for change in tax rate and party systems indicate the unconditional effects of these characteristics on the likelihood of incumbent re-election. Once the interaction term is introduced to test hypothesis 3 in Model 2, this interpretation is no longer valid because coefficients show conditional effects of these characteristics on the likelihood of incumbent re-election (Brambor, Clark, and Golder 2006).

10 Omitted variable bias is likely to be a major problem in this kind of analysis. This is why the study includes more than one election. For the sake of example, imagine that municipalities that reduce the tax rate in election years are those in which the economy is doing relatively well, whereas in the others, mayors are forced to increase taxes to keep municipal revenues at a reasonable level. If voters do not respond to the tax rate but only to the general economic environment, one would still find a positive effect of lowering taxes, but this would not be enough to conclude that it is a response to a tax cut. Bagues and Esteve-Volart (2015) showed that electors can demonstrate this type of behaviour during elections at lower levels of government.

REFERENCES

Aidt, Toke S., Francisco J. Veiga, and Linda G. Veiga. 2011. "Election Results and Opportunistic Policies: A New Test of the Rational Political Business Cycle Model." *Public Choice* 148(1): 21–44.

Alesina, Alberto, Nouriel Roubini, and Gerald D. Cohen. 1999. *Political Cycle and the Macroeconomy*. London: MIT Press.

Balaguer-Coll, Maria T., Marìa I. Brun-Martos, Anabel Forte, and Emili Tortosa-Ausina. 2015. "Local Governments' Re-election and Its Determinants: New Evidence Based on a Bayesian Approach." *European Journal of Political Economy* 39: 94–108.

Barro, Robert J. 1973. "The Control of Politicians: An Economic Model." *Public Choice* 14(1): 19–42.

Besley, Timothy, and Stephen Coate. 1997. "An Economic Model of Representative Democracy." *Quarterly Journal of Economics* 112(1): 85–114.

Bherer, Laurence, and Sandra Breux. 2012. "L'apolitisme municipal." *Bulletin d'histoire politique du Québec* 21(1): 170–84.

Boyne, George A., Oliver James, Peter John, and Nicolai Petrovsky. 2009. "Democracy and Government Performance: Holding Incumbents Accountable in English Local Government." *The Journal of Politics* 71(4): 1273–84.

Brambor, Thomas, William Robert Clark, and Matt Golder. 2006. "Understanding Interaction Models: Improving Empirical Analyses." *Political Analysis* 14(1): 63–82.

Breux, Sandra, Jérôme Couture, and Laurence Bherer. 2014. "Les candidats sortants: atouts ou obstacles à la participation électorale." *Canadian Journal of Urban Research* 23(2): 59–78.

Cadigan, John. 2005. "The Citizen-Candidate Model: An Experimental Analysis." *Public Choice* 123(1): 197–216.

Cancela, João, and Benny Geys. 2016. "Explaining Voter Turnout: A Meta-analysis of National and Subnational Elections." *Electoral Studies* 42: 264–75.

Carr, Jared B., and Antonio Tavares. 2014. "City Size and Political Participation in Local Government: Reassessing the Contingent Effects of Residential Location Decisions within Urban Regions." *Urban Affairs Reviews* 50(2): 269–302.

Clingermayer, James C., and Richard C. Feiock. 1993. "Constituencies, Campaign Support, and Council Member Intervention in City Development Policy." *Social Science Quarterly* 74(1): 199–215.

Crowder-Meyer, Melody, Shana Kushner Gadarian, and Jessica Trounstine. 2015. "Electoral Institutions, Gender Stereotypes and Women's Local Representation." *Politics, Groups and Identities* 3(2): 318–34.

Downs, Anthony. 1957. *An Economic Theory of Democracy*. New York: Harper.

Drazen, Allan, and Marcela Eslava. 2010. "Electoral Manipulation via Voter-Friendly Spending: Theory and Evidence." *Journal of Development Economics* 92(1): 39–52.

Elmendorf, Christopher S., and David Schleicher. 2012. "Informing Consent: Voter Ignorance, Political Parties and Election Law." *University of Illinois Law Review* 2013(2): 363–432.

Erikson, Robert S., and Gerald C. Wright, Jr. 1980. "Policy Representation of Constituency Interest." *Politic Behavior* 2(1): 91–106.

Ferejohn, John. 1999. "Accountability and Authority: Toward a Theory of Political Accountability." In *Democracy, Accountability and Representation*, edited by Adam Przeworski, Susan C. Stokes, and Bernard Manin, 131–53. Cambridge: Cambridge University Press.

– 1986. "Incumbent Performance and Electoral Control." *Public Choice* 50(1): 5–25.

Fiorina, Morris P. 1981. *Retrospective Voting in American National Elections.* New Haven, CT: Yale University Press.

Foremny, Dirk, and Nadine Riedel. 2014. "Business Taxes and Electoral Cycle." *Journal of Public Economics* 115: 48–61.

Foucault, Martial, and Abel François. 2005. "La politique influence-t-elle les décisions publiques locales? Analyse empirique des budgets communaux de 1977 à 2001." *Politiques et management public* 23(3): 1–22.

Fox, Richard, and Jennifer Lawless. 2004. "Entering the Arena? Gender and the Decision to Run for Office." *American Journal of Political Science* 48(2): 264–80.

Franco, Luciane Maria Gonçalves, Nestor Baptista, Marcia dos Santos Bertolocci Espejo, Luciano Marci Scherer, and Cristiano do Nascimento. 2014. "Determinants of Electoral Budget Cycles and Its Relationship with the Likelihood of Re-election of Mayor in State of Parana (Brazil)." *Public Administration Research* 3(2): 107–20.

Gerstlé, Jacques. 2003. "Démocratie représentative, réactivité politique et imputabilité." *Revue française de science politique* 53(6): 851–8.

Good, Kristin R. 2017. "Municipal Political Parties: An Answer to Urbanization or an Affront to Traditions of Local Democracy." In *Canadian Parties in Transition*, 4th ed., edited by Alain Gagnon and Brian Tanguay, 432–64. Toronto: University of Toronto Press.

Goodman, Christopher B., and Suzanne M. Leland. 2013. "Cost Shocks and Their Relationship to the Creation, Consolidation and Dissolution of US Local Governments." *Public Finance and Management* 13(2): 58–79.

Goodman, Nicole J., and Jack Lucas. 2015. "Policy Priorities of Municipal Candidates in the 2014 Local Ontario Elections." Paper prepared for presentation at the annual meeting of the Canadian Political Science Association, University of Ottawa, 2–4 June.

Großer, Jens, and Thomas R. Palfrey. 2014. "Candidate Entry and Political Polarization: An Antimedian Voter Theorem." *American Journal of Political Science* 58(1): 127–43.

Imbeau, Louis M., and Jérôme Couture. 2010. "Pouvoir et politiques publiques." In *L'analyse des politiques publiques*, edited by Stéphane Paquin, Luc Bernier, and Guy Lachapelle, 37–72. Quebec: Les Presses de l'Université Laval.

Jacobson, Gary C., and Samuel Kernell. 1981. *Strategy and Choice in Congressional Elections.* New Haven, CT: Yale University Press.

Key, Valdimer O. 1966. *The Responsible Electorate: Rationality in Presidential Voting*. Cambridge, MA: Belknap Press.

Kramer, Gerald. 1971. "Short-Term Fluctuations in U.S. Voting Behavior." *American Political Science Review* 65(1): 131–43.

Krebs, Timothy B. 1998. "The Determinants of Candidates' Vote Share and the Advantages of Incumbency in City Council Elections." *American Journal of Political Science* 42(3): 921–35.

Lago-Peñas, Ignacio, and Santiago Lago-Peñas. 2008. "Explaining Budgetary Indiscipline: Evidence from Spanish Municipalities." *Public Finance & Management* 8(1): 36–69.

Lee, David S., Enrico Moretti, and Matthew J. Butler. 2004. "Do Voters Affect or Elect Policies? Evidence from the U.S. House." *The Quarterly Journal of Economics* 119(3): 807–59.

Lewis-Beck, Michael S. 1990. *Economics and Elections: The Major Western Democracies*. Ann Arbor: University of Michigan Press.

McGregor, Michael, and Zachary Spicer. 2016. "The Canadian Homevoter: Property Values and Municipal Politics in Canada." *Journal of Urban Affairs* 38(1): 123–39.

Mévellec, Anne. 2011. "Les élections municipales de 2009 dans les villes moyennes du Québec: entre changement et reconduction." In *Les élections municipales au Québec: enjeux et perspectives*, edited by Sandra Breux and Laurence Bhérer, 289–310. Quebec: Presses de l'Université Laval.

Mouritzen, Poul E. 1989. "The Local Political Business Cycle." *Scandinavian Political Studies* 12(1): 37–55.

Nordhaus, William D. 1975. "The Political Business Cycle." *The Review of Economic Studies* 42(2): 169–90.

Oliver, Eric J., and Shang E. Ha. 2007. "Vote Choice in Suburban Elections." *American Political Science Review* 101(3): 393–408.

Osborne, Martin J., and Al Slivinski. 1996. "A Model of Political Competition with Citizen-Candidates." *The Quarterly Journal of Economics* 111(1): 65–96.

Parodi, Jean-Luc. 2004. "Les élections intermédiaires du printemps 2004: entre structure et événement." *Revue francaise de science politique* 54: 545–53.

Persson, Torsten, and Guido Tabellini. 2003. "Do Electoral Cycles Differ across Political Systems?" *IGIER Working Paper* 232: 1–23.

Remmer, Karen L., and François Gélineau. 2003. "Subnational Electoral Choice: Economic and Referendum Voting in Argentina, 1983–1999." *Comparative Political Studies* 36(7): 801–21.

Rogoff, Kenneth. 1990. "Equilibrium Political Budget Cycles." *The American Economic Review* 80(1): 21–36.

Rogoff, Kenneth, and Anne Sibert. 1988. "Elections and Macroeconomic Policy Cycles." *Review of Economic Studies* 55(1): 1–16.

Sakurai, Sergio N., and Naercio A. Menezes-Filho. 2008. "Fiscal Policy and Reelection in Brazilian Municipalities." *Public Choice* 137(1): 301–14.

Sedminradskà, Lucie, Rudolf Kubìk, and Jakub Hass. 2011. "Political Business Cycle in Czech Municipalities." *Prague Economics Papers* 1: 59–70.

Slack, Enid, and Richard M. Bird. 2015. "How to Reform the Property Tax: Lessons from around the World." Paper prepared by the Institute on Municipal Finance & Governance 21.

Trounstine, Jessica. 2008. *Political Monopolies in American Cities: The Rise and Fall of Bosses and Reformers*. Chicago: University of Chicago Press.

– 2011. "Evidence of a Local Incumbency Advantage." *Legislative Studies Quarterly* 36(2): 255–80.

Tufte, Edward R. 1978. *Political Control of the Economy*. Princeton, NJ: Princeton University Press.

Wooldridge, Jeffrey M. 2010. *Econometric Analysis of Cross Section and Panel Data*. Cambridge, MA: MIT Press.

3

Political Accountability and Responsiveness: What Is the Role of Municipal Political Parties?

Jérôme Couture, Sandra Breux, and Laurence Bherer

INTRODUCTION

Political parties are seen by many as the primary mechanism of accountability at the national level (Mainwaring and Torcal 2006). According to this view, the presence of competing parties over a series of elections encourages belonging among the electors with regard to issues and political dynamics. In addition, it is seen to allow for the development of a stable political environment, which reduces the cost of information for the electors. In a political party context, electors have a greater likelihood of knowing their parties and platforms and are better able to assess the performance of incumbent candidates, which reinforces accountability. The stability provided by political parties running for election also creates closer ties between the parties and civil society. When these ties exist, electoral volatility is reduced, and political parties are in a better position to understand the needs and concerns of citizens. This interplay is called responsiveness.

However, what might we say about a non-partisan context? Is such a political environment conducive to responsibility? Is it possible for candidates to develop and demonstrate a true understanding of citizens' preferences without partisan support? How can citizens judge the performance of their elected officials when electoral promises made in this context tend to be looser than those made in a partisan system? In other words, how is political accountability exercised in a non-partisan system? To answer these questions, we will examine the political lives of Canadian municipalities, which are characterized by a weakly institutionalized party system. There, political parties, in addition to their scarcity, often claim to be politically neutral and to have no ideological ties with higher-level political parties (Bherer and Breux 2012). According to the institutionalization theory of partisan systems, this political context fosters poor consistency in electoral competition and high electoral volatility as well as a strong personalization of politics. The goal of this chapter is to understand how electoral teams operate at the Canadian municipal level and to make hypotheses about the environment of accountability created in a non-partisan context. The discussion aims to establish a typology for Canadian non-partisan municipalities.

To accomplish this, we begin by reviewing the definition of a political party, including its origins and the role it plays in a system of electoral competition. In so doing, we seek to identify the ties that these political formations have with the notions of accountability and political responsiveness. In addition, we seek to address the specificities of municipal political parties and the way in which accountability and political responsiveness play out at this level. These theoretical elements will then open up a channel for reflecting on the Canadian situation as a whole. Based on a review of the municipal political parties that existed during the last elections in the ten largest cities of Quebec and British Columbia, we will develop a typology of electoral competition systems. In our conclusion, this typology will allow us to detail the ways in which accountability and political responsiveness are expressed in the presence of municipal political formations and the different questions these relationships raise.

POLITICAL PARTIES: DEFINITIONS, ORIGINS, AND ROLE IN A SYSTEM OF ELECTORAL COMPETITION

Defining political parties allows us to establish the individual characteristics of political formations and their rationales. There are actually three distinct and yet complementary rationales that can be identified among political parties (Lemieux 2012). First, with regard to internal organization, partisan actors aim to ensure that party members' mobilization activities help to provide them with all of the human, financial, and information resources they need. Second, when elections are concerned, the political party's actions are focused on obtaining the highest possible number of votes and elected positions through the democratic process. Lastly, governmental activities carried out by political parties may be nomination and coordination activities that concern positions of political authority, or they may be actions related to opposition parties. Political parties can be defined in different ways: by formulating the criteria that allow us to distinguish political parties from other political entities, by looking at the origin of these political formations, and by identifying the role they play within a political system of electoral competition. However, before expanding on these three types of analyses, we first need to consider other important factors.

Most works that attempt to define political formations use specific criteria to accomplish this goal. While these criteria tend to be similar across studies, they may also vary from author to author. For example, La Palombara and Weiner (1966) make use of four criteria to differentiate a party from other political entities: 1) a visible organization; 2) the desire to exercise power; 3) interest in keeping popular support; and 4) the life expectancy of the organization surpasses those of the directors who are currently in place. For Key (1942), however, political parties have three distinct characteristics: 1) political parties are organizations in a relationship with the electorate; 2) their mission is to direct government; and 3) like all organizations, they have an internal dynamic. Many of these researchers, especially those studying the US context, developed and tested their theories by focusing on the first two aspects – namely, understanding the objectives of these formations and the nature of their organization.

As a result, there is a wealth of analyses that aim to explain how partisan affiliation and identification with a party contribute to shaping the choice of electors (Bartels 2000; MacKuen, Erickson, and Stimson 1989). Other studies look at the way in which parties organize the public policy development process (Cox and McCubbins 1993; 2005). There is also a stream of research that defines political parties according to their function within the democratic system. Lemieux (1985), for example, differentiates between candidate selection functions, the functions of representation within the legislative body, and the functions of government. Webb, Farell, and Holliday (2002), by contrast, prefer to classify parties according to how they organize their electoral and legislative activities as well as how they develop their political platforms, nominate candidates, and appoint to other positions within their governance.

The internal dynamics and organization of political parties, along-side the concentration of leadership in political parties, is generally described in two opposing theories. One is the oligarchical model of Michels (1971), which posits that power is concentrated in the hands of a small number of professional leaders; the other is the stratarchical structure of Eldersveld (1964), which presumes that power is shared between various party instances. The different assumptions underlying these theories beg a closer inspection of the origin of these formations.

Research on the origins of political parties tends to fall into two main camps. In the first camp, a connection is established between the development of representative democracy and parties. From this perspective, Duverger (1969), for example, distinguishes two types of parties. The first revolves around electoral and parliamentary creations, with parliamentary groups organizing to provide structure for the arrival of new electors via the extension of universal suffrage. The second type of party was created by pre-existing institutions whose activities were located outside of the electoral playing field, such as unions and farmers' and church associations. In the second camp, the origin of parties is linked to the economic and social development process. Here, Lipset and Rokkan (1967), for example, maintain that parties emerged from four major divisions produced by national and industrial revolutions. According to them, political parties represent the political divisions between owners and workers, industrial and rural societies, and the church and the state and the separation between the political centre of a state and its peripheral regions.

For still others, political parties are nothing other than a conglomerate of candidates and elected officials (Aldrich 1995; Aldrich and Rodhe 2001), though new propositions have recently been put forward on the subject (Bawn et al. 2012; Cohen et al. 2008). In their view, political parties can also be coalitions of interest groups or advocacy groups whose goal is primarily to put their own policies into action. As a result, such groups are not as focused on the election or re-election of candidates under a party banner as one might expect. Conversely, these formations do not seek to win elections in order to establish policy choices. This scenario, insofar as it takes place, has clear consequences for political responsiveness. These new propositions, however, run counter to the theory of Downs (1957), who posited that political parties define policy choices with the aim of winning elections.

If a political party is not, as Cohen et al. (2008) and Bawn et al. (2012) propose, deemed to be driven primarily by the need or desire to please the median elector, then it need not necessarily be inclined to respond to the preferences of electors. From a normative standpoint, this is a huge difference, since parties dominated by interest and advocacy groups – in other words, those less sensitive to electoral preferences – can take advantage of a blind spot in the attention and information of electors in order to win seats in the legislative assembly. These possibilities lead us to question the role played by political parties within a competitive system.

Several typologies have been developed to describe electoral competition systems. Together, they form a third type of analysis for defining a political party. The typologies, many of which date back some time, refer to one and the same criterion – that is, the number of parties in the system. Almond and Coleman (1960) distinguish competitive systems with several parties from non-competitive ones in which a single party holds a political monopoly. For La Palombara and Weiner (1966), however, it is not the number of parties that is of importance but rather the hegemonic or alternating character of governmental control by a single party. A party can, for example, be dominant and hold a monopoly on governance inside a system where several parties coexist. These authors also isolate the ideological and pragmatic character of parties that make up a partisan system.

To our knowledge, Jupp (1968) was the first to add the non-partisan system to this typology, with reference to authoritarian regimes that forbid the very existence of political parties. For Jupp, partisan systems can also be distinguished by party discipline and by whether they are rigid or loose. This means that partisan systems can be distinguished along a single ideological division. In other words, in some systems the platforms are less important than the immediate issues, while in others ideology and the party platform are the pulse and driving force of the political parties.

In a similar vein, Sartori's typology (1976) points to the presence of non-partisan systems in a de jure version: parties can be prohibited or discouraged by law. This stands out from de facto non-partisan systems where no law precludes or limits the formation of political parties but where no parties exist. Aside from the numerical criteria, which are evaluated based on the level of fragmentation in the partisan system, Sartori's typology takes into account more qualitative elements, such as the relationships between parties. As a result, parties can be more or less distanced ideologically and may, or may not, be able to form coalitions. This last point regarding the presence, or absence, of a coalition in a partisan system is also found in the typology developed by Lemieux (2012), albeit alongside the added dimension of openness to third parties. This latter dimension is drawn from the cartel party idea developed by Mair (1990), based on which established parties have a vested interest in maintaining the established partisan system and as a result of which they push for regulations that impede or obstruct the emergence of new parties.

For more than half a century, much research has been dedicated to defining and delineating the role of political parties. Essentially focusing on the national level, these analyses tend to overlook those formations that fail to meet all the criteria that define political parties as well as the formations operating at the municipal scale.

MUNICIPAL POLITICAL PARTIES: DEFINITIONS, ORIGINS, AND ROLE IN A SYSTEM OF ELECTORAL COMPETITION

Studies performed for the European context have shown that since 1945 national political parties have progressively worked their way into the field of municipal politics – namely, by creating local branches that present their candidates at municipal elections (Kjaer and Elklit 2010). This phenomenon, more commonly called the "nationalization of local elections," is a process by which national parties transform the local political arena by prioritizing national issues to the detriment of more local ones (Rokkan 1996). The nationalization of local elections has a negative effect on accountability. As a result, local elections become an opportunity to punish the party governing at the national level rather than for judging the performance of locally elected officials. For some, this turns local elections into second-order elections (Parodi 2004).

The nationalization of local elections has slowed down somewhat in several European countries with the more recent emergence of strictly local political parties. These parties have appeared as a response to the increasing dissatisfaction of electors with national parties and to respond to local community needs. According to Copus et al. (2012), this dissatisfaction is tied in part to national parties using the local level for their own purposes, such as creating a space for patronage, and to the maladjustment of national electoral platforms with local priorities. Additionally, these authors note that national parties tend to homogenize local issues and to overlook the individual concerns of the respective municipalities. Overall, the nationalization of local elections is seen to have a negative effect on political responsiveness.

Nonetheless, this cohabitation between the nationalization of local elections and local independent parties can also have a beneficial effect on the politicization of local issues (Breux and Bherer 2013). Where local independent political parties do exist, they are integrated into a highly politicized context that is largely dominated by the ideological directions of parties from higher levels. This politicization of the local level then contributes to the success of local independent political parties in that it allows them to position themselves differently, particularly from an ideological and program point of view.

These conclusions, however, take on new meaning in the North American municipal context. There, the majority of municipal elections are non-partisan in the sense that the political affiliations of the candidates are not indicated on the ballot (Anzia, Sarah, and Meeks 2016; Breux, Couture, and Koop 2017). In the United States, research focusing on big cities has shown that national-level political parties have been slowing down their activity at the local scale since the 1960s (Bridges 1997; Trounstine 2008). Whether this might apply to the Canadian context as well is difficult to say, given the dearth of studies on this aspect for Canada (Fillon 1999).

Nevertheless, recent analyses of the municipal level in the United States and Canada have offered a few pointers to understanding the role of municipal political parties and their place in the system of electoral competition. According to Oliver, Ha, and Callen (2012), there is a connection between the size of a city and the presence of political parties. According to these authors, there may well be less of a need for formal political organizations in smaller cities, where electors often know the candidates personally and where connecting with electors requires less effort and fewer resources. However, in larger cities, political parties have an important role to play in the organization of elections. In the same vein, Anzia (2015) holds that larger cities are more likely to have political parties because of the scale of the issues they face.

The activity of parties varies from city to city, and this variation provides an opportunity to compare systems of electoral competition with and without political parties, as was done by Couture and Breux in the preceding chapter. Recently, similar comparative approaches have been used to study the contributions of political parties to the US municipal political level (Bonneau and Cann 2015; Caladarone, Canes-Wrone, and Clark 2009; Schaffner, Streb, and Wright 2001).

A similar strategy is to assess the impact of municipal competitiveness on electoral participation and highlight the ties between electoral mobilization and the concepts of responsiveness and accountability. There are two main explanations for these relationships: either voters choose representatives who share their preferences and/or elected officials are sensitive to the preferences of electors simply to ensure their re-election (Griffin and Newman 2005). In a similar vein, Hajnal and Trounstine (2005) show that electoral participation is higher when electors are sanctioning the municipal government currently in power, thereby associating electoral participation with accountability. It should be noted, however, that these studies do not appear to offer any consensus concerning the impact of non-partisan elections on the rate of participation (Alford and Lee 1968; Breux, Couture, and Goodman 2016; Caren 2007; Couture, Breux, and Bherer 2014; Karnig and Walter 1983; Lublin and Tate 1995; Marschall 2010).

Behind these analyses lies the idea that a non-partisan environment makes the cost of voting higher, which should reduce electoral participation. In truth, voters do not necessarily have all the information required to be able to make a perfectly rational choice between different political alternatives (Althaus 2003). Here, the presence of party names reveals its importance insofar as they can also serve as a heuristic shortcut, simplifying the act of voting (Chong and Druckman 2007). More specifically, these heuristic shortcuts essentially serve as problem-solving strategies used by voters who want to make a decision in a context where access to the information required to make such an enlightened choice is highly limited (Elmendorf and Schleicher 2012; Schneider et al. 1999). The goal is to limit the required cognitive process as much as possible and reduce the quantity of information that is used to choose among the different alternatives. For example, voters can decide to use a likability-type shortcut. In other words, they can choose to vote for a candidate who can provide them with direct and personal benefits, as illustrated in chapter 2. If they do not have easy access to such information, electors can also reduce the information they need to make a decision by engaging in a retrospective evaluation of the outgoing government's performance (Fiorina 1981). This performance can be evaluated by using the current economic situation as a heuristic shortcut. Partisan-type heuristics can also be used to assess candidate performance. In this case, voters simply choose the candidate representing their party of preference. As stated by Stephenson, McGregor, and Moore in the first chapter of this book, in the absence of a political label electors have no choice but to turn to other heuristic shortcuts.

That said, party labels are not the only shortcut that allows for a reduction in the cost of voting. This point is directly tied to the concepts of accountability and responsiveness as well as the system of political competition at the municipal level. In fact, the capacity of political competition to encourage accountability and responsiveness is directly connected to the clarity of responsibility (Powell and Whitten 1993). More specifically, it is possible for electors to assign the results of public action to those elected officials who are responsible for it. According to Hobot, Tilley, and Baducci (2013), this clarity has two aspects: the formal dispersion of governmental power and the cohesion of the incumbent government. In other words, the system shows clarity of responsibility when only one party forms the government, when the government is a majority, when there is strict party discipline, and when there is an ideological coherence in the party's programs and actions.

However, these elements are a problem for non-partisan systems. As stated by Großer and Palfrey (2014), accountability and responsiveness are two notions that are difficult to apply in a non-partisan context when there is no outgoing candidate up for re-election – in other words, when there is no one to reward or punish. A non-partisan system has the same tendency to favour candidates located on the periphery of the political spectrum in the absence of an incumbent.

In non-partisan systems, there can also be different cohabitation mechanisms between independent elected officials. These mechanisms can range from informal coalitions and issue-focused collaborations to logrolling. It is also possible that in certain contexts electors are informed about the mechanisms of cohabitation, especially given the findings stated in Sancton's chapter (chapter 5). If this is the case, electors can punish or reward members of an informal majority coalition as they would do with a political party in power. In the absence of a visible party label, which is one criterion put forth by La Palombara and Weiner (1966), coalitions may exist that could be called a "quasi-party." The same also applies to candidates who are known for their political affiliations with higher levels, as is the case stated in the chapter by Stephenson, McGregor, and Moore (chapter 1). This affiliation can be used by electors as a heuristic shortcut for situating candidates in relation to one another.

Additionally, at the municipal level it is possible that political formations have only a few traits in common with political parties. Nonetheless, their mere presence on the electoral scene has the effect of allowing these organizations to give shape to a specific system of competition. Indeed, the Canadian municipal level is a perfect example of this phenomenon.

SYSTEMS OF MUNICIPAL ELECTORAL COMPETITION IN CANADA

The systems of municipal electoral competition in Canada are an interesting case for research. Canada is one of the rare countries where purely local municipal-level party organizations exist. In fact, municipal political parties in Canada are not branches of parties present at higher levels of government because the partisan systems of each political level (municipal, provincial, and federal) are independent of each other. This propensity for local parties was encouraged by provinces such as Quebec and British Columbia, which adopted legislation over a period of thirty years that promoted the development of municipal political parties.

To properly identify these systems of electoral competition, a census was conducted of the existing political parties in the ten largest cities in Quebec and British Columbia over the last series of elections. This census found a total of sixty-one formations. Despite this number, we should keep in mind that non-partisan systems are dominant in both provinces and that they are non-existent in the eight other provinces.

As shown in the two tables in the appendix, we counted twenty-eight political parties in the ten largest cities of British Columbia, twelve of which won at least one seat on city council during the 2014 elections. We found thirty-three parties in the ten largest cities of Quebec, nineteen of which won at least one seat on the municipal council in the 2013 elections. The major difference between the two provinces was determined to concern the origin of the parties. This is particularly noticeable with regard to party labels.

In Quebec, parties appear to be created by candidates and elected officials in particular. In fact, eighteen of the thirty-three political parties use the name of the candidate running for mayor in the party name. This phenomenon does not exist in British Columbia, where the vast majority of party names are more likely to be citizens' movements, which do not always present themselves as parties. There are even coalitions of independent candidates that reject all forms of party discipline in their political platform. British Columbia was also shown to have parties with names that advocate a specific cause, a phenomenon not seen in Quebec. We also noted that the Green Party runs candidates in the City of Vancouver. This is the only case where a municipal party has the same name as another party from a higher level of government.

The common trait between the two provinces is the presence of several parties for which the city name is part of the party name. However, British Columbia is unique in that movements use a similar name in several municipalities. The First Movement, for example, is found in Vancouver, Surrey, Burnaby, and Richmond. This phenomenon does not exist in Quebec.

Table 3.1 analyzes the system of competition in greater detail for these twenty cities. To begin, there were five occasions when the outgoing mayor's mandate was not renewed. In two cases (Surrey and Lévis), the party in power appointed a new leader and successfully took the election as the only party present on the city council and with a strong majority in terms of the number of city councillors elected. In two other cases (Montreal and Laval), the resignation of the incumbent mayors and the disappearance of their party led to the emergence of new parties. In Montreal, for example, a new mayor with a new party held a minority in the city council. In Laval, the mayor's new party won a strong majority in a two-party system. The last case is Kelowna, where the independent incumbent mayor did not present himself for re-election and two new political parties on the ballot did not manage to nominate a candidate. As a result, the political scene there is dominated by independent elected officials.

A minority uni-partisan system occurs when an incumbent mayor is beaten in the election. This took place in two cities – Abbotsford and Gatineau – and in each the outgoing mayor who lost was an independent. In Abbotsford, the new mayor was a previously elected city councillor. The new city council includes four re-elected incumbent councillors and four newcomers who are members of the same party. In Gatineau, the new mayor (previously elected city councillor in 2009) formed a party in 2012, which was the only party represented

Table 3.1
Elements of the British Columbia (2014) and Quebec (2013) party systems

	Incumbent mayor re-elected	Change in party mayor's candidate	Number of parties elected	Mayor chief of a party	Council majority for the mayor's party	Council majority for another party
Vancouver	Yes	–	3	Yes	Yes	No
Surrey	–	Yes	1	Yes	Yes	–
Burnaby	Yes	–	1	Yes	Yes	–
Richmond	Yes	–	3	No	–	No
Abbotsford	No	–	1	No	–	No
Coquitlam	Yes	–	1	No	–	No
Kelowna	–	–	0	No	–	–
Saanich	No	–	0	No	–	–
Langley	Yes	–	0	No	–	–
Delta	Yes	–	2	Yes	No	No
Montreal	–	–	8	Yes	No	No
Quebec	Yes	–	2	Yes	Yes	No
Laval	–	–	2	Yes	Yes	No
Gatineau	No	–	1	Yes	No	No
Longueuil	Yes	–	2	Yes	Yes	No
Sherbrooke	Yes	–	1	Yes	Yes	No
Saguenay	Yes	–	1	No	–	No
Lévis	–	Yes	1	Yes	Yes	–
Trois-Rivières	Yes	–	0	No	–	–
Terrebonne	Yes	–	1	Yes	Yes	No

on city council in 2013. The party held a minority, succeeding in electing only four councillors. Additionally, only five incumbent independent candidates were re-elected as councillors. The remaining eighteen members of the city council were all new independent councillors.

When an incumbent mayor is re-elected, two main scenarios present themselves. One, if the incumbent mayor is the head of a political party, the party almost always holds a majority in the city council. Occasionally, that party is also the only represented party (Burnaby, Sherbrooke, Terrebonne), or if there are other parties, they are (Vancouver, Quebec, Longueuil). This scenario strongly resembles the case of a party in power that has successfully found a new leader, such as in Lévis and Surrey. In fact, only Delta did not fit into this scenario. There, the incumbent mayor's party does not hold a majority in the city council, nor does the other party. In the second scenario, an incumbent independent mayor is re-elected. Here, the incumbent independent mayor does not have to face a majority from another political party in the city council. Sometimes, the situation remains non-partisan (Saanich, Langley, Trois-Rivières), and in others it becomes uni-partisan (Coquitlam, Saguenay) or multi-partisan (Richmond). This scenario is similar to the situation in Abbotsford, where a new independent mayor was elected with a party that is in the minority on city council.

A brief analysis of these twenty cities reveals three elements: 1) The departure of an incumbent mayor contributes to the appearance of new political parties. 2) Incumbent mayors that lead a party tend to dominate the political scene and are seemingly difficult to beat – this dominance also appears to be equally applicable for incumbent political parties when there is a leadership transition. 3) Incumbent independent mayors can be beaten, though this phenomenon is rare. The creation of political parties for the purpose of running against an incumbent independent mayor does not appear to be the most efficient means of beating said candidate. Overall, such parties tend to remain very marginal or hold a minority on city council.

Table 3.2 summarizes the systems of competition in the ten largest cities in Quebec and British Columbia based on the number of parties present on their respective city councils. The two provinces run the full gamut with non-partisan, uni-partisan, and multi-partisan systems. The uni-partisan system is the most common, with five cities in Quebec and four in British Columbia. In six of these nine cases, the mayor's party is the only one present on city council. The mayor, as party leader, holds the majority in four out of six cases. This means there are only two cases of cohabitation between a mayor and a city council composed of independent city councillors. The three uni-partisan cases were cities where parties held a minority with an independent mayor.

For the multi-party systems, in five of the seven cases the mayor was the head of a party, with a majority in city council. The mayor was independent and cohabitated with several other parties in one other case. In that case, the mayor's party held a minority and cohabitated with another party that did not have a majority either. Regarding the four non-partisan systems, there were two cities where political

Table 3.2
Competition systems in the ten biggest cities in British Columbia and Quebec

	Non-partisan	*Uni-partisan*	*Multi-partisan*
Quebec	1	5	4
British Columbia	3	4	3

parties presented candidates, but neither managed to have those candidates elected. In the two other cases, there were no political parties running for election.

These diverse descriptive elements aptly demonstrate the specificity of municipal political parties in Canada. In practical terms, this means that the first and fourth criteria of La Palombara and Weiner's typology are not easily applicable to such organizations. Nevertheless, these formations contribute to forming systems of competition and influence the accountability–responsiveness relationship.

RESPONSIVENESS, ACCOUNTABILITY, AND POLITICAL MUNICIPAL COMPETITION IN CANADA

By re-using previously collected data on the number of political parties present in the same system of competition, we can develop a few hypotheses about their influence on accountability and responsiveness (figure 3.1). The municipal level is a quasi-presidential system in which the mayor is directly elected by the entire populace. Though the process does involve different parties, the mayor nonetheless remains the central figure of the system. There is essentially a personalization of power (Karvonen 2010), so much so that it is possible to think that the incumbent mayor influences the choices of the electors, even at the district level. From this perspective, a multi-partisan system is preferable to a uni-partisan system or to a system with no parties at all. In a multi-partisan context, electors have a choice between several alternatives. The presence of an alternating option in power can accentuate accountability for the elected officials in power. Additionally, the presence of several parties should, in principle, push them toward being more responsive to the preferences of citizens. In practice, however, there remain several nuances to note. For one, the parties nevertheless need clarity of responsibility in each of the systems of competition. As we have seen, the cohabitation between the political

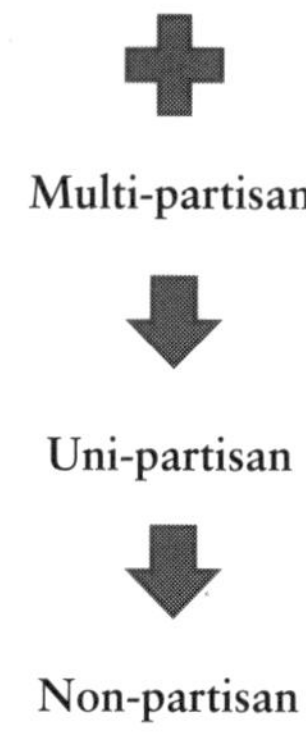

Multi-partisan

Uni-partisan

Non-partisan

Figure 3.1 Hierarchy of responsiveness
and accountability according to the partisan
competition system

parties and independent elected officials is governed by several structures at once. This type of hybrid structure does not necessarily align with figure 3.1.

Table 3.3 presents a typology of the systems of competition that are found in Canadian municipalities. As a reminder, this table is based on our observations. It attempts to delineate the systems of competition in a municipal partisan context. For each of the categories, there are a number of cities in parentheses that have been previously analyzed. The idea behind this first typology is to distinguish between systems of competition according to clarity of responsibility. Clarity is highest when the mayor is the leader of a party that holds a majority in city council. The left-hand column shows the presence, or absence, of a majority for political parties in their city councils. The second aspect of the typology, which is the status of the mayors and whether they are the leader of a political party. This diagram has four boxes allowing for a distinction between several possible modes of municipal-level political competition in Canada. We opted to use four models of competition, which can be situated in more than one box for the typology. Belonging to more than one typology box indicates influence on the clarity of responsibility. Figure 3.2 presents the broad strokes of this model.

Table 3.3
Political competition system typology

	Mayor is a party leader	*Mayor is independent*
One party has majority in council	Majority government party (9)	Cohabitation with a majority opposition party (0)
	Cohabitation with a majority opposition party (0)	
No party has majority in council	Cohabitation with a fragmented council (3)	Cohabitation with a fragmented council (4)
		Non-partisan (4)

It is important that we distinguish between majoritarian government parties where the mayor is the head of a party with a majority. This is the most common case, with nine cities fitting this model. We next have a cohabitation between a mayor and one or two parties in a minority. Seven cities fit this scenario. In four cases the mayor is an independent candidate, and in three other cases the mayors lead a party with a minority. There is also, conceivably, cohabitation between a mayor and an opposition party with a majority, yet none of the cities analyzed had this scenario. In 2005, the City of Quebec had this scenario with an independent mayor and then again in 2007 with another independent mayor who was seated with an opposition party holding a majority. The last case is a non-partisan system, which was found in four cities.

The majoritarian government party model is the one that presents the most obvious clarity of responsibility. In principle, this model shows that the cohesion of the incumbent government in reaction to the electorate is highest. Additionally, it is precisely in this type of government that formal dispersion is least important, since only one party is singled out in decision-making. However, the examples of Laval and Montreal show that a majority party can dissolve. If a majoritarian government party does not run for election, no accountability is possible, since there is no cohesion with regard to the electorate. Hence, we see the importance of transfers of leadership within municipal parties. As we will discuss later, cohesion and dispersion of power can also depend on the type of political party.

Regarding cohabitation structures, this clarity is theoretically lower than in a majoritarian government party structure. Varying types of cohabitation can also exist within city councils. These mechanisms

Majoritarian government

Independent mayor cohabitation

Mayor's party cohabitation

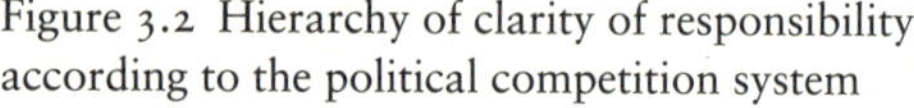

Figure 3.2 Hierarchy of clarity of responsibility
according to the political competition system

affect the level of dispersion and cohesion of power. This can range from a government coalition all the way to confrontation and blame avoidance (Weaver 1986). A simple hypothesis, which remains to be tested, appears to support the case that cohabitation and clarity of responsibility are highest when there is an independent mayor. In fact, according to the above figure, there most likely will be a formal or even informal coalition government. In essence, this means that an independent mayor cannot act alone and must instead find support within the city council. As a result, coalition members, if they are known to the electors, can be associated with responsibility for the actions that have been taken. In this coalition scenario there is a certain level of cohesion rather than dispersion. A priori, a formal coalition presents more clarity than an informal one. The presence of a minority political party in a coalition with an independent mayor could also strengthen clarity by minimizing dispersion. If the independent mayor does not run in the following election, because of cohesion the incumbent coalition members will be accountable. Therefore, accountability would be impossible if there are no incumbents in the running. In the case when an independent mayor is isolated by a majority party that refuses to collaborate, it is the opposition that risks being attributed with responsibility for the actions or inactions of the government.

Table 3.4
Municipal non-partisan system typology

	Link to other level	*No link to other level*
Informal coalition	Quasi-partisan (cohesion + electoral cue)	Quasi-partisan (cohesion)
No informal coalition	Quasi-partisan (electoral cue)	Purely non-partisan

By the same logic, we hypothesize that the level of clarity decreases when the mayor leads a party with a minority on city council, since the mayor must then find allies from independent councillors or other parties. However, mayors who belong to a party have less chances of forming alliances. In this case, more dispersion leads to less cohesion. In fact, a coalition led by a party could be given credit for success or blamed for government actions performed by elected officials who are not members of the party. By the same token, when the mayor, as party leader, cohabitates with another, majority party in city council, clarity could be at its lowest. This is a fairly common occurrence in minority governments. Partisan confrontation and strategies of blame avoidance should therefore be commonplace for this configuration of a city council.

Non-partisan systems, for their part, show the least cohesion and, in particular, the most dispersion of power. However, not all non-partisan systems are purely non-partisan, in the sense that elected officials are not always entirely independent. Thus, alliances of varying sustainability can exist; thus, the level of cohesion in non-partisan city councils varies. For example, mayors can be isolated by their own councillors, can succeed in eking out a majority for most issues, or can develop alliances in piecemeal fashion. While this remains a simple hypothesis, the presence of logrolling by its very nature favours informal coalitions in non-partisan systems. In table 3.4, we list what we believe to be the fundamentals to understanding what encourages or discourages responsiveness and accountability in non-partisan systems. This typology can also apply in cases where an independent mayor is seated with third parties on city council. As with table 3.3, this table aims at providing a definition and model for the reality we observed and offering a typology for systems of competition in a non-partisan context.

This typology presents two aspects. The first aspect is how it relates to the presence or absence of an informal coalition. An informal coalition exists when a group of elected officials in a majority vote in solidarity on the vast majority of issues. The presence of such a coalition generally translates into more coherence in the exercise of power and more cohesion before the electorate. In summary, the success or failure of government actions are more easily attributed to an incumbent candidate if the latter is aligned with the majority than if she or he is not. In this scenario of informal coalition, mayors can either participate or not in such a coalition. If they do not, they are isolated by city council. It is this risk of isolation that can incite candidates to create political parties.

The second aspect of the table indicates the ties maintained between elected officials and higher levels of government. In fact, elected officials are not members of a municipal political party. However, they can still be sympathetic, passive or active members, or even former elected officials of a political party at the federal or provincial level. The presence of a party connection, its intensity, and the public's level of awareness can also serve as a heuristic shortcut for electors, as was shown by Stephenson, McGregor, and Moore in chapter 1. This partisan tie facilitates the choice for electors by reducing ideological dispersion.

Overall, the typology of table 3.4 allows us to differentiate between what we call quasi-partisan and purely non-partisan systems. The quasi-partisan expression simply means that despite the absence of a party label, a certain coherence of actions can be attributed to a party regarding the actions of a government made up of independent elected officials. Figure 3.3 presents our reflections on the effect of quasi-parties on clarity of responsibility. Clarity is greater when there is an informal coalition and a partisan tie.

For the Canadian municipal level, it is possible to categorize the different systems of electoral competition and to schematically show the consequences of these systems in terms of accountability and responsiveness. To conclude this reflection, we will take a closer look at the way in which municipal political parties can have an influence on political accountability and responsiveness.

CONCLUSION: CANADIAN MUNICIPAL PARTIES REGARDING ACCOUNTABILITY AND RESPONSIVENESS

The purpose of this chapter was to attempt to understand the way in which mechanisms of accountability and political responsiveness are

Cohesion + electoral cue

Cohesion / electoral cue

Pure non-partisan

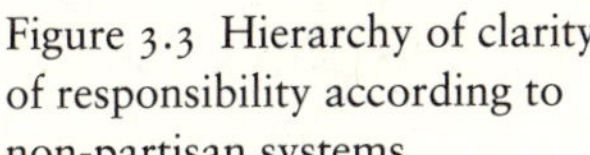

Figure 3.3 Hierarchy of clarity
of responsibility according to
non-partisan systems

expressed in a context in which political parties do not meet the generally established criteria for qualifying as either partisan or non-partisan. We began by reviewing the definition of a national political party, followed by an examination of the specificities of municipal political parties. By focusing on two Canadian provinces that have had legislation favourable to the formation of municipal political parties, we categorized the different types and systems of parties in order to better understand their possible influences on the mechanisms of accountability and responsiveness.

Over the course of our reflection, we used case studies to develop a typology for Canadian municipal parties and their relationships with the terms of accountability and responsiveness. Table 3.5 presents this typology for political parties. Again, as a reminder, this was a first attempt to more accurately capture the municipal political scene. The type of party we described was developed through observations of these parties as well as partisan (table 3.3) and non-partisan contexts (table 3.4). The aspects listed on the left column refer to the party's origins. In accordance with what we described in the first section of this chapter, we consider parties to have originated from candidates and elected officials or from advocacy or interest groups. The aspects listed on the top row of the table refer to party discipline, which can be strict or relaxed.

Table 3.5
Municipal political party typology

	Strong coordination	*Flexible coordination*
Created by advocates or interest groups	Programmatic party	Citizen movement
Created by candidates or elected officials	Coalition to govern	Electoral coalition

These two aspects allowed us to distinguish four types of parties. When party discipline is rigid and the party is the creation of an external group, we consider it to be a program party. If discipline is more relaxed, then we consider it to be a citizens' movement. It is the existence of a more formalized organization in programmatic parties that allows us to make the distinction between program parties and citizens' movements. Additionally, if the party is the creation of elected officials or candidates and if the party line is rigid, then we consider it to be a governing coalition. Finally, if party discipline is relaxed, then it is considered an electoral coalition. The party life between two elections allows us to make the distinction between these two types of parties. An electoral coalition is less likely to be active between elections, with few caucus meetings and little financing activity, for example.

This typology appears to correspond well with the parties present in British Columbia and Quebec. Governing coalitions are more present in Quebec, although British Columbia has electoral coalitions, especially independent candidate associations, as well as several citizens' movements. The presence of program parties is also likely. Montreal's Projet Montréal would appear to fall into this category.

Additionally, in light of the above statements, we could even push this typology further by connecting it with the notions of accountability and responsiveness. Table 3.6 presents the different ways in which accountability and responsiveness can be expressed as a function of each party type.

As a result, from a program party perspective, accountability would be strong and responsiveness weak, since the main goal of this type of party is the application of its platform rather than being responsive to the preferences of citizens. In the case of citizens' movements, responsiveness is likewise weak, yet accountability is too, given the absence of party discipline. A governing coalition, for its part, shows

Table 3.6
Accountability and responsiveness according to municipal political party type

	Accountability	*Responsiveness*
Programmatic party	+	–
Citizen movement	–	–
Governing coalition	+	+
Electoral coalition	-	+

the most accountability and responsiveness, whereas an electoral coalition, which is less active between elections, would most likely be less accountable.

As with any typology, the one proposed in this chapter is mechanical and restrictive, putting ideal-types to the forefront. In addition, the typology admittedly still needs further testing. Nonetheless, it serves as a useful tool in our reflection while also giving us pointers as to future research paths – for example, by raising important research questions. Among these questions are: How can parties that are external to both elected officials and candidates be susceptible to diminishing responsiveness? What are the conditions that allow for a transfer of leadership while respecting the criteria established by La Palombara and Weiner (1966) for ensuring that municipal political parties are true political parties? And how do dominant parties manage to form political monopolies, which remain a reality at this level of government (Bherer 2011; Trounstine 2008)?

APPENDIX

Table 3.7
Parties in each city

Party name	*City*	*Mayor candidate vote share*	*Mayor candidate elected*	*Number of candidates as councillors*	*Number of councillors elected*
Vision Vancouver	Vancouver	46.0	Yes	8	6
Non Partisan Association	Vancouver	40.4	No	8	3
Green	Vancouver	–	–	3	1

Table 3.7
Parties in each city (*continued*)

Party name	City	Mayor candidate vote share	Mayor candidate elected	Number of candidates as councillors	Number of councillors elected
Coalition of Progressive Electors	Vancouver	9.2	No	8	0
Vancouver First	Vancouver	–	–	4	0
Cedar Party	Vancouver	–	–	4	0
Stop Party	Vancouver	0.3	No	0	–
Hotel Workers	Vancouver	–	–	1	0
idea	Vancouver	–	–	1	0
One City Vancouver	Vancouver	–	–	1	0
Surrey first	Surrey	48.2	Yes	8	8
One Surrey	Surrey	21.0	No	7	0
Safe Surrey Coalition	Surrey	27.0	No	4	0
Team Surrey	Surrey	–	–	1	0
Burnaby Citizen Association	Burnaby	68.9	Yes	8	8
Burnaby First	Burnaby	21.7	No	8	0
Richmond Citizen Association	Richmond	–	–	6	2
Rite	Richmond	–	–	1	1
Richmond First	Richmond	–	–	5	3
Richmond Reform	Richmond	27.4	No	1	0
Renew Richmond	Richmond	–	–	2	0
Abbotsford First	Abbotsford	–	–	5	4
Coquitlam Citizen Association	Coquitlam	–	–	5	2
Prosper Kelowna	Kelowna	–	–	2	0
Tax Payer First	Kelowna	–	–	4	0
Delta Independent Voter Association	Delta	100.0	Yes	3	2
Independents Working for You	Delta	–	–	2	2
Delta Connect	Delta	–	–	2	0
Équipe Denis Coderre pour Montréal	Montreal	32.2	Yes	63	27
Vrai changement pour Montréal – Équipe Mélanie Joly	Montreal	26.5	No	35	4

Party name	City	Mayor candidate vote share	Mayor candidate elected	Number of candidates as councillors	Number of councillors elected
Projet Montréal – Équipe Bergeron	Montreal	25.5	No	64	20
Coalition Montréal – Marcel Côté	Montreal	12.8	No	62	6
Intégrité Montréal	Montreal	1.4	No	22	0
Équipe Anjou	Montreal	–	–	2	2
Équipe Dauphin Lachine	Montreal	–	–	2	2
Équipe Barbe Team – Pro Action LaSalle	Montreal	–	–	3	3
Équipe Conservons Outremont	Montreal	–	–	1	1
Parti alternatif LaSalle	Montreal	–	–	3	0
Équipe Savard – Option Verdun / Montréal	Montreal	–	–	3	0
Équipe Andrée Champoux pour Verdun	Montreal	–	–	3	0
Équipe Richard Bélanger	Montreal	–	–	1	0
Équipe Labeaume	Quebec	74.4	Yes	21	18
Démocratie Québec	Quebec	25.6	No	21	3
Alliance de Québec	Quebec	–	–	3	0
Mouvement lavallois	Laval	44.2	Yes	21	17
Action Laval – Équipe Jean Claude Gobé	Laval	24.3	No	21	2
Option Laval	Laval	12.4	No	21	0
Parti au service du citoyen – Équipe Robert Bordeleau	Laval	10.9	No	21	0
Nouveau Parti des Lavallois – Équipe Guy Landry	Laval	1.3	No	3	0
Action Gatineau	Gatineau	52.6	Yes	18	4
Action Longueuil – Équipe Caroline St–Hilaire	Longueuil	87.3	Yes	15	13
Option Greenfield Park	Longueuil	–	–	1	1

Table 3.7
Parties in each city (*continued*)

Party name	City	Mayor candidate vote share	Mayor candidate elected	Number of candidates as councillors	Number of councillors elected
Équipe Bernard Sévigny – Renouveau sherbrookois	Sherbrooke	73.4	Yes	19	10
Comme une eau Terre	Sherbrooke	5.9	No		
Équipe Paul Grimard – Équipe du renouveau démocratique	Saguenay	37.0	No	18	2
Lévis Force 10 – Équipe Lehouillier	Lévis	38.9	Yes	15	14
Renouveau Lévis	Lévis	16.4	No	15	0
Action Lévis	Lévis	5.2	No	8	0
Force 3R	Trois-Rivières	2.3	No	10	0
Équipe Robitaille	Terrebonne	62.4	Yes	16	14
Renouveau Terrebonne	Terrebonne	37.6	No	9	0

REFERENCES

Aldrich, John H. 1995. *Why Parties? The Origin and Transformation of Political Parties in America*. Chicago: University of Chicago Press.

Aldrich, John H., and David W. Rodhe. 2001. "The Logic of Conditional Party Government: Revisiting the Electoral Connection." In *Congress Reconsidered*, edited by Lawrence C. Dodd and Bruce I. Oppenheimer, 269–92, Washington: CQ Press.

Alford, Robert, and Eugene Lee. 1968. "Voting Turnout in American Cities." *The American Political Science Review* 62(3): 796–813.

Almond, Gabriel A., and James S. Coleman. 1960. *The Politics of the Developing Areas*. Princeton, NJ: Princeton University Press.

Althaus, Scott L. 2003. *Collective Preferences in Democratic Politics: Opinion Surveys and the Will of the People*. Cambridge: Cambridge University Press.

Anzia, Sarah F. 2015. *City Policies, City Interests: An Alternative Theory of Interest Group Systems*. Goldman School of Public Policy. Accessed 28 July 2017. https://gspp.berkeley.edu/assets/uploads/research/pdf/Anzia_CityInterestGroups_Aug2015.pdf.

Anzia, Sarah F., and Olivia M. Meeks. 2016. "Political Parties and Policy Demanders in Local Elections." Paper presented at the University of Maryland–Hewlett Foundation Conference on Parties, Polarization and Policy Demanders.

Bartels, Lary M. 2000. "Partisanship and Voting Behavior 1952–1966." *American Journal of Political Science* 44: 35–50.

Bawn, Kathleen, Martin Cohen, David Karol, Seth Masket, Hans Noel, and John Zaller. 2012. "A Theory of Political Parties: Groups, Policy Demands and Nominations in American Politics." *Perspectives on Politics* 10(3): 571–97.

Bherer, Laurence. 2011. "Pourquoi un sixième mandat pour le maire de Laval en 2009? Les sources d'un monopole politique." In *Les élections municipales au Québec en 2011: enjeux et perspectives*, edited by Sandra Breux and Laurence Bherer, 233–65. Quebec: Presses de l'Université Laval.

Bherer, Laurence, and Sandra Breux. 2012. "L'apolitisme municipal." *Bulletin d'histoire politique* 21(1): 170–84.

Bonneau, Chris, and Damon Cann. 2015. "Party Identification and Vote Choice in Partisan and Nonpartisan Elections." *Political Behavior* 37(1): 43–66.

Breux, Sandra, and Laurence Bherer. 2013. "The Democratic Contributions on Local Political Parties: A View from Canada." Paper presented at the Political Studies Association, Cardiff, UK.

Breux, Sandra, Jérôme Couture, and Nicole Goodman. 2016. "Fewer Voters, Higher Stakes? The Applicability of Rational Choice for Voter Turnout in Small Quebec Municipalities." *Environment and Planning C.* Published online before print, 4 November. doi:10.1177/0263774X 16676272.

Breux, Sandra, Jérôme Couture, and Royce Koop. 2017. "Turnout in the 100 Biggest Canadian Cities (2004–2014)." *Canadian Journal of Political Science.* Published online before print, 3 July. doi:https://doi. org/10.1017/S0008423917000018X.

Bridges, Amy. 1997. "Textbook Municipal Reform." *Urban Affairs Review* 33(1): 97–119.

Caladarone, Richard, Brandice Canes-Wrone, and Tom S. Clark. 2009. "Partisan Labels and Democratic Accountability: An Analysis of State Supreme Court Abortions Decisions." *The Journal of Politics* 71(2): 560–73.

Caren, Neal. 2007. "Big City, Big Turnout? Electoral Participation in American Cities." *Journal of Urban Affairs* 29(1): 31–46.

Chong, Dennis, and James Druckman. 2007. "Framing Public Opinion in Competitive Democracies." *American Journal of Political Science Review* 101(4): 637–55.

Cohen, Marty, David Karol, Hans Noel, and John Zaller. 2008. *The Party Decides: Presidential Nominations before and after Reform*. Chicago: University of Chicago Press.

Copus, Colin, Melvin Wingfield, Kristof Steyvers, and Herwig Reynaert. 2012. "A Place to Party? Parties and Nonpartisanship in Local Government." In *The Oxford Handbook of Urban Politics*, edited by Karen Mossberger, Susan E. Clarke, and Peter John, 211–30. Oxford: Oxford University Press.

Couture, Jérôme, Sandra Breux, and Laurence Bherer. 2014. "Analyse écologique des déterminants de la participation électorale municipale au Québec." *Canadian Journal of Political Science* 47(4): 787–812.

Cox, Gary W., and Mathew D. McCubbins. 1993. *Legislative Leviathan: Party Government in the House*. Berkeley: University of California Press.

– 2005. *Setting the Agenda: Responsible Party Government in the US House of Representatives*. Cambridge: Cambridge University Press.

Downs, Anthony. 1957. *An Economic Theory of Democracy*. New York: Harper and Row.

Duverger, Maurice. 1969. *Les partis politiques*. Paris: Colin.

Eldersveld, Samuel J. 1964. *Political Parties: A Behavioral Analysis*. Chicago: Rand McNally.

Elmendorf, Christopher, and David Schleicher. 2012. "Informing Consent: Voter Ignorance, Political Parties and Election Law." *UC Davis Legal Studies Research Paper* 285: 1–70.

Fillon, Pierre. 1999. "Civic Parties in Canada: Their Diversity and Evolution." In *Local Parties on Political and Organizational Perspective*, edited by Martin Saiz and Hans Geser, 77–100. Boulder, CO: Westview Press.

Fiorina, Morris P. 1981. "Retrospective Voting in American National Elections." New Haven, CT: Yale University Press.

Griffin, John D., and Brian Newman. 2005. "Are Voters Better Represented?" *The Journal of Politics* 67(4): 1206–27.

Großer, Jens, and Thomas R. Palfrey. 2014. "Candidate Entry and Political Polarization: An Antimedian Voter Theorem." *American Journal of Political Science* 58(1): 127–43.

Hajnal, Zoltan, and Jessica Trounstine. 2005. "Where Turnout Matters: The Consequences of Uneven Turnout in City Politics." *Journal of Politics* 67(2): 515–35. doi:10.1111/j.1468-2508.2005.00327.x.

Hobot, Sara, James Tilley, and Susan Baducci. 2013. "Clarity of Responsibility: How Government Cohesion Conditions Performance Voting." *European Journal of Political Research* 52(2): 164–87.

Jupp, James. 1968. *Political Parties*. London: Routledge and Kegan Paul.

Karnig, Albert, and Oliver Walter. 1983. "Decline in Municipal Voter Turnout: A Function of Changing Structure." *American Politics Quarterly* 11(4): 491–505.

Karvonen, Lauri. 2010. *The Personalization of Politics*. Colchester: ECPR Press.

Key, Valdimer O. 1942. *Politics, Parties and Pressure Groups*. New York: Crowell.

Kjaer, Ulrik, and Jørgen Elklit. 2010. "Local Party System Nationalisation: Does Municipal Size Matter?" *Local Government Studies* 36(3): 425–44. doi:10.1080/03003931003730451.

La Palombara, Joseph, and Myron Weiner. 1966. *Political Parties and Political Development*. Princeton, NJ: Princeton University Press.

Lemieux, Vincent. 2012. *Les partis et leurs transformations*. Quebec: Presses de l'Université Laval.

– 1985. *Systèmes partisans et partis politiques*. Sillery: Presses de l'Université du Québec.

Lipset, Seymour, and Stein Rokkan. 1967. *Party System and Voters Alignments*. New York: Free Press.

Lublin, David I., and Katherine Tate. 1995. "Racial Group Competition in Urban Elections." In *Classifying by Race*, edited by Paul E. Peterson. Princeton: Princeton University Press.

MacKuen, Michael, Robert S. Erickson, and James A. Stimson, 1989. "Macropartisanship." *American Political Science Review* 83(4): 1125–42.

Mainwaring, Scott, and Mariano Torcal. 2006. "Party System Institutionalization and Party System Theory after the Third Wave of Democratization." In *Handbook of Party Politics*, edited by Richard S. Katz and William J. Crotty, 204–27. London: Sage.

Mair, Peter. 1990. *The West European Party System*. Oxford: Oxford University Press.

Marschall, Melissa J. 2010. "The Study of Local Elections in American Politics." In *The Oxford Handbook of American Elections and Political Behavior*, edited by Jan. E. Leighley, 471–92. Oxford: Oxford University Press.

Michels, Robert. 1971. *Les partis politiques: essai sur les tendances oligarchiques des démocraties*. Paris: Flammarion.

Oliver, Eric, Shang Ha, and Zachary Callen. 2012. *Local Elections and the Politics of Small-Scale Democracy*. Princeton, NJ: Princeton University Press.

Parodi, Jean-Luc. 2004. "Les élections 'intermédiaires' du printemps 2004." *Revue française de science politique* 54(4): 533–43.

Powell, G. Bingham, and Guy D. Whitten. 1993. "A Cross-National Analysis of Economic Voting: Taking Account of the Political Context." *American Journal of Political Science* 37(2): 391–414.

Rokkan, Stein. 1996. *Citizens, Elections, Parties*. Oslo: ECPR Press.

Sartori, Giovanni. 1976. *Parties and Party Systems*. New York: Cambridge University Press.

Schaffner, Brian F., Matthew J. Streb, and Gerald C. Wright. 2001. "Teams without Uniforms: The Nonpartisan Ballot in State and Local Elections." *Political Research Quarterly* 54(1): 7–30. doi:10.1177/106591290105400101.

Schneider, Mark, Melissa Marschall, Christine Roch, and Paul Teske. 1999. "Heuristics, Low Information Rationality, and Choosing Public Goods: Broken Windows as Shortcuts to Information about School Performance." *Urban Affairs Review* 34(5): 729–41.

Trounstine, Jessica. 2008. *Political Monopolies in American Cities: The Rise and Fall of Bosses and Reformers*. Chicago: University of Chicago Press.

Weaver, R. Kent. 1986. "The Politics of Blame Avoidance." *Journal of Public Policy* 60(4): 371–98.

Webb, Paul, David Farell, and Ian Holliday, eds. 2002. *Political Parties in Advanced Industrial Democracies*. Oxford: Oxford University Press.

PART TWO

Discussing the Career and Function of Elected Officials

4

Responsiveness, Accountability, and the Long-Term Development of Local Political Careers in Calgary and Edmonton

Jack Lucas and Anthony Sayers

INTRODUCTION

Our theories of responsiveness and accountability at the local level of government are centred around elected municipal politicians. The preferences and goals of these politicians – their hopes for re-election, their ambitions to move up to higher levels of government, their understanding of the municipal office as either a part-time service or full-time career – shape how they will respond to constituent preferences and the extent to which they can be held accountable for their decisions while in office. By focusing our attention on their political career, an aspect of municipal government that has largely been neglected in Canada, we can learn a great deal about accountability and responsiveness in Canadian municipalities.

In this chapter, we present a comparative analysis of the long-term development of local political careers in the Canadian cities of Edmonton and Calgary. Drawing on a new dataset containing the full career trajectory of each of the 604 individuals elected to municipal office in the two cities, we describe career lengths, council stability and turnover, and rates of incumbent success. We then draw on the Canadian Elections Database to provide a survey of local political careers as a whole, including periods of provincial or federal office, to understand how municipal political service fits into larger career trajectories in Canada. We conclude with some reflections on the implications of our findings for our understanding of local accountability and responsiveness in Canadian local government.

ACCOUNTABILITY, RESPONSIVENESS, AND CAREERS

To get a preliminary sense of the possible relationships between accountability and responsiveness, imagine a simple two-by-two table. Along one dimension, we distinguish between high and low levels of accountability, understood as the extent to which politicians are either rewarded or punished by their constituents for their actions while in office (Dutton 1975; Prewitt 1970). Along the second dimension, we distinguish between high and low responsiveness, understood as the extent to which politicians act in the interests of their constituents and respond to their policy preferences and needs (Pitkin 1967; Eulau and Karps 1977).

Plotting these dimensions across one another, as we have done in table 4.1, produces four highly simplified but nonetheless useful accountability–responsiveness regimes. The top-left and bottom-right corners of the table (types 1 and 4) are the familiar categories: these are the regimes in which accountability and responsiveness are closely correlated and both are either high or low. In the two other cells, however, we find some less intuitive possibilities.

Type 2, in the top-right corner of the table, is a regime characterized by high responsiveness and low accountability. In this regime, politicians work hard to respond to constituents, but they are largely immune to traditional forms of electoral accountability: the proverbial politician who "returns every phone call." In these situations, accountability levels can be low – high incumbency rates, an inattentive public, poor media coverage of issues and council decisions, and so on – while some politicians nevertheless continue to respond quickly and consistently to their constituents' needs.

The final remaining type – type 3, in the bottom-left corner of the table – is characterized by high levels of accountability and low responsiveness. In this regime, individual politicians do little to understand or address their own constituents' preferences, but levels of accountability remain high. The most plausible environment in which such a regime might develop is probably one of highly disciplined political parties, with politicians held accountable not so much for their own

Table 4.1
Four responsiveness/accountability regimes

		Responsiveness	
		Low	High
Accountability	Low	1	2
	High	3	4

specific actions as for the collective decisions of the parties to which they belong. Political scandals in low-information contexts – as described by Andrew Sancton in chapter 5 – may also produce environments in which accountability "tornados" occur that are unrelated to ongoing levels of responsiveness.

What factors determine whether a local political system falls into one or another of these four types? The list of potential variables that we might consider is practically endless: electoral systems and voting rules, party structures and policy debates, the local media landscape, levels of education and engagement among the voting public, and so on. Some of these factors are explored in other chapters of this volume. In this chapter, our focus is on the long-term development of the local political career, as well as the political institutions in which those careers take place. Our goal is to describe the large-scale, long-term factors that shape accountability and responsiveness in Canadian local politics. To this end, we identify four features of each city's political development that are particularly relevant for our understanding of accountability and responsiveness regimes.

The first is *career duration*. As Joseph Schlesinger famously argued, the short-term, amateur career – in which men and women briefly take up the noble yoke of office, like Cincinnatus, and then quietly return to private life – may not actually stimulate high levels of accountability or responsiveness (Schlesinger 1966). Since the amateur politician will retire after a term or two of service, constituents cannot "punish" an incumbent politician for poor performance. And while a particularly selfless amateur might work hard to address the needs of her constituents, her motivation to do so is largely altruistic, there being no career-based incentives to build up a reputation for responsiveness. Thus, we may find some clues about the nature and development of a city's accountability–responsiveness regime simply by tracking the *length* of local political careers over time.

A second relevant consideration is *incumbency*. Among the key features of municipal politics in Canada, as many observers have noticed, is the exceptional electoral power of local incumbents: as Andrew Sancton's chapter explains, those who are currently in office are likely to remain in office for as long as they wish to do so (Kushner, Siegel, and Stanwick 1997). While it is possible that high rates of incumbency might reflect nothing more than ongoing public satisfaction with politicians, we might legitimately worry about accountability when incumbency rates remain high over extended periods of time. Exceptionally high incumbency rates can mean that a politician is unlikely to even face a serious challenger – who is unlikely to sign up for an impossible electoral battle – making the incumbent less accountable to constituents for her or his actions.

Closely related to incumbency is the question of council *turnover*. While incumbency rates provide a picture of the likelihood that a particular politician will be defeated, turnover rates offer a view of the council as a whole, including the proportion of new faces in the council chamber each year. These turnover rates may be useful for understanding council's capacity to develop coherent and responsive policies over time. An institution with a very high turnover rate may find it rather difficult to maintain a coherent policy agenda or sufficient institutional memory to develop and implement new policies. Similarly, an institution with an exceptionally low turnover rate may signal some of the same problems of accountability and responsiveness noted in our discussion of incumbency above. Our analysis of turnover rates can thus provide us with some clues about institutional capacity, and the potential for sustained and responsive policy agendas, in Canadian city councils.

A final consideration is *career trajectory*. Do local politicians remain in one office for their entire political careers? Do they move from one institution to another – and if so, do they tend to move through political offices in a consistent direction? Since Joseph Schlesinger's pathbreaking work in the 1960s, political scientists have recognized that responsiveness may vary in important ways depending on a politician's career path; those who harbour ambitions for higher office, for instance, are likely to look for opportunities to distinguish themselves as innovative policy leaders (Borchert 2011; Hibbing 1999; Schlesinger 1966). Our data on political careers will allow us to provide an overview of these career trajectories and career types over time and to reflect on their implications for local responsiveness in Canada.

LOCAL CAREERS: AN OVERVIEW

We begin with a survey of the first three factors mentioned above: career duration, incumbency, and turnover. Our analysis below is based on a new dataset containing the full political career of every councillor and mayor ever elected in the cities of Edmonton and Calgary from the time of their incorporation in the nineteenth century up to the present. We constructed the municipal portion of the dataset using materials provided to us by the Calgary and Edmonton archives. We then used the Canadian Elections Database – a new database created by Anthony Sayers containing constituency-level data on every provincial and federal election in Canadian history – to add additional career data for Calgary and Edmonton politicians who also served at the provincial or federal levels. The result is a dataset containing the full political career of each of the 604 individuals who have served on Calgary and Edmonton councils. While this dataset is inspired by previous studies of municipal, provincial, and federal careers in Canada (Barrie and Gibbins 1989; Docherty 2011; Lucas 2015), it is, to our knowledge, the first comprehensive and comparative dataset on local political careers assembled in Canada. The full dataset, along with tables, figures, replication files, and a methodological appendix, is available to interested researchers on our website.[1]

Career Duration

Figure 4.1 provides a first look at career lengths on Edmonton and Calgary city councils; the figures capture the average career length of the men and women who sat on council in a particular year. Because the careers of those who have been elected very recently are truncated at the present, average career lengths take a significant plunge in the most recent period; this is an artifact of our inability to see into the future and is therefore best ignored.

Setting aside the most recent period, then, what we can see in both figures is a clear increase in average career lengths over time. In both cities, the average political career in the late nineteenth and early twentieth century hovers at or below five years, reaches ten years by

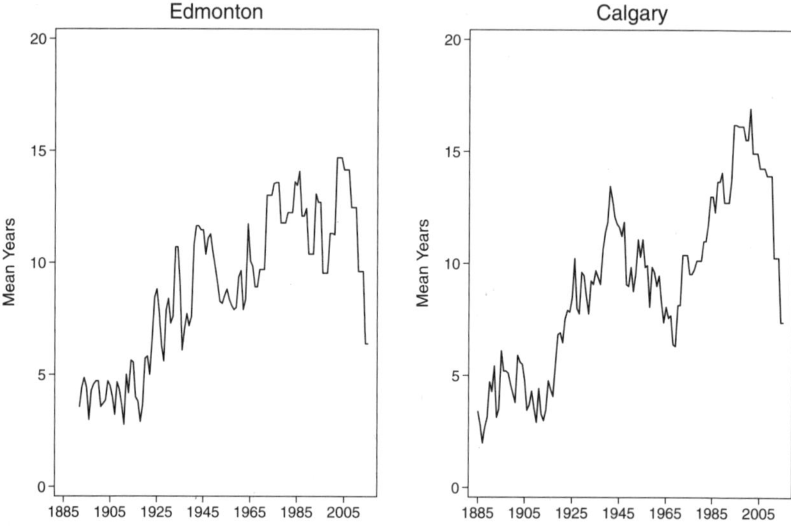

Each year's value is the average career length of the politicians who sat on council in that year. Note that the significant drop at the right-hand side of each figure is best ignored; it results from the truncation of recent political careers at the present.

Figure 4.1 Average career lengths in Calgary and Edmonton

the end of the Second World War, and is now in the neighbourhood of fifteen years in both cities. In Edmonton, this increase appears to have been slightly more gradual than in Calgary, but the general story in both cities is similar.

Figure 4.2 offers a disaggregated look at the same data; each mark represents an individual career (Calgary politicians are circles, and Edmonton politicians are pluses). The horizontal axis marks the year in which the politician's career began, and the vertical axis records total career length. Notice, first, the relative absence of marks above the ten-year mark in the late nineteenth and early twentieth century as well as the high density of marks in the zero-to-five-year range up to the early 1960s; for the first half of both cities' histories, most careers clearly tended to be quite short. Notice also the much more dispersed appearance of the marks in the post-1965 period, suggesting a larger range in career durations in more recent decades. Taken as a whole, the figure illustrates that changes to career durations have occurred both at the bottom and the top ends of the distribution: longer careers have become more common, while very short careers

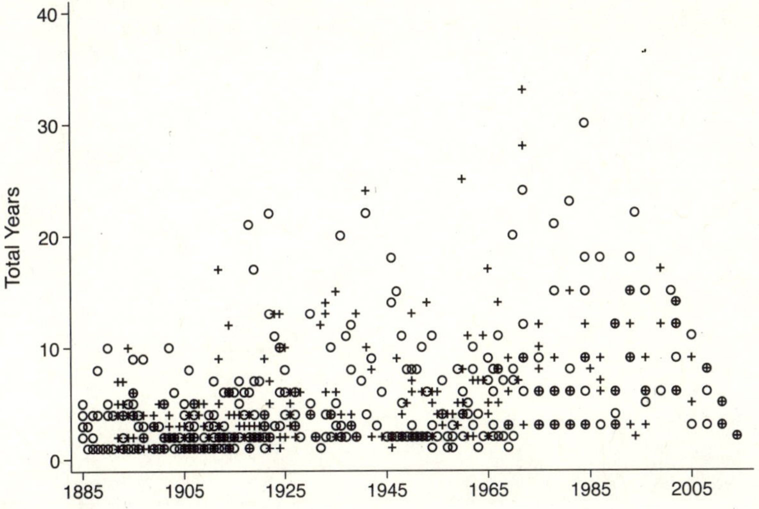

Figure 4.2 Calgary and Edmonton careers by length and first year

have become less common, producing an overall pattern of increasing average career lengths over time.[2]

Incumbency

Given that career lengths have increased in Calgary and Edmonton over time, we might assume that incumbent candidates have had more success at re-election in recent years than in the past. But this relationship is not strictly necessary: it may be, for instance, that candidates in the pre-war years retired more frequently than in recent years rather than being more frequently defeated at the polls. We therefore need to examine incumbency rates separately from the question of career length and council turnover.

Measuring incumbency rates requires that we have access not only to lists of city councillors and mayors over time but also to municipal election results. Our analysis in this section is therefore based on a separate dataset in which we recorded the number of incumbents who ran for office, and the proportion of those incumbents who were re-elected, for each of the municipal elections in Calgary and Edmonton's history.

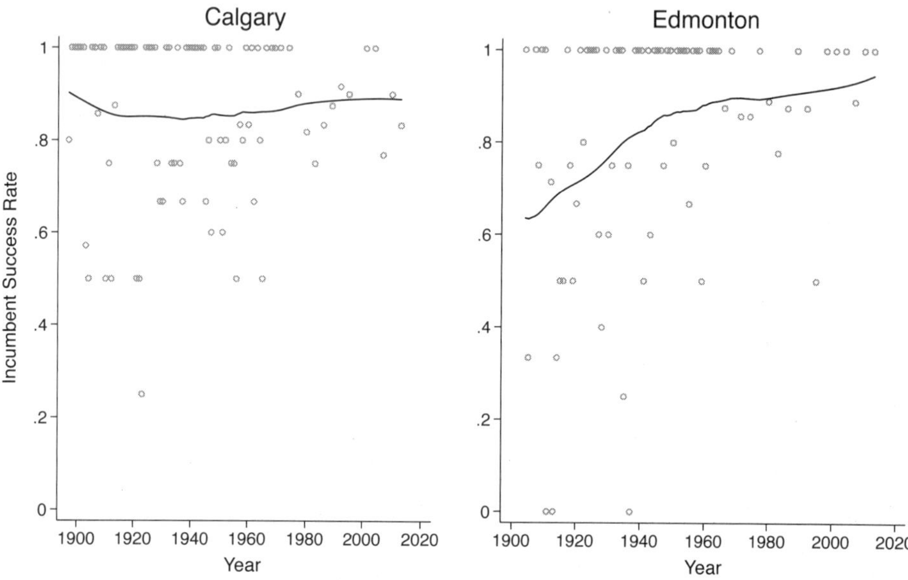

Figure 4.3 Incumbent candidate success in Calgary and Edmonton

The election-by-election results of our analysis are reported in figure 4.3, with the raw re-election rates represented by gray circles and an overall trend line (lowess) in black. The figure suggests considerable volatility in incumbency success rates, ranging from elections in which all incumbents were defeated to those in which every incumbent was successfully re-elected. The overall message in the figures, however, is clear: incumbents have always enjoyed substantial advantages in Calgary and Edmonton, and if anything, that advantage has only grown stronger in recent years.

The most recent period in these figures is particularly remarkable. Since the 2001 election, nearly every incumbent in Edmonton who has chosen to run for office again in the subsequent election has been successfully re-elected. While these individuals represent only about two-thirds of available municipal positions in the past two decades, it is still very important to recognize the enormous advantage of municipal incumbents in contemporary municipal elections. Much the same is true in Calgary: since the 1980s, incumbent success rates in the 80–100 per cent range have been the norm.

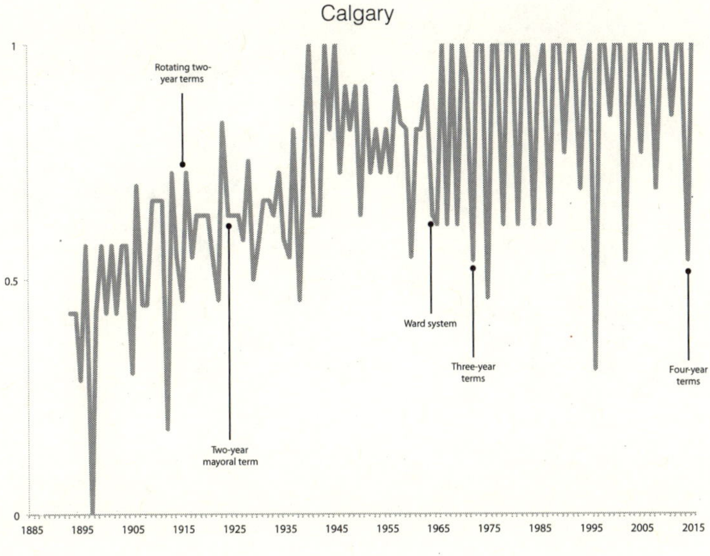

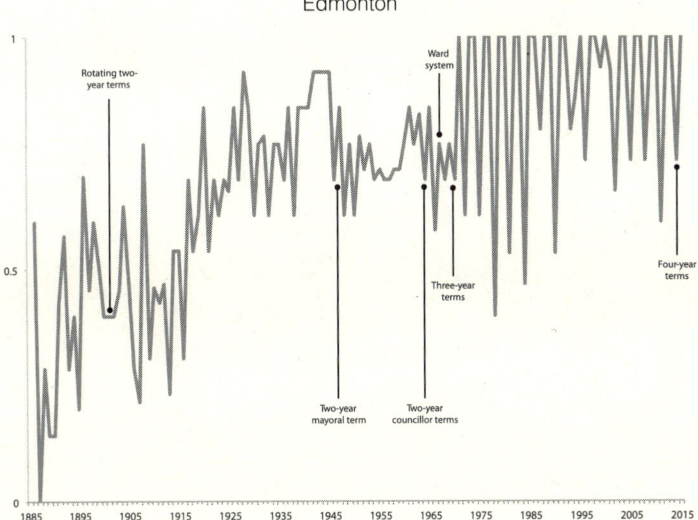

Figure 4.4 Year-by-year stability rates, Calgary and Edmonton

Turnover

We now turn from the individual-level question of career length and incumbency to the institution-level question of turnover: the proportion of the council as a whole that remains constant over the years.

Calgary

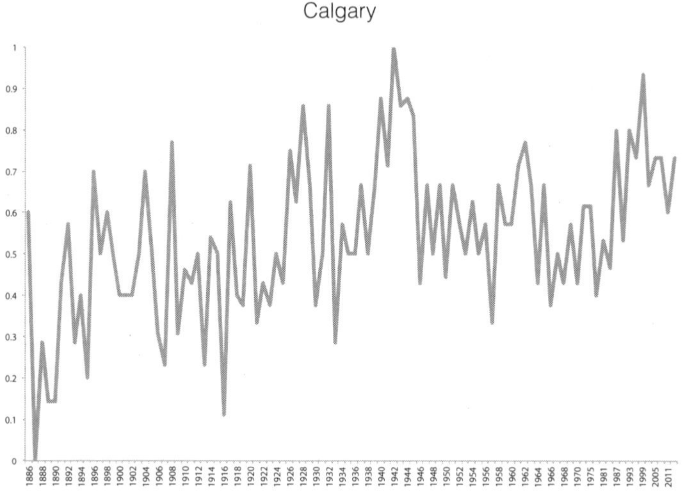

Edmonton

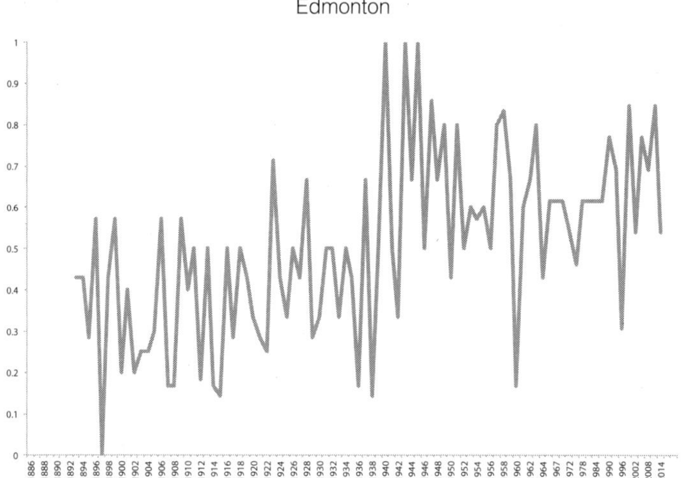

Figure 4.5 Term-by-term stability rates, Calgary and Edmonton

Figure 4.4 provides a comprehensive picture of "stability rates" (the proportion of councillors who remain on council over the years) in Calgary and Edmonton. The figure also notes key institutional changes in Calgary and Edmonton over time.

Beginning with figure 4.4, what is most notable are the nearly identical trajectories in the long-term development of turnover rates in the two cities. The individual city profiles in figure 4.4 suggest that these similarities are driven by similar institutional changes over time. Both Calgary and Edmonton began with one-year terms of municipal office and then shifted to two-year overlapping terms, with half of the city council up for election each year (1899 in Edmonton, 1913 in Calgary). Edmonton then moved to non-overlapping two-year terms for mayors in 1947 and for councillors in 1962 and then to three-year terms for all municipal politicians in 1968. Calgary retained two-year overlapping terms until 1971, when it shifted to three-year terms. Both cities then moved to four-year terms of office beginning in 2013. The impact of these institutional changes is quite clear in the figures. Notice, for instance, how the introduction of rotating two-year terms induces a gradual increase in the year-to-year stability of the councils in both cities; notice also the obvious shift to much higher stability rates after the introduction of three-year terms.

Much of this stability is of course driven directly by the term length itself: provided that councillors do not retire in the midst of their term, turnover levels will be at zero in non-election years. Figure 4.5, which ignores term lengths and records council stability on an election-by-election basis, demonstrates that electoral turnover has changed very little since the end of the Second World War. In both figures, we can see a gradual increase in stability rates up to the middle of the twentieth century, followed by rates just below 60 per cent from that point onward.

CAREER TRAJECTORY

In the discussion above, our dataset has enabled us to provide an overview of career duration, incumbency, and turnover rates on Calgary and Edmonton city councils over time. But political careers are not fully contained within a single political institution or level of government. Thus, in this section we explore the full careers of Calgary and Edmonton municipal politicians, including any time they spent in political life at the provincial or federal levels.

Provincial and Federal Careers: An Overview

Table 4.2 provides a broad look at provincial and federal careers among municipal politicians in Calgary and Edmonton. The proportions are similar in both cities: about 20 to 25 per cent of those who

Table 4.2
Municipal politicians with provincial/federal careers (%)

City	Provincial candidate	Provincially elected	Federal candidate	Federally elected
Calgary	20	11	9	2
Edmonton	26	12	11	4

Table 4.3
Direction of political careers

Stage 1	Stage 2	Frequency
Municipal		86%
Municipal	Provincial	8%
Municipal	Federal	1.5%
Provincial	Municipal	1.5%
Federal	Municipal	0.5%

have served municipally have run as candidates in a provincial election, and about 10 per cent have run in federal elections. Of these candidates, roughly 10 per cent of municipal politicians were successfully elected to provincial office, while considerably fewer – just 2 per cent in Calgary and 4 per cent in Edmonton – have been elected federally.

In what order do politicians in Calgary and Edmonton move through these offices? As table 4.3 shows, politicians in the dataset almost always begin their careers at the municipal level and then move on to provincial or federal office. Just 1.5 per cent of the politicians in the dataset began their careers at the provincial level and then went on to a municipal career, and fewer than 1 per cent were elected federally before entering municipal politics. Among their many roles, municipal institutions continue to serve as "schools of democracy," institutions in which politicians gain legislative experience before moving on to provincial and federal politics.

At this point, then, we know that a substantial portion of municipal politicians in Calgary and Edmonton also serve at the provincial level and that a much smaller proportion of them serve federally; we also know that those who *do* serve at another level of government tend to do so after they have been elected to municipal office. The task at hand, then, is to survey these general patterns over time. Since most of those who have gone on to further political office have done so at

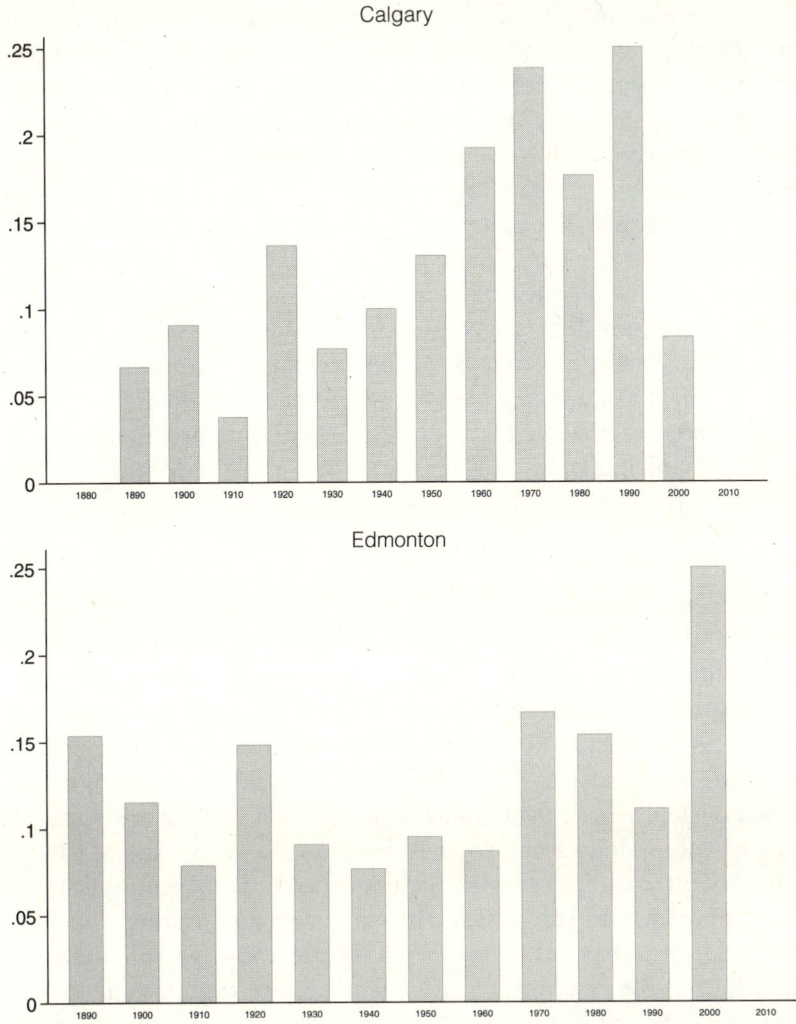

Figure 4.6 Proportion of councillors elected provincially, by decade

the provincial level, we will focus our attention on the provincial side of the story. Figure 4.6 provides a decade-by-decade overview of the proportion of municipal councillors who went on to serve provincially. The figure suggests that while Calgary and Edmonton have similarities in overall *rates* of election, they may nevertheless differ with regard to the proportion of those rates in time. Namely, the proportion in Calgary has followed an upward trajectory while that in Edmonton has remained mostly steady throughout most of its history. This intriguing difference may be attributed to the history of provincial development in Alberta. We conjecture that whereas provincial government has always been highly visible in Edmonton, the capital city, politicians in Calgary may not have started taking provincial politics more seriously until the city began having a more significant weight within the growing province. The amenities of life and work in Calgary – better highways, more up-to-date communication systems, and so on – may also have made a provincial career more attractive to politicians in Calgary over time. These speculations merit further research, since this may offer insight into the extent and timing of provincial political development in Canada. However, whatever the cause of the city-by-city differences, the overall rate of participation in provincial politics among municipal politicians is very similar in the two cities.

Sequence Analysis

To deepen our analysis of career trajectories in Calgary and Edmonton and uncover additional patterns of similarity and dissimilarity among the political careers, we used a sequence analysis tool known as optimal matching. Optimal matching was first used in biology to compare distances between DNA sequences and was introduced into the social sciences by the sociologist Andrew Abbott in the 1980s (Abbott and Forrest 1986). Since then, it has been used in a wide range of studies (see Aisenbrey and Fasang 2010; Abbott and Tsay 2000; and MacIndoe and Abbott 2004 for reviews), including political science applications to turnout, mayoral careers, and urban governance (Buton, Lemercier, and Mariot 2014; Lucas 2016; MacKenzie 2009; Wilson 2014). As a technique for descriptive analysis and pattern recognition, optimal matching algorithms hold considerable promise for revealing patterns of similarity and dissimilarity among sequences, including political careers.

The basic purpose of sequence analysis is to provide a tool with which to systematically compare similarities and differences among sequences – in our case, political careers – within a dataset. For sequence-analytic purposes, "distance" between two careers is measured as the number of insertion, deletion, and substitution operations required to transform one sequence into another. For instance, transforming the sequence "CC" (a two-year council career) into "CCCC" (a four-year council career) would require the insertion of two instances of "C" and thus a distance score of (2). Using insertion, deletion, and substitution operations, sequence analysis algorithms are able to identify differences in career *duration*, career *elements*, and the *order* in which each element occurs in a particular sequence. (A more detailed description of the operation of the sequence analysis technique is available upon request.)

To accurately capture the range of possible differences between one career and another requires that we make two basic decisions: first, we must set the relative "cost" involved in substituting one office for another, and second, we must assign the "cost" of an insertion or deletion operation relative to a substitution. In our case, we developed a substitution cost matrix in which transitions within a level of government (such as a switch from municipal council to municipal mayor) have a substitution cost of (1) while transitions across levels of government (such as a move from municipal to federal office) have a substitution cost of (2). We then assigned a cost of (1) to each insertion or deletion operation. Each of these decisions is in keeping with methodological recommendations in the sequence analysis literature and also aligns with our theoretical interest in career trajectories in this paper. (A more detailed description of these cost settings, including a demonstration of the robustness of our findings to alternative cost settings, is available upon request.)

Optimal matching analyses produce a "distance matrix," akin to the distance table on a road map, which allows us to read the distance or dissimilarity between any pair of careers in the dataset. In our case, the sequence analysis produces a 604 x 604 matrix (one row and column for each distinct career), producing a total of just over 182,000 distinct pairwise distance scores.

We used two basic statistical tools to interpret the distance matrix. First, we used regression analysis to understand how the *distance scores* (our dependent variable) are related to shared characteristics of particular politicians. For instance, it may well be the case – based on a substantial literature review on gender differences in recruitment and political ambition (Fox and Lawless 2014) – that men and women have political careers that tend to look different from each other. It may also be the case that careers in a given city tend to resemble each other more than those across different cities. Finally, it seems plausible, in light of our analysis of career lengths above, that careers that begin around the same time will tend to resemble each other more than those that begin at very different time periods.

To test these possibilities, we coded each of the 182,106 pairwise observations in the distance matrix for three dichotomous variables: whether the members of the pair belong to the same gender, the same city, or the same time period (measured as having begun their careers within five years of one another).[3] Since the dependent variable in the regression is the *distance score* between pairs, a negative coefficient indicates reduced distance and thus a more similar career. For ease of interpretation, we converted *distance scores* to a 100-unit scale; the regression analysis can therefore be interpreted as estimating how many units closer a particular pair of careers is likely to be if the individuals in that pair belong to the *same gender*, the *same city*, or the *same time period*.

The results of the regression analysis are summarized in table 4.4. Both *shared city* and *shared time period* produce statistically significant reductions in distance score. Starting one's career within five years of another person in the dataset is associated with a reduced *distance score* of about three units, a modest but nonetheless conspicuous effect. This finding aligns nicely with our summary of the figures above: careers in Calgary and Edmonton have clearly changed over time, and we should not be surprised that careers tend to resemble each other simply by virtue of having begun around the same time. In the case of careers in the same city, the magnitude of the coefficient is much smaller – a distance reduction of just 0.1 units. Taken as a whole, then, the regression analysis suggests that *time* is an important variable for understanding similarities and differences among local political careers in Calgary and Edmonton, while *shared city* and *shared gender* are not.

This leads us to a second, more descriptive data-reduction technique: cluster analysis. A cluster analysis of the 604 x 604 distance matrix allows us to seek out patterns in the data that may be associated with particular career *types*. Determining the exact number of types to extract from a cluster analysis involves a combination of science and art; while there are statistical tools that we can and do use to narrow down the list of possibilities, our choice among the remaining alternatives must trade off the simplicity of a smaller number of clusters against the precision of a larger number. (A more detailed description of these trade-offs, as well as the stopping rules that we used to select an appropriate number of clusters, is available upon request.)

In the case of political careers in Calgary and Edmonton, we believe that it is most informative to divide the distance matrix into three

Table 4.4
Impact of shared gender, city, and time period
on sequence distance

	Distance
Same city	−0.167*
	[−0.309, −0.0246]
Same gender	0.104
	[−0.0816, 0.290]
Same time period	−3.371***
	[−3.617, −3.124]
Constant	34.97***
	[34.78, 35.15]
Observations	182,106

95% confidence intervals in brackets

* $p <0.05$;   **$p<0.01$;   ***$p<0.001$

distinct career types. We summarize these types in table 4.5.[4] For ease of interpretation, we highlighted what we consider to be the decisive components – the aspects of the cluster that differentiate it most clearly from the others – for each type. At the right-hand side of table 4.5, we provide a description and an example of each of the career types. Clusters 1 and 2 are primarily municipal careers; nearly all of these individuals spent their entire political careers at the municipal level of government. What distinguishes the two clusters is career length. In the first cluster, composed of "municipal professionals," careers are quite long, averaging about a decade, while careers in the second cluster, composed of "municipal amateurs," careers average just over three years.[5] Izena Ross, for instance, who was the first woman ever elected to city council in Edmonton, is a member of cluster two, having served for just a single year in 1922. Janice Reimer, on the other hand, who was the first woman to be elected mayor of Edmonton, had a fifteen-year municipal career beginning in 1980 and belongs to cluster one. While both women's careers took place exclusively at the municipal level, the difference in length between the two separates them into two distinct clusters.

Cluster three is distinguished by the provincial political component: all of the forty-one individuals in this cluster were elected at some point to provincial office. In nearly every case, as we noted above, those who have served as elected government officials at the provincial or federal levels had been voted into office at those levels of

Table 4.5
Summary of career types in Calgary and Edmonton

Clus.	N	El.	Yrs.	May. (%)	Prov. (%)	Fed. (%)	Description	Example
1	200	1.4	9.3	11	4	0.50	Municipal professional	CCCCCMM
2	363	1.4	3.3	11	5	4	Municipal amateur	CCC
3	41	2.5	15.4	14	100	0	Provincial climber	CCCPPPPP

Note: Columns in this table, from left to right: cluster number (Clus.), number of individuals (N), career elements (El.), average number of years (Yrs.), proportion of individuals in the cluster with mayoral service (May.), proportion of individuals in the cluster with provincial service (Prov.), proportion of individuals in the cluster with federal service (Fed.), description, and example of a sequence from each cluster.

government *after* their time at the municipal level. We therefore label this cluster the "provincial climbers" to capture their movement from the municipal to the provincial level of government. Ralph Klein, for example, began his career at the municipal level, serving as mayor of Calgary for nearly ten years; he was then elected to the Alberta legislature in 1989 from where he went on to serve as premier of Alberta for more than a decade. Klein's career is a good example of the "provincial climber" trajectory in cluster three.

How have these three career types developed over time? Figure 4.7 provides a historical overview of each career in the dataset organized by career type, career starting year, and city. Notice, first, the basic similarities between the circles (Calgary and Edmonton careers) in each of the three categories, confirming what the regression analysis had already suggested: political careers in Calgary and Edmonton have been very similar both in the distribution of career types and in their development across time. Second, notice how the "municipal amateur" category at the top of the figure is more densely populated in the earlier decades of the timeline. These careers began to fade somewhat in the 1960s as both cities moved toward longer terms of office and more sustained careers for local politicians.

The final observation that emerges from the figure is the lack of any obvious temporal patterns in the two career types at the bottom of the figure. Both the "municipal professional" and the "provincial climber" have been common throughout both cities' histories. As the shorter municipal careers faded, these career types grew in prominence

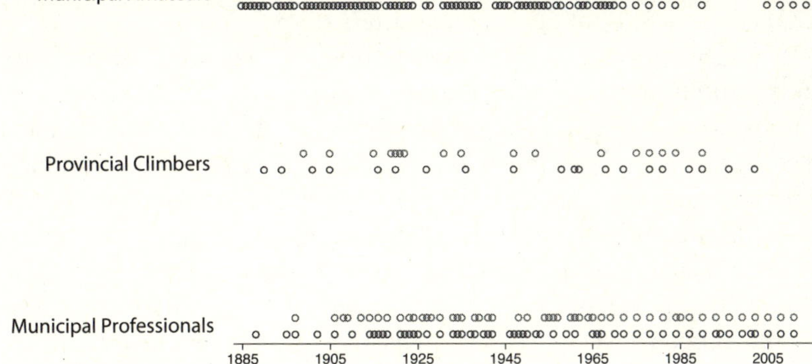

Frequency of each career type over time, marked by year in which career began. Edmonton careers on top, Calgary below.

Figure 4.7 Career types in Calgary and Edmonton, 1885–2015

as a proportion of the overall total. However, at any period in the development of Calgary and Edmonton we can find examples of those who were serving extended local careers with no additional service at the provincial or federal levels (the bottom type in the figure) as well as those who would eventually move on to a career at the provincial level.

DISCUSSION

The findings that we have reported in this paper offer a first comparative look at the long-term development of local political careers in Canada. They provide a foundation for further comparison in other cities and provinces and ultimately in other countries as well. The findings also suggest several implications for our understanding of local accountability and responsiveness in Canadian municipalities.

First, our findings point to the obvious impact of institutional changes on patterns of local careers in Canadian cities. Our analysis of career duration and council turnover suggests that the shape and character of municipal careers has been directly affected by institutional changes to term lengths on city council, both by making very short careers less likely and by making it easier for councillors to continue in office for extended periods of time. The relative absence of "municipal amateur" careers after the adoption of three-year terms of office in the 1960s also speaks to the importance of institutional changes on local political career patterns.

This institutional impact has clear implications for accountability and responsiveness. Simply put, municipal voters today have fewer opportunities to hold local politicians accountable than in the past. Yet the result has been much longer political careers and thus municipal politicians who are arguably much more familiar with local policy and administration than in the past. Our findings suggest that politicians in Calgary and Edmonton today are much more likely to be "municipal professionals" or "provincial climbers" than in the past – politicians whose own career goals may incline them toward policy leadership and responsiveness to constituent preferences. Thus, it may be the case that municipal politicians in Edmonton and Calgary have become more responsive to their constituents over time, even as opportunities to hold those politicians accountable have declined. Contemporary municipal politicians appear to operate in the top row of table 4.1, with generally low levels of accountability and varying responsiveness.

A second important feature of our findings is the layered character of political careers in Calgary and Edmonton. In neither city do we find periods in which one career type clearly predominates. We therefore describe political careers in Calgary and Edmonton as being differentially *layered* over time. In the first period, running from the late nineteenth century to the First World War, three career types coexisted in both cities: municipal professionals, municipal amateurs, and provincial climbers. After the 1960s, as short municipal careers became less common, municipal institutions in Calgary and Edmonton tended to feature two main career types: municipal professionals and provincial climbers.

Over the long term, then, the structure of local political careers in Calgary and Edmonton has become simpler, reflecting the gradual disappearance of "amateur" careers. For those who emphasize the accessibility of local government to relative amateurs – its ability to provide meaningful, short-term opportunities for political participation – this development may seem to be a normative loss. From the standpoint of accountability and responsiveness, however, the professionalization of local political careers has probably driven local politicians to be more determined to demonstrate their responsiveness to local residents and to consider their actions in light of their potential electoral consequences. The threat of electoral defeat means more to the "municipal professional" and the "provincial climber" than it did to municipal politicians who had little interest in prolonging their careers beyond a term or two.

If the increased professionalization of local politicians has meant that they have become increasingly interested in avoiding electoral defeat, our analysis of incumbency rates in Edmonton suggests the possibility, from the perspective of accountability, that the local professionalization process can go too far. For more than two decades, vanishingly few incumbent councillors in Edmonton have lost an election. In a non-partisan environment, highly professionalized incumbent politicians in Edmonton appear to enjoy massive advantages over their challengers, which only grow larger as potential challengers recognize the long odds they face and choose not to contest an election in the first place. Further comparative research will help us to better understand how the local incumbent advantage operates in Canadian municipalities, but our findings from Edmonton suggest that the increasing professionalization of municipal politicians, amidst a non-partisan local environment, may have produced politicians who are exceptionally skilled at remaining in office for as long as they wish to do so.

A final finding in our analysis is the deep similarity in political career development in Calgary and Edmonton. The stories of political career development in Calgary and Edmonton do not appear to be peculiar to individual cities: both the development of careers and the array of career types are deeply similar in Calgary and Edmonton. From the standpoint of accountability and responsiveness, this suggests that we need to think about the broader, non-localized determinants of professionalization and career development, including the ways that provincial policy decisions about the shape of local institutions affect local accountability and responsiveness regimes. While we can undoubtedly learn a great deal about local accountability and responsiveness by studying specific democratic innovations in particular cities, our findings in this paper suggest that the basic structure of local political careers is largely determined at broader spatial and temporal scales.

CONCLUSION

Our aim in this paper has been to provide a comparative preliminary description of the long-term development of political careers in the cities of Calgary and Edmonton and to reflect on the implications of this development for accountability and responsiveness in both cities. We have argued that individual political careers and local political institutions have stabilized over time as careers have lengthened, council turnover has declined, and incumbency rates have grown increasingly formidable. We have also examined the broader career trajectories of municipal politicians, finding many who have gone on to lengthy political careers at the provincial level (and a handful who have done the same at the federal level) after their municipal careers. We introduced three descriptive labels for the career patterns that we found in the two cities – municipal professionals, municipal amateurs, and provincial climbers – and discussed how each career type developed over time.

From the perspective of political careers, then, these findings suggest that electoral accountability in Calgary and Edmonton has been limited. Incumbent politicians enjoy an immense advantage over their challengers, one that has only grown stronger over time. Combined with increasing career lengths and declining numbers of "municipal amateurs," this suggests that, barring scandal or other unusual circumstances, municipal politicians are quite free to determine how long their municipal careers will last. However, the constant presence of "provincial climbers" among municipal politicians may help to ensure that low levels of accountability are *not* always linked to similarly low levels of responsiveness. As Schlesinger (1966) has suggested, politicians who hope to move on to careers at other levels of government often try to distinguish themselves in office by devoting themselves to a handful of high-profile achievements. Of course, factors other than a distinguished municipal career may well be more relevant to provincial or federal candidate selection. Indeed, the linkages between officially non-partisan municipal candidates and their subsequent partisan efforts at the provincial or federal levels are often opaque and merit further research. To the extent that future career goals *do* incentivize high-profile responsiveness in municipal politicians, they may help to pull municipal politics in Calgary and Edmonton away from a low-accountability, low-responsiveness environment.

Our study suggests a number of issues that are worthy of further study in Canada. We suggested, for instance, that increasing career lengths, and the increased professionalization of incumbent politicians, may create trade-offs between responsiveness and accountability. For example, politicians will tend to develop the capacity and incentives for responsiveness but be less likely to encounter a meaningful electoral challenge. These findings could be usefully combined with Canadian research on part-time and full-time municipal careers (Sancton and Woolner 1990) and with more intensive case studies of the responsiveness patterns of local politicians (Koop 2016). Similarly, additional research on other dimensions of political professionalization – staff sizes, politicians' salaries, and so on – would nicely supplement the portrait of political career development that we have outlined here. Finally, and perhaps most obviously, our findings could be extended to cities in other provinces, allowing us to test the relative impact of factors such as provincial legislative context or regional patterns of party support on the long-term development of local political careers. In all of these areas, we believe that careful attention to local politicians themselves – the men and women whose actions are at the core of our theories of accountability and responsiveness – will teach us a great deal about the concrete operation and development of local democratic institutions in Canada.

NOTES

Our thanks to Adrian Raddatz for his excellent research assistance and to Carol Stokes for providing us with archival materials on Calgary's city councils. We also gratefully acknowledge the financial support of the University of Calgary School of Public Policy.

1 For further information, see http://jacklucas.pennyjar.ca/careers.html.

2 The interquartile range of the observations for each year provides a more quantitative summary of the same pattern: since incorporation in both cities, the 25th percentile has risen from about 1–2 to about 6–8, while the 75th percentile has increased from 5–10 to about 20.

3 The findings reported below are robust to alternative time settings, including three-year, seven-year, and ten-year time windows.

4 The structure of this table is inspired by MacKenzie (2009).

5 Municipal amateur careers can also involve long spells in which a politician is out of politics. John Alexander McDougall, for instance, served for two years as a councillor in Edmonton in the early 1890s, withdrew from politics for two years, served for a year as mayor, withdrew again for a decade, served another year as mayor, and was then elected to the provincial legislature for four years. Careers like McDougall's were remarkably common in the early decades of Calgary and Edmonton.

REFERENCES

Abbott, Andrew, and John Forrest. 1986. "Optimal Matching Methods for Historical Sequences." *The Journal of Interdisciplinary History* 16(3): 471–94.

Abbott, Andrew, and Angela Tsay. 2000. "Sequence Analysis and Optimal Matching Methods in Sociology: Review and Prospect." *Sociological Methods & Research* 29(1): 3–33.

Aisenbrey, Silke, and Annette E. Fasang. 2010. "New Life for Old Ideas: The 'Second Wave' of Sequence Analysis Bringing the 'Course' Back into the Life Course." *Sociological Methods & Research* 38(3): 420–62.

Barrie, Doreen, and Roger Gibbins. 1989. "Parliamentary Careers in the Canadian Federal State." *Canadian Journal of Political Science* 22(1): 137–45.

Borchert, Jens. 2011. "Individual Ambition and Institutional Opportunity: A Conceptual Approach to Political Careers in Multi-Level Systems." *Regional & Federal Studies* 21(2): 117–40.

Buton, François, Claire Lemercier, and Nicolas Mariot. 2014. "A Contextual Analysis of Electoral Participation Sequences." In *Advances in Sequence Analysis: Theory, Method, Applications*, edited by Philippe Blanchard, Felix Buhlmann, and Jacques-Antoine Gauthier, 191–211. New York: Springer International Publishing.

Docherty, David. 2011. "The Canadian Political Career Structure: From Stability to Free Agency." *Regional & Federal Studies* 21(2): 185–203.

Dutton, William H. 1975. "The Political Ambitions of Local Legislators: A Comparative Perspective." *Polity* 7(4): 504–22.

Eulau, Heinz, and Paul D. Karps. 1977. "The Puzzle of Representation: Specifying Components of Responsiveness." *Legislative Studies Quarterly* 2(3): 233–54.

Fox, Richard L., and Jennifer L. Lawless. 2014. "Uncovering the Origins of the Gender Gap in Political Ambition." *American Political Science Review* 108(3): 499–519.

Hibbing, John R. 1999. "Legislative Careers: Why and How We Should Study Them." *Legislative Studies Quarterly* 24(2): 149–71.

Koop, Royce. 2016. "Institutional- and Individual-Level Influences on Service Representation and Casework in Canadian Cities." *Urban Affairs Review* 52(5): 808–31.

Kushner, Joseph, David Siegel, and Hannah Stanwick. 1997. "Ontario Municipal Elections: Voting Trends and Determinants of Electoral Success in a Canadian Province." *Canadian Journal of Political Science* 30(3): 539–53.

Lucas, Jack. 2015. "How Hydro Ontario Went Local: The Creation of Local Districts and the Ontario Central System." *Scientia Canadensis: Canadian Journal of the History of Science, Technology and Medicine* 37(1): 19–59.

– 2016. "Patterns of Urban Governance: A Sequence Analysis of Long-Term Institutional Change in Six Canadian Cities." *Urban Affairs Review*. Published online before print, 23 December. doi:10.1177/1078087415620054.

MacIndoe, Heather, and Andrew Abbott. 2004. "Sequence Analysis and Optimal Matching Techniques for Social Science Data." In *Handbook of Data Analysis*, edited by Melissa Hardy and Alan Bryman, 387–406. London: Sage.

MacKenzie, Scott A. 2009. "For Mayors, the Future Is Now: The Effects of Political Experience on Mayoral Election and Retirement." Working paper, University of California, Davis.

Pitkin, Hanna. 1967. *The Concept of Representation*. Los Angeles: University of California Press.

Prewitt, Kenneth. 1970. "Political Ambitions, Volunteerism, and Electoral Accountability." *American Political Science Review* 64(1): 5–17.

Sancton, Andrew, and Paul Woolner. 1990. "Full-Time Municipal Councillors: A Strategic Challenge for Canadian Urban Government." *Canadian Public Administration* 33(4): 482–505.

Schlesinger, Joseph. 1966. *Ambition and Politics: Political Careers in the United States*. Chicago: Rand McNally.

Wilson, Matthew Charles. 2014. "Governance Built Step-by-Step: Analysing Sequences to Explain Democratization." In *Advances in Sequence Analysis: Theory, Method, Applications*, edited by Philippe Blanchard, Felix Buhlmann, and Jacques-Antoine Gauthier, 213–30. New York: Springer.

5

What Happened to Incumbent Councillors in Greater Sudbury and London, Ontario, in 2014? The Role of the Ontario Ombudsman's Reports on Alleged Secret Meetings

Andrew Sancton

INTRODUCTION

Students of urban politics have frequently observed that incumbent councillors in non-partisan local elections are almost invariably re-elected. For example, in the 2014 elections in the City of Toronto, which has forty-four council seats, thirty-six of the thirty-seven incumbents in the race were re-elected – despite the fact that there was no incumbent running for mayor and that the mayoral victor (John Tory) was quite a different type of politician from his predecessor (Rob Ford). However, the flipside to this perceived notion of the incumbent advantage is that incumbents who have drawn negative attention to themselves while in office are likely to be easy prey for challengers. As a result, for many incumbents the optimal strategy for electoral longevity is to avoid negative publicity at all costs.

Negative publicity might concern personal misbehaviour and/or the taking of political positions that are manifestly unpopular. In the 2014 Ontario municipal elections in the cities of Greater Sudbury and London, only seven of twenty-six incumbents were returned to office. Nine incumbents who contested the 2014 council elections lost; two other incumbent councillors ran for mayor and lost; the other eight incumbents did not present themselves for re-election. The shared feature of those who were defeated was that that they had been denounced by the Ontario ombudsman for having attended closed, informal council or committee meetings that were illegal. The ombudsman's findings about such meetings were widely reported in the local media in both cities.

Building on another article (Sancton 2015) in which I analyzed the ombudsman's position, I seek in this chapter to analyze the political implications of that position. My argument is that the elections demonstrated that media and voters *were* paying close attention to publicized findings of an authoritative figure that groups of councillors had acted illegally by congregating in secret to lay the groundwork for decisions relating to council business. In other words, the electoral system did indeed hold incumbents responsible for actions that were arguably inappropriate. The ombudsman himself and local media were quick to underline this point.

But what was lost in the finger-pointing frenzy about these informal, "secret" meetings of some municipal councillors was that there was no Ontario law, regulation, or judicial determination that defined such meetings as illegal. Thus, the ombudsman's claim in 2008 that such meetings were illegal was generally accepted at face value as though it were perfectly obvious that municipal councils could not be accountable and transparent if some councillors discussed municipal business with each other outside council meetings.

Many have argued that municipal councils would be more accountable in Ontario if elections were contested by organized political parties such that a party (or coalition of parties) could potentially govern in a way that is similar to parliamentary systems or to municipal systems in major cities in Quebec and British Columbia.[1] These systems are all based on the premise that elected politicians talk with each other outside formal meetings about what they are going to do.[2] It appears that incumbents in Greater Sudbury and London were punished electorally for doing precisely what we expect politicians at other levels of government to do. How can this advance the cause of municipal accountability?

The conventional model for such accountability involves attentive voters informed by journalists about the actions of local elected members of council. It is easy to see how this model fails. Even before the decline of intensive political reporting by local media in mid-sized cities such as Greater Sudbury and London, it was difficult for voters to monitor the actions of their local non-partisan council. This is why, as long as there appeared to be competent management of local affairs, incumbents generally won local elections with little difficulty – unless, of course, they had somehow attracted a great deal of negative publicity. Another official way of ensuring accountability is to take recourse to the courts or other types of legal remedies. However, these options are usually expensive and are therefore generally available only to individuals or corporations that are significantly invested in particular municipal decisions. In this chapter, I aim to show that yet another option – the mandating of an ambitious and creative provincial ombudsman to intervene – resulted in significant negative unintended consequences.

The first section of this paper examines past research relating to the performance of incumbents in non-partisan local elections, with a particular focus on what we know about why some incumbents lose. The second section looks at events in the City of Greater Sudbury since the Ontario ombudsman first intervened there in 2008. The third section looks at the City of London since 2012. Finally, the conclusion examines the implications of these events for our understanding of municipal accountability and responsiveness.

INCUMBENTS IN NON-PARTISAN LOCAL ELECTIONS

There is a considerable literature, especially regarding the US Congress, on the effects of incumbency on election outcomes. There also exists a broad body of literature emphasizing the apparent importance of incumbency in determining outcomes of non-partisan local elections in the United States. However, as Jessica Trounstine (2011) has pointed out, much of this literature assumes that the main factor for electoral success is incumbency rather than allowing for the possibility that incumbents might win for the same reasons they won their initial elections: better qualifications, more popular positions on issues, better communications skills. Nonetheless, by analyzing local election results in three US cities over many decades, she is also able to show that incumbency itself has a significant independent effect on election outcomes. In Canada, two recent academic articles examine incumbency in local elections. Breux, Couture, and Bherer (2014) find no direct link between the presence of incumbents and voter turnout in Quebec municipal elections. Moore, McGregor, and Stephenson (2017) determined that in the 2014 Toronto municipal elections, voters who paid closer attention to the election campaigns were less likely to vote for their incumbent councillor than those who paid less attention.

For the purposes of this article, however, we need to know more about the rare circumstances in which incumbents actually lose local non-partisan elections. In these cases, we are faced with much less published research. However, Oliver, Ha, and Callen (2012) have attempted to determine the factors associated with incumbent losses in smaller US municipalities, generally suburbs and small towns. Most of these places are what Oliver calls "managerial democracies" in that they contain fewer major political cleavages than the major US cities. The Canadian cities of Greater Sudbury and London are clearly not managerial democracies in this sense, even though they can hardly be compared meaningfully to such places as New York, Chicago, and Los Angeles. Oliver notes the ubiquity of incumbent success at all levels and pays attention to population size as a variable.

One of Oliver's initial observations about incumbency is highly relevant to what happened in Greater Sudbury and London: "As long as basic operations run smoothly and incumbents avoid being on the wrong side of a very visible issue or caught in a scandal, voters in most localities will probably not need to seek any more information and incumbents should have an easy time getting elected" (2012, 31). The data for Oliver's subsequent analysis was derived from surveys conducted in 1986, 1991, 1996, 2001, and 2006 by the International City Management Association (ICMA) among its member municipalities with populations between 2,500 and 100,000. The data came from 7,000 different places and contained more than 14,000 cases of elections in which at least one incumbent lost (2012, 123–4). Even in these cases (elections in which at least one incumbent lost), it is almost certain that most incumbents actually won.

Oliver's general conclusion from his analysis of the ICMA data is as follows:

Local elections are a curious mixture of the mundane and the unexpected. For the overwhelming majority of local elections, incumbents are likely to win. This is because they either run unopposed or because they are able to convince voters that they are doing a good enough job to stay in office. All things being equal, the single most powerful predictor of whether someone will win an election is whether they are already in office. Yet for all their advantages, incumbents do not always win. The ICMA data suggest that in any given year at least one incumbent city council member will lose an election in about one quarter of all municipalities. This number grows higher for places that are large in size, that are lower in income, and that have strong mayors, greater municipal responsibilities, and district [i.e., ward] elections for council members. For a local politician, re-election becomes more hazardous as one's responsibilities grow, resources and powers diminish, and opponents have easier access to mounting challenges. (2012, 147)

In the final chapter of his book, Oliver reflects on the incumbency issue within managerial democracies by looking at a context that goes well beyond the ICMA data:

Like tornado strikes, the politics of managerial democracy, vacillating between periods of general calm and brief tumult, are hard to describe with a general theory of politics simply because the precise periods of tumult are so unpredictable. Just as we know the general conditions of when tornados are likely to hit, we might anticipate general conditions where incumbents are more likely to lose, but knowing where and when tornados hit or incumbents lose is going to be extremely hard to specify with any accuracy. (2012, 193)

In the cases of Greater London and Sudbury in the municipal elections of 2014, the Ontario ombudsman was a tornado, wreaking havoc on incumbent councillors.

THE CITY OF GREATER SUDBURY

Effective 1 January 2008, new mechanisms were put in place for Ontario citizens to file complaints about meetings of municipal councils that were alleged to have been illegally closed to the public.[3] The problem being addressed was that many municipal councils were meeting *in camera* for long periods of time for reasons that were either unclear or that were not authorized by the Ontario Municipal Act. The only remedy for concerned citizens was to launch costly and complicated court actions. Then, starting in 2008, citizens could complain about closed meetings to a designated independent "closed meeting investigator" appointed by the council itself or, if no such person had been appointed, to the Ontario ombudsman. Neither the ombudsman nor the investigator had the legal authority to do anything other than to declare publicly that the council (or one of its committees or commissions) had acted improperly and then to recommend alternative courses of action for the future.

The Sudbury story began with a concert by Elton John at a municipal arena. Because stars of his magnitude rarely perform in Sudbury, his February 2008 concert was a big event, and the demand for tickets far outstripped supply. The thirteen members of council reserved 120 tickets for themselves for which they intended to pay the full price. Nevertheless, as soon as citizens learned about the council tickets, there was public outrage. After a council meeting on 20 February, ten of the councillors, not including the mayor, gathered informally in their lounge to talk about how they could respond to the mayor's promise to return up to seventy of the council tickets. They summoned the general manager for community development, who was in charge of the arena, to ask about how the return process could be implemented. On 26 February, the Ontario ombudsman received a complaint stating that this gathering in the councillors' lounge was an illegally closed meeting of the city council (Ontario Ombudsman 2008).

The ombudsman delivered his report on 25 April. In it he stated that the ten councillors in the lounge "had a quorum and therefore the legal authority to make decisions. This was a meeting of the council, period" (2008, 7). On the surface at least, this was a most unusual statement. How could the ten councillors possibly make legally binding decisions in the absence of any of the formal apparatus of an official meeting (e.g., a summons, an agenda, a clerk taking minutes, a presiding officer)? The significant part of the decision was the ombudsman's statement that a council meeting could take place if members met together "for the purpose of doing the groundwork necessary" to exercise the council authority (2008, 7). Even this statement, however, went well beyond anything set forth by Ontario law, jurisprudence, or ordinary practice. In another part of his ruling, he stated that "even if a quorum is not present, those who attend might still begin to lay the groundwork necessary to exercise the body's power" (2008, 18–19). In the final analysis, the ombudsman ruled that the meeting of the ten councillors did not constitute a meeting but only because they were merely talking about how to return their tickets; they were not talking about exercising council authority. The ruling was much more significant outside Greater Sudbury than within it. Henceforth in Ontario, municipal lawyers and clerks would warn councillors not to talk about municipal business in informal groups because they might in fact be holding illegally closed meetings. A new era in Ontario municipal government had begun.

The next Ontario municipal elections were held on 25 October 2010. All nine incumbent councillors who presented themselves were re-elected, including eight who attended the informal meeting about the Elton John tickets in the councillors' lounge. However, the incumbent mayor, John Rodriguez, a former New Democratic Party (NDP) member of Parliament (MP), was surprisingly defeated by Marianne Matichuk, who had never previously held any political office. Matichuk's victory reflected much dissatisfaction about a number of local issues, including the Elton John ticket "scandal" over which Mayor Rodriguez had presided. But the ombudsman's report in itself was not much of a concern, which presumably helps to explain the incumbent councillors' electoral success.

In February 2012, the ombudsman received complaints that the Greater Sudbury council had held *in camera* meetings in late 2011 to discuss the performance of the city's auditor general, Brian Bigger. The discussion had more than usual political relevance because Bigger was subsequently elected mayor in 2014, when Matichuk did not run. The issue for the ombudsman was whether the meeting was about the office of the auditor general (in which case the meeting should have been public) or whether it was about the personal performance of Bigger (a circumstance that allows *in camera* meetings). The ombudsman ruled in August that the *in camera* meeting was justified. Yet other aspects of the report turned out to be more important (Ontario Ombudsman 2012a).

All of the thirteen councillors whom the ombudsman's investigators wanted to interview initially insisted that they be accompanied by the city solicitor. But the ombudsman ruled that he would not proceed on this basis because the city solicitor was an official municipal representative and that his presence might prevent whistle-blowing on the part of any or all of the councillors. In the end, two of the councillors were interviewed without any legal support being present, and the other eleven were not interviewed at all. The mayor and the city clerk were accompanied by their own personal lawyers, whose fees were paid by the city (MacDonald 2013a). The ombudsman claimed in his report that legal counsel was not necessary for anybody.

> My investigations are not adversarial in nature, but fact-finding
> exercises. My Office's authority does not extend to finding
> individuals personally at fault or issuing sanctions for any
> procedural or substantive violations. I can only issue recom-
> mendations, and in the closed meeting context, my recommen-
> dations normally address future best practices for holding
> closed meetings. (Ontario Ombudsman 2012a, 4–5)

Later in his report, he stated that the "council for the City of Greater
Sudbury now has the dubious distinction of being the least cooperative body we have ever investigated" (2012a, 11).

In December 2012, the ombudsman received two complaints about
illegally closed meetings in June of that year. Once again, the complaints were that the council had acted illegally by holding *in camera*
meetings to discuss the auditor general. On 14 February, the ombudsman ruled for the first time that the council actually did act illegally,
but the ruling was based on a technicality about exactly what kinds
of motions were allowed to be held in closed meetings (Ontario
Ombudsman 2013a). The ruling was much less significant than
another controversy that was brewing at the same time.

At a public meeting on 12 February, Councillor Claude Berthiaume
moved that the ombudsman, as the city's closed meeting investigator,
be replaced by LAS Ltd, a company which, owned by the Association
of Municipalities of Ontario (AMO), delegated its closed meeting
investigations to another company, Amberley Gavel Ltd. The motion
was supported by all members of council except Mayor Matichuk
(Greater Sudbury 2013a). A local newspaper reported that "the speed
and consensus with which the decision was made sparked public
suspicions that councillors had met beforehand to discuss the matter"
(MacDonald 2013b).

Sure enough, the ombudsman received a number of complaints
about an illegal closed meeting of councillors that took place sometime
before the official council meeting on 12 February. The ombudsman
stated that he could not deal with the complaints because he was no
longer the closed meeting investigator. Amberley Gavel, for its part,
stated that it could investigate only if the complainants agreed to
officially redirect their complaints from the ombudsman to Amberley
Gavel. Five complainants agreed, and one more launched a new complaint about the same incident directly to Amberley Gavel. Meanwhile,
the ombudsman stated that he would do all in his power to have the

law changed to prevent future municipal councils from doing what the Sudbury council did (MacDonald 2013b).

At the next formal meeting on 26 February, a motion was moved to reconsider the council's decision about the ombudsman that it had taken at the previous meeting. This time, three councillors – Cimino, Belli, and Craig – joined the mayor in wanting to maintain the ombudsman as the closed meeting investigator (Greater Sudbury 2013b). None of them was a candidate in the 2014 election: Belli had died; Cimino had resigned in order to run (successfully) for the NDP in the 2014 provincial election; and Craig had retired from municipal politics. Of the nine who voted against reconsideration, only two were re-elected in 2014. One (Dupuis) ran for mayor and finished fourth with 9 per cent of the vote; two others did not present themselves for re-election; and four others were defeated.[4] It was this council vote on 26 February 2013 that provides the clearest public indication of which members of council supported the ombudsman and which did not.

The Amberley Gavel report on the alleged illegal closed meeting held "on or before" 12 February was released in August 2013. In its substance, it provides a partial contrast to the ombudsman's approach to informal meetings of councillors. It acknowledges that such meetings can be deemed illegally closed meetings, but only if a quorum is present and only if the meeting "materially advances the business or decision-making of the council" (Amberley Gavel 2013, 8). This wording is different from the ombudsman's use of "laying the groundwork" and mimics both judicial decisions on the subject and the Ontario Municipal Act's provision that councils can conduct closed educational sessions as long as such decisions do not materially advance the conduct of council business. Amberley Gavel found ample evidence that Councillor Berthiaume had been in individual contact, both by email and in conversations, with different councillors prior to moving his motion about dispensing with the ombudsman's services. However, the company found no evidence that any illegally closed meeting (according to its definition) had taken place.

Not surprisingly, this conclusion drew heated reactions. They were fuelled by the ombudsman himself, who told local media that the "e-mails, phone and one-on-one discussions initiated by [...] Coun. Claude Berthiaume constituted a gathering of councillors to further city business, which effectively is a prohibited closed meeting" (MacDonald 2013c). Mayor Matichuk, a continuing supporter of the ombudsman, went so far as to say that "she won't talk to other councillors to try and get their support because it may break the rules" (MacDonald 2013c). In any event, Amberley Gavel's ruling – and the ombudsman's reaction to it – fuelled local suspicions that the majority on the city council had dispensed with the ombudsman's services precisely so that they would no longer be subject his more stringent interpretation of the closed meeting rules. There was little question that the ombudsman's position as a crusading independent officer of the Ontario legislature placed him in an apparently far more legitimate position than that of a consulting company doing work delegated to it by an arm of the AMO.

During the period after the ombudsman was replaced as closed meeting investigator, "the Greater Sudbury Taxpayers Association collected 8,000 postcards demanding the ombudsman be reinstated" (MacDonald 2014). It is therefore not surprising that councillors who had voted to dispense with the ombudsman did so poorly in the 2014 elections. Table 5.1 shows this. The six incumbents who had rejected the ombudsman in 2013 collectively ended up running against eight more candidates in 2014 than they did in 2010. Their vote totals within their wards declined by 27.1 per cent. It is unfortunate, however, that we cannot compare this number to votes received by incumbents who had voted in council to maintain the ombudsman as the closed meeting investigator. We cannot do this because none of the four were running for re-election. However, it is no doubt significant that in 2010, ten of twelve incumbent councillors ran for re-election. Two were acclaimed. All of the remaining eight were re-elected, *increasing* their total votes by 19.0 per cent. Based on our general knowledge of the success of incumbents in non-partisan elections, and our particular knowledge of the previous election in Greater Sudbury, the implication of this is clear: the 2014 election was an anomaly.

LONDON

The City of London had no experience with closed meeting investigations prior to the 2010 municipal election. At that election, a former federal Liberal cabinet minister, Joe Fontana, defeated the incumbent mayor. Given his own recent parliamentary experience and his ambitious local plans to implement property-tax freezes, it is perhaps not surprising that Mayor Fontana worked hard to mobilize councillor

Table 5.1
Election results for 2014 incumbent councillors in Greater Sudbury, 2010 and 2014 elections

Ward	Councillor	2010 votes	2010 % votes	2010 # of candidates	2014 votes	2014 % votes	2014 # of candidates	Loss of votes	Decrease in %	Won 2014?
2	Barbeau	3,689	75.2	2	2,190	39.3	5	1,499	40.6	No
4	Kutrisac	2,614	63.9	2	2,112	48.1	3	502	19.2	Yes
6	Rivest	2,400	53.3	3	1,663	32.3	4	737	30.7	No
7	Kilgour	2,078	51.5	3	1,525	31.2	5	553	26.6	No
11	Kett	1,971	39.2	5	1,700	31.7	5	271	13.7	No
12	Landry-Altmann	2,844	71.2	2	2,179	53.0	3	665	23.1	Yes
	Totals	15,596	58.7	17	11,369	38.6	25	4,227	27.1	

Source: Calculated from data at: https://www.greatersudbury.ca/inside-city-hall/election-2014.

support for his political objectives. It soon became obvious that the council was almost evenly divided between the mayor's supporters and his opponents. Eventually, local media began referring to the "Fontana Eight," a group of council members including the mayor who often voted together on the fifteen-person council. The Fontana Eight were to become a target of the ombudsman's investigations of closed informal meetings, and none was re-elected in 2014. What follows is an account of the ombudsman's findings. It must be recognized, however, that London voters had other reasons to become dissatisfied with the Fontana Eight, especially in the case of voters whose political views were more generally favourable to maintaining existing levels of government spending and regulation. Even more significantly, Mayor Fontana was convicted of fraud during his fourth year in office for expense claims he made while a federal cabinet minister. He resigned as mayor prior to sentencing. Being associated in voters' minds with a disgraced former mayor was obviously not good for the remaining "Fontana Seven." While no one suggested that any of them had the remotest connection with mayor's prior criminal actions, they were, however, considered responsible for their own behaviour with respect to closed informal meetings. This behaviour, as reported and assessed by the ombudsman, received a great deal of publicity in local media.

The ombudsman's first encounter with the London city council was the result of a complaint that six council members were seen lunching at a downtown buffet restaurant prior to an important budget meeting on 21 February 2012. The six councillors were identified on a local website on 23 February.[5] The ombudsman included the names of the six councillors in his report, presumably because they were already public knowledge (Ontario Ombudsman 2012b). He also reported, as he did in his Sudbury report at about the same time, that it was not appropriate for the city solicitor to be present when individual councillors were being interviewed. The city solicitor's presence was not an issue in London, perhaps because, unlike the contested meeting in Sudbury, the London "meeting" comprised councillors sitting around a table in a restaurant. There was no member of the City of London staff, including lawyers, who had any direct knowledge whatsoever of what went on at the restaurant. In any event, despite the council's willingness to pay for personal legal representation, "no London city council members attended with legal counsel in the interviews conducted in this investigation" (Ontario Ombudsman

2012b, 3). The ombudsman claimed that "typically, there is no legal interest at stake in an Ombudsman investigation that would warrant legal representation" (2012b, 3). There might not be a "legal interest" at stake but, as we shall see, political interests can be very much at stake when an ombudsman names individual councillors as transgressors in a formal, public report.

Despite the fact that the lunch lasted for about an hour, the mayor and five of his council allies claimed only to have socialized and to have exchanged limited information about an item in the local newspaper, the funding of social housing, and a constituent call about wading pools. They "explained that there were no issues discussed at the lunch relating to matters before any committees of council, nor was there any further consideration of matters connected indirectly or directly to council business" (2012b, 6). There were presumably no other witnesses who were in a position to provide contrary evidence. But the absence of contradictory evidence did not prevent the ombudsman from providing his own further commentary by quoting local media accounts of critical statements by the lunch attendees about the anonymous complainants and the ombudsman's investigatory practices. Mayor Fontana was quoted as calling the law "ridiculous" (2012b, 7). In fact, the "law" in question makes no reference at all to informal meetings of groups of councillors, and nobody in Ontario ever suspected them of being illegal until the ombudsman's report on Greater Sudbury and the Elton John tickets.

Towards the end of his report, the ombudsman stated the following:

> Even after concerns were raised publicly, about the luncheon meeting from various sources, a number of the lunch participants dismissed them out of hand, and further inflamed the situation by labelling the critics as politically motivated and sore losers. The histrionics and criticism by some councillors also muddied the waters, was singularly unhelpful, and demonstrated an ignorance of the nature of the closed meeting investigations carried out by my office. (2012b, 12–13)

In his conclusion, the ombudsman recommended that "Having audio and/or video recordings of closed meetings would significantly reduce the time and resources necessary to respond to a closed meeting complaint investigation, and would also provide the citizens of London with a measure of assurance that there is a complete record of what transpires behind closed doors" (2012b, 14).

But the next time Mayor Fontana and his allies met in a restaurant, they failed to make any recordings.

On 23 February 2013, five days before another important budget vote, seven council members of the Fontana Eight met for lunch again. (In popular parlance, they became known as the "Fontana Ate.") This time they chose a private dining area of a popular restaurant on the outskirts of the city, referred to by the ombudsman as a "back room" (Ontario Ombudsman 2013b). Unfortunately for the diners, someone tipped off the local media, causing reporters to surround the restaurant and council members to attempt to depart before they were intercepted. Sixty separate complaints were made to the ombudsman about an illegal closed meeting.

In his report, the ombudsman identified the seven council members "who were issued summonses to give testimony under oath, in interviews on March 20, 2013" (2013b, 6) and again on 19 June. Each council member was accompanied by the same two lawyers paid for by the City of London at a total cost of $97,148 (Maloney 2014). According to the ombudsman's report, the participants claimed that "the mayor-with-six-councillors gathering was a happenstance convergence of councillors for social purposes" (2013b, 8). The report contains detailed, amusing, and contradictory accounts by the different council members of how they all happened to be there at the same time. The ombudsman used the full resources of his office for the detective work, including the examination of cellphone records and interviews with restaurant employees.

The ombudsman did not accept the evidence of the council members that seven of them happened to end up in the same "back room" at the same time by chance. Instead, he concluded "that it is more likely than not that the gathering [...] was both purposeful and planned" (2013b, 26). Various participants testified that some particular subjects of city business were discussed in different small-group conversations at different times, but they all claimed there was no single conversation about any topic involving them all. Nevertheless, the ombudsman concluded that an illegally closed meeting of the council's Investment and Economic Prosperity Committee had taken place (2013b, 29). Exactly which councillors were members of this committee was a technicality. All seven participants were deemed to have attended an illegally closed meeting (2013b, 32) and, by implication, to have lied under oath to the Ontario ombudsman. The ombudsman's report received huge local publicity when he released it in person in London in October 2013.

Of the seven members of council condemned by the ombudsman, four ran for re-election to their same council seats in 2014, and all of them lost. Mayor Fontana had already resigned and did not run again. Another of the seven ran for mayor and finished third with 4.2 per cent of the total vote. Of the remaining eight councillors in 2010 who did not attend the 2013 illegal lunch meeting, three did not run again in 2014. One ran for mayor and was elected with 57.8 per cent of the vote.[6] Only one of the remaining four lost, considered one of the Fontana Eight – Councillor Denise Brown attended the lunch meeting in 2012 but not the illegal one in 2013.

As in Greater Sudbury, it is not surprising that those councillors condemned by the ombudsman fared poorly in the 2014 election. The details can be seen in table 5.2. The four condemned incumbents who ran again collectively had three more candidates running against them in 2014 than they did in 2010. Their vote totals within their wards declined by 41.1 per cent. This is a greater decline than that experienced by the comparable group of councillors in Greater Sudbury. In London's case, we are fortunate that there were four councillors not condemned by the ombudsman in 2013 who did present themselves for re-election in the same council seats. Their total votes decreased by only 6.1 per cent (see table 5.3). In London in 2010, nine out of fourteen councillors ran for re-election; only one lost. Collectively, the incumbents in 2010 *increased* their total vote by 23.7 per cent. London voters were obviously dissatisfied with all incumbents in 2014 in a way that they were not in 2010. Moreover, in 2014 they were significantly more dissatisfied with those who had been condemned by the ombudsman than with those who were not.

The situation proved particularly problematic for Councillor Denise Brown. In 2010, she was the only candidate to defeat an incumbent (a former NDP MPP during the Rae government in the early 1990s). After being elected, she became one of the Fontana Eight and, as noted earlier, attended the lunch meeting in 2012 that was *not* found to be illegal by the ombudsman. Significantly, she did *not* attend the 2013 lunch and therefore was considered, as stated in table 5.2 and in the calculations above, as being one of the incumbents *not* condemned by the ombudsman. But Brown *was* defeated in 2014; her vote decreased by 40.6 per cent, by almost exactly the same amount as

Table 5.2
Election results for 2014 incumbent candidates for London council condemned by ombudsman in 2013, elections of 2010 and 2014

Ward	Councillor	2010 votes	2010 % votes	2010 # of candidates	2014 votes	2014 % votes	2014 # of candidates	Loss of vote	Decrease in %	Won in 2014?
1	Polhill	3,904	61.7	5	1,818	30.3	4	2,086	53.4	No
4	Orser	3,020	50.7	4	1,424	22.6	6	1,596	52.9	No
10	Van Meerbergen	6,166	79.2	2	3,827	45.0	3	2,339	37.9	No
14	White	1,721	26.6	5	1,649	24.8	6	72	4.1	No
	Totals	14,811	55.8	16	8,718	31.7	19	6,093	41.1	

Source: Calculated from data at: http://www.london.ca/city-hall/elections/Pages/default.aspx.

Table 5.3
Election results for 2014 incumbent candidates for London council not condemned by ombudsman in 2013, elections of 2010 and 2014

Ward	Councillor	2010 votes	2010 % votes	2010 # of candidates	2014 votes	2014 % votes	2014 # of candidates	+ or – vote	+ or – in %	Won in 2014?
2	Armstrong	3,196	50.1	3	2,499	39.0	3	–697	–21.8	Yes
8	Hubert	5,678	71.7	3	7,408	83.1	2	+1,730	+30.5	Yes
11	D. Brown	4,267	50.3	3	2,531	28.4	6	–1,736	–40.7	No
12	Usher	3,800	52.4	6	3,475	48.4	3	–325	–8.6	Yes
	Totals	16,941	56.4	15	15,913	50.6	14	–1,028	–6.1	

Source: http://www.london.ca/city-hall/elections/Pages/default.aspx.

the ones who *did* attend the 2013 lunch. If she were not to be included in table 5.2, we would see that the remaining three councillors who did not attend the 2013 lunch and who ran for council in 2014 lost only 1.3 per cent of their total vote compared to 2010.

This suggests that membership in the Fontana Eight, and not condemnation by the ombudsman, was perhaps the essential problem for incumbents in 2014. In the real world of politics, everything is connected to everything else, and independent variables can rarely be totally isolated from each other. Many left-leaning voters in London no doubt followed local politics sufficiently closely to know that there was a Fontana Eight and presumably did not agree with its political agenda. But for many others, the well-publicized ombudsman reports were most likely the significant sources of reference for defining the Fontana Eight, to associate them all (not just Fontana) with illegality, and to cause them to take corrective action at the ballot box.

CONCLUSION

Immediately following the 2014 municipal elections, the ombudsman was quoted in the local media in both Greater Sudbury and London about how pleased he was that voters in both cities had rejected incumbents with whom he had crossed swords about informal closed meetings. He also used his official Ontario Ombudsman Twitter account to express similar sentiments. Even in the official annual report for 2013–14 from the Ombudsman's Open Meeting Law Enforcement Team (OMLET) he went as far as to state: "In a few places where closed meetings were a hot topic – notably London, Ont. and the City of Greater Sudbury – voters elected almost entirely new councils, replacing politicians who had violated the open meeting rules or resisted co-operating with our investigations in the past" (Ontario Ombudsman 2015, 5).

It is almost impossible to believe that the ombudsman, a supposedly politically neutral officer of the Ontario legislature, would boast in an official annual report about the apparent connection between his reports and the defeat of incumbent councillors in municipal elections. We hypothesize that such behaviour was part of a broader pattern that helps to explain why André Marin's application to be reappointed in 2015 for an unprecedented third five-year term as ombudsman was ultimately rejected by the legislature.[7] But it also raises larger questions about the mechanisms by which incumbent municipal councillors are to be held accountable for their actions.

In the past, the most significant cases relating to the definition of meetings of municipal councils have emerged from companies owning newspapers that have successfully argued in court that councils should not be allowed to exclude the press and public from off-site meetings organized as "retreats" to discuss long-term objectives and strategic planning.[8] It is hard to imagine in today's strained circumstances that owners of local newspapers would engage in such costly legal endeavours. Indeed, one of the main arguments made in 2006 for creating the office of "closed meeting investigator," and for having the ombudsman as the default investigator, was to avoid the necessity of launching court action by anyone challenging official meetings that were improperly held *in camera*. Not much attention was paid to procedural protection for councils being investigated, because the investigators were given no authority other than to declare that a meeting had been improperly closed and to suggest improved procedures to modify future behaviour. No sanctions were available; anyone wanting to nullify a by-law on the grounds that it had been illegally considered by the council *in camera* would still have to take the matter to a court of law. Significantly, the ombudsman has frequently complained about his lack of authority to levy any formal sanctions against offending municipal councillors.

The results of the 2014 municipal elections in Greater Sudbury and London demonstrated that in practical terms the ombudsman in fact possessed considerable political power. This power was derived from what we know about both the strengths and vulnerabilities of incumbent non-partisan municipal councillors. They are safe if they stay out of trouble but are subject to quick electoral defeat by any form of political "tornado." An incumbent found guilty of just about anything in a court of law is likely to be in severe political jeopardy. However, the occasional public battle with other politicians or with the local media is unlikely to be fatal. In those cases, at least everyone is on a level playing field.

In 2008, the Ontario ombudsman entered the fray as the default closed meeting investigator with the authority to pass judgment on the behaviour of local councillors. At the time, everyone assumed that this new authority related only to councils and their committees as collectivities. Either they were holding meetings *in camera* according to the rules or they were not. No one anticipated that the ombudsman (or any other closed meeting investigator) would create a new definition of "meeting" to include informal gatherings of a few municipal councillors discussing municipal business. Everything changed in 2008 when the ombudsman investigated complaints about councillors meeting informally in Sudbury to try to figure out what to do with their Elton John tickets.

It was extremely difficult for any incumbent councillors who wanted to fight back. Defending "secret" informal meetings (especially if held in a "back room" of a restaurant) is difficult. Claiming that a crusading officer of the legislature is going beyond his authority in interpreting the law is equally difficult, especially when local media are happy to report uncritically on a story pitting openness against secrecy.[9] Incumbent councillors suffered no penalties that they could contest in a court of law. In Greater Sudbury and London, they were instead tried in the court of public opinion in 2014. They lost; there is no appeal court.

Incumbent councillors do not have a right to be free of unfair criticism. However, if we are concerned about effective and accountable municipal government, we should reconsider the idea of providing opportunities for high-profile but nevertheless unaccountable provincial officials (who are not subject to judicial constraint) to pass judgment on people who are elected to our local councils.

NOTES

1 See, for example, the Toronto Party, 2016, "Vote Toronto Party 2014 Home," accessed 10 August 2017, http://thetorontoparty.com.

2 For evidence that members of the same political grouping do talk to each other prior to municipal council meetings in British Columbia, see Jeff Lee, "Councillors Who Meet Privately Likely Breaking the Rules, Says Lawyer," *Vancouver Sun*, 24 September 2015, http://www.vancouversun. com/news/Councillors+meet+privately+likely+breaking+rules+says+lawyer/ 11385689/story.html, and Urbanizta, "Significant: Councillors Who Meet Privately Likely Breaking the Rules, Says Lawyer (by Jeff Lee, *Vancouver Sun*, 23-Sept-2015)," *City Hall Watch* 24 September 2015, https://cityhallwatch. wordpress.com/2015/09/24/vision-vancouver-illegal-meetings. The British Columbia ombudsman has provided guidelines relating to informal meetings of councillors but never stipulated that informal meetings of municipal political groups on council are illegal. See BC Ombudsperson, "Open

Meetings: Best Practices Guide for Local Governments," 20 September 2012, https://www.bcombudsperson.ca/documents/open-meetings-best-practices-guide-local-governments.

3 See Section 239 of the Ontario Municipal Act, at: Ontario, 2001, *Municipal Act*, 1 June 2017, https://www.ontario.ca/laws/statute/01m25.

4 This information derived from material available at https://www.greater sudbury.ca/inside-city-hall/election-2014, accessed 8 August 2016.

5 Kate Dubinski, "Ombudsman 'Disturbed' by Lunches," *London Free Press*, 3 August 2012, accessed 14 August 2017, http://www.lfpress.com/news/london/2012/08/03/20063061.html.

6 This information was derived from material of the City of London.

7 In reality, it was rejected by the majority party, the Liberals. The third party, the NDP, apparently supported Marin's bid for re-appointment, while the official opposition, the Progressive Conservatives, were neutral. A new ombudsman was appointed by the Ontario legislature on 16 February 2016 without a recorded vote.

8 See *Southam Inc. v. Hamilton-Wentwoth (Regional Municipality) Economic Development Committee.* [1988] O.J. No. 1684, and *Southam Inc., Eade and Aubry v. Council of the Corp. of the City of Ottawa et al.* [1991] O.J. No. 3659 (Ont. Div. Ct.)

9 It is less difficult for academics to do so, which helps to explain why I have felt free to criticize the former Ontario ombudsman on this issue. In fairness to local reporters, they have occasionally reported my views. For example, see MacDonald (2013c) and Maloney (2013).

REFERENCES

Amberley Gavel Ltd. 2013. *Report to the Council of the City Of Greater Sudbury Regarding an Investigation into Complaints about an Alleged Closed Meeting of Members of Council Held on or before February 12, 2013.*

Breux, Sandra, Jérôme Couture, and Laurence Bherer. 2014. "Les candidats sortants: atout ou obstacle à la participation électorale." *Canadian Urban Research* 23: 59–78.

Greater Sudbury. 2013a. Council. *Minutes*, 12 February 2013.

– 2013b. Council. *Minutes*, 26 February 2013.

MacDonald, Darren, 2013a. "Can't Do More Investigations in Sudbury, Ombudsman Says." *Sudbury Northern Life*, 10 April.

– 2013b. "Marin Takes Aim at 'Rogue' Sudbury City Council." *Sudbury Northern Life*, 15 February.

– 2013c. "Mayor, Council Clash Again." *Sudbury Northern Life*,
   16 September.
– 2014. "Matichuk to Marin: Welcome Back to Sudbury." *Sudbury
   Northern Life*, 8 March.
Maloney, Patrick. 2013. "Western Prof Takes on the Ombudsman." *The
   London Free Press*, 20 September.
– 2014. "Cost of Inquiry Kept under Wraps." *The London Free Press*,
   18 January.
Moore, Aaron A., R. Michael McGregor, and Laura B. Stephenson. 2017.
   "Paying Attention and the Incumbency Effect: Voting Behavior in the
   2014 Toronto Municipal Election." *International Political Science
   Review* 38(1): 85–98.
Oliver, J. Eric, Shang E. Ha, and Zachary Callen. 2012. *Local Elections
   and the Politics of Small-Scale Democracy*. Princeton, NJ: Princeton
   University Press.
Ontario Ombudsman. 2008. "Don't Let the Sun Go Down on Me:
   Opening the Door to the Elton John Ticket Scandal," Investigation into
   the City of Greater Sudbury Council Closed Meeting of February 20,
   2008. 25 April.
– 2012a. "Investigation into Closed Meetings Held by the Council for
   the City of Greater Sudbury on October 3 and 12, November 9 and
   December 14, 2011." August.
– 2012b. "Investigation into Whether Council for the City of London
   Held an Improper Closed Meeting at Harmony Grand Buffet on
   February 21, 2012." August.
– 2013a. "Re: Ombudsman Review of Closed Meetings Held June 12 and
   June 26, 2012." Letter to City of Greater Sudbury, 14 February.
– 2013b. "'In the Back Room,' Investigation into Whether the Council for
   the City of London Held an Improper Closed Meeting on 23 February
   2013." October.
– 2015. OMLET, *Annual Report, 2013–14*.
Sancton, Andrew. 2015. "What Is a Meeting? Municipal Councils and the
   Ontario Ombudsman." *Canadian Public Administration* 58: 426–43.
Trounstine, Jessica. 2011. "Evidence of Local Incumbency Advantage."
   Legislative Studies Quarterly 36: 255–80.

6

Accountability and Local Politics: Contextual Barriers and Cognitive Variety

Anne Mévellec

INTRODUCTION

Some of the questions explored in this book address accountability for decisions, asking "Who decides?" and "Who does what?" The book also examines the accountability of elected officials by asking "To whom are they accountable?" and "What are they accountable for?" These are important issues in the municipal context because they challenge certain preconceived notions. One such notion is the idea that the municipal level, compared to other levels of government, is closest to citizens and that, consequently, local elected officials are under more scrutiny from citizens. However, certain contextual elements invalidate this presupposition. For instance, as discussed in other chapters of this book, municipal electoral participation is relatively weak in Quebec (as well as in other Canadian provinces), with an average voter turnout of nearly 45 per cent (Champagne and Patry 2004; Sancton and Young 2009). Nevertheless, this situation has improved since 2013, when, for the first time, fewer than half of the mayors were elected by acclamation. These figures highlight how the direct relationship between elected officials and the electors affects only a small number of electors. In his definition of the municipality, Vandelli emphasizes that for the average citizen this frontline public institution is "the point of reference for all their problems, needs, expectations and drama. Independent of all the legal jurisdictions attributed to it, a municipality is where individuals address all their social requests and protestations" (2000, 7). The proximity of municipal government prevents neither a lack of interest on the part of citizens nor confusion among the electorate regarding its jurisdiction. In that context, the questions of accountability are of resounding importance.

In this chapter, I propose to address accountability using the municipal political system itself from the dual point of view of the ordinary citizen and the elected official. I will apply Mansbridge's (2009) conception of a sanctions model on the one hand and a selection model on the other. Both models use the principal–agent perspectives as represented by the elector and elected official. The sanctions model presupposes that the interests of these two parties are divergent and that therefore the monitoring and sanctioning of the behaviour of agents is done by way of an election. In other words, electors evaluate outgoing elected officials in terms of their delivery of public policy and consequently vote to reward or punish them for their performance (Pitkin 1967). The selection model, on the other hand, presumes that the principal and the agent share a certain number of similar objectives. As a result, the struggle for power in this model is determined beforehand, at the moment elected officials are chosen by the electors. The community of interests also allows for a form of accountability that is essentially narrative and that cannot prevent the mechanism of sanctions. Mansbridge also insists that the two models are not mutually exclusive and that the moment of the election is the instrument of both selection and sanction.

Building on this discussion, I then adopt the relevance of seeing accountability as something other than a form of sanction and of instead focusing on the material and cognitive conditions that support the day-to-day functioning of municipal democracy. More specifically, accountability is here addressed under two main questions: accountability to whom and of whom. Following Mansbridge's argument, I propose to address the question of sanctions and monitoring in the Quebec municipal context. More specifically, I address the issue of monitoring city councillors via clarity and transparency in the municipal system. Indeed, new mechanisms that attempt to ensure greater transparency in the functioning of municipal instances do not always fulfill their task of making the complexity of the institutional landscape and the process of public policy-making more understandable and clear. In addition to the material conditions of local democracy, I am also interested in the representations that elected officials have of themselves. For example, Christian Le Bart (1992) looks at the strategies of elected officials as they attempt to take credit (positive

self-assessment) or put the blame (negative hetero-assessment) on
their competitors for a series of actions or public decisions. Examining
accountability as practised by elected officials over the course of their
mandates leads me to examine the manner in which they maintain
variable notions of their claims of accountability. This allows me to
make a connection between emerging works from Canada that are
not simply concerned with the stakes of elections but rather with
what is happening between elections. Though municipal elections in
Canada are receiving increasing research attention (e.g., Cutler and
Matthews 2005; Goodman 2014; Tremblay and Mévellec 2013; Siegel,
Kushner, and Stanwick 2001; Taylor and McEleney 2015), very few
of the studies explicitly detail the manner in which mandates are
actually exercised (Koop 2015; Mévellec and Tremblay 2016).

The goal of this chapter is to offer a reflection on accountability in
a context of municipal practices as observed in the medium and large
cities of Quebec. Institutional complexity coupled with multiple conceptions of the role of local elected officials leads me to examine the
fundamental conditions of accountability that go beyond the theoretical models of democracy. I will begin by arguing that despite institutional reforms that led to more focus on the activity of local members,
the average citizen faces an institutional context that obscures the
clarity of municipal politics, potentially reducing the ideal conditions
for accountability sanctioning (Mansbridge 2009). Additionally, using
a study on the conceptions of the role played by city councillors in
Quebec, I will show that there is no unanimous view of accountability.
Individual and collective registers colour local elected officials' understanding and practice of accountability, which makes for some added
layers of analysis. Moreover, looking at councillors adds some complexity because it constantly poses the issue of scale between ward
and city focus. By looking at city councillors rather than mayors, I
then target the relationship between the electors at the most minute
electoral level, which is rarely considered in Canadian studies. The
diversity of ideas regarding the role of municipal politics also allows
me to shed more light on the conditions of accountability.

THE THORNY ISSUE OF CLARITY
IN MUNICIPAL POLITICS

The municipal level is often considered "the base cell for all democracies" (Vandelli 2000) or the school of democracy. The geographic

proximity of the municipal level to citizens seems to characterize it as being easily accessible. Several studies on the term *proximity* in the socio-political context have shown that it tends to be used more as a catch-all term than with a critical or historical perspective (Le Bart and Lefebvre 2005). To the extent that the municipal level embodies spatial and social proximity, this means that proximity is also a natural location for scrutiny – in other words, for constant surveillance by the public. However, this scrutiny remains limited, since institutional reforms have muddied the socio-political landscape (Lefebvre 2010) and because forms of territorial governance have entailed a complex horizontal arrangement between public and private actors (Pinson 2010). Additionally, though other contexts have allowed us to specify the importance of journalism in local scrutiny (Ekström, Johansson, and Larsson 2006), the Canadian context is characterized by a situation of information deficit (Bherer and Breux 2011; Cutler and Matthews 2005). I should take this opportunity to specify that clarity is not a prerogative of the municipal level – as Cutler (2008) has aptly proved by pointing to the confusion electors have regarding the Canadian provincial and federal levels.

Among other elements that likewise blur clarity at the municipal level, in particular in Quebec, is an accumulation of institutional reforms that have transformed (but by no means simplified) the politico-administrative landscape. In more general terms, these reforms reinforce the multilevel character of governance, which makes it even more difficult to identify the locus of decision-making for observers and citizens alike.

INSTITUTIONAL REFORMS AND TOOLS OF ACCOUNTABILITY

Since the end of the 1990s, the Quebec municipal system has been marked by several institutional upheavals, the first of which was structural reform. Following in Ontario's footsteps, the smaller cities that comprise the province's largest metropolises were merged, and their supra-local instances were restructured (Collin, Léveillée, and Poitras 2002; Sancton 1999). The choice was made by the Parti Québécois government to amalgamate many smaller municipalities to create six new cities of 100,000 inhabitants in Quebec.[1] To prepare for opposition to this reform, several measures were made by the legislature. Some were implemented through instruments that contributed to transparency, while others made the municipal and metropolitan system rather more complex.

As of 2001, one of these measures was the obligatory hiring of a municipal auditor general (MAG) for cities with more than 100,000 inhabitants. The implementation of the municipal amalgamations provoked serious opposition, which the government tried to address with Bill 29, passed on 21 June of the same year. New measures were implemented regarding the simultaneity of polls, wages, and auction contract terms. Until then only Montreal (1993), Quebec City (1997), and Laval had such stipulations in their respective charters, with external auditing being the practice elsewhere. Thus, from 2001 on, the position of MAG became obligatory by law. The measure also included evaluating and monitoring the effects of the mergers on municipal management. Yet even though the amalgamation reform transformed the municipal landscape (organizational charter mergers, the harmonization of collective agreements, financial consolidation, etc.), its impacts have not yet been systematically evaluated. In Quebec, like other provinces, the financial and organizational aspects of municipalities have not been adequately investigated. However, the creation of the MAG position, intended to raise awareness of the state of city finances and its organization, did allow for a certain level of assessment. In Quebec City, the MAG took a proactive role by leading the municipality through the merger process. Elsewhere, MAGs assumed a more reactive role by restoring order in post-amalgamation organizational charters. Via integrated auditing (finances, conformity, performance auditing), the MAG is required to question the work done as part of this amalgamation. By doing so, MAGs performed a new role in Quebec's big cities. The position also serves as an additional tool used by the government to create transparency and improve public management. Though the implementation varies from city to city (see Mévellec and Audet 2014), it is clear that the legislative spirit was to implement, municipally at least, a tool that had been proven in the provincial and federal systems. Once the municipal mergers were "absorbed" by the municipal systems, the mandates of MAGs became more concerned with the proper management of administrative apparatuses, in addition to engaging in decision-making of a more political nature, such as matters regarding foreign missions or the functioning of mayoral offices. The accountability was not only legislative and fiscal (from administration to city council) or political (from elected officials to electors) but also the object of external control for the benefit of the electors. The MAG, like provincial and federal officers of Parliament, acts on behalf of citizens and provides advice in municipal practices as a whole. The position is designed as a tool for transparency and control, with annual reports relayed to the public via local media.

Other arrangements were made by the legislator to attenuate protest against the municipal mergers, which muddied the clarity of the municipal level from above and from below. To appease certain opponents, the merged cities gave their newly minted "boroughs" broader fiscal scope and new powers. In the case of Montreal, neighbourhood leaders even became "borough mayors." In 2003, with the arrival in power of Jean Charest's Liberal government, the door was opened to citizen disputes in the form of a referendum. This new approach allowed forty-one municipalities that had been fused in 2001 to opt out of the new cities – though without returning to their previous full and complete autonomy. These "demerged" cities retained power over local services while the agglomeration councils were responsible for collective interest jurisdictions such as public transit, water supply and wastewater treatment services, policing, and promoting tourism. To ensure a measure of cooperation with the merged cities, eleven agglomeration councils were created, including for the largest cities such as Montreal, Quebec, and Longueuil.[2] In addition to this new municipal entity, there is also a metropolitan level in the case of Montreal (Tomàs 2012). The Montreal case is exemplary in the sense that it allowed us to observe the municipal reorganization process at the turn of the 2000s. This Quebec institutional layer cake thereby veered away from a simplified system, and in several locations it even went as far as becoming extremely complex. The clarity of public governance in the Montreal region became a guessing game, even for its most keen observers. In Toronto, Kushner and Siegel (2003) evaluated the effects of municipal mergers on the accessibility of elected officials. They concluded that only a small portion of the population declared that they had more difficulty reaching their municipal councillor and that these people represented the people most opposed to municipal mergers to begin with. To our knowledge, no similar work has been conducted in Quebec that would allow us to evaluate the mergers in terms of the relationship between elected officials and electors. However, we should highlight that fifteen years after the municipal mergers, several cities have attempted to simplify their structure by reducing the number of boroughs (Sherbrooke) or by reorganizing their committees and commissions (Gatineau).

MUNICIPALIZATION AND THE INCREASING ACCOUNTABILITY OF ELECTED OFFICIALS

While the municipal mergers and their legislative avatars tended to make the Quebec institutional landscape more complex and less transparent, other more recent reforms have increased the accountability of elected officials to the detriment of the other partners involved in public action – at least according to Simard and Leclerc (2008), who studied the transformations taking place at the Quebec regional scale. Though Quebec is the only province with a regional makeup characterized by a tripartite partnership governance (political–economic–social), the 2003 reforms transformed the regional development councils into regional conferences of elected officials as the primary political actors. Not only were municipal elected officials consequently in the majority, they also set the parameters for representation by the other components of society (Chiasson and Robitaille 2004). The 2003 regional reform was, in a manner of speaking, a first step toward the "development of municipalization" (Simard and Leclerc 2008). In 2014, new reforms confirmed the "municipalization" trend. Two new measures shook up the territorial structures: 1) the disappearance of regional institutions ended the development relocalization movement in the municipal portfolio, and 2) the revision of financing, as part of the financial pact, strengthened the positions of the municipalities and the extended regional county municipalities as the main stakeholders (Mévellec, Chiasson, and Fournis 2017). In terms of institutional clarity, the disappearance of the regional scale can be seen as a factor for simplification whereby municipal political personnel become the main stakeholders of territorial development policies, including the principal as well as the accountable stakeholders.

Finally, the clarity of the municipal political system is greatly affected by the demands placed on Quebec's elected municipal officials. The legislators did not simply transfer responsibility to the elected officials but rather demanded it. The Union of Quebec Municipalities (UMQ) has, in line with Alberta and Ontario's experiences, borne a political vision for the role of municipalities looking to be recognized as a level of government unto themselves and has profoundly renegotiated the parameters of municipal taxation (UMQ 2013). The provincial government partially responded to these demands in its partnership with the municipalities (2016–19) by offering special status to the cities of Quebec and Montreal, for example, by announcing a new legislative framework for local governance, and by decentralizing certain collective bargaining processes.

MULTILEVEL AND TRANSPARENT GOVERNANCE

Clarity is not just a structural affair; it is also important to multilevel governance. In Quebec, not only are exclusive municipal jurisdictions the exception, the means of taxation also make the production of public policy extremely complicated. Canadian infrastructure programs are also extremely revelatory in this regard. Created in 1994, these programs bear witness to the federal involvement in municipal affairs, despite the fact that they are supposedly the exclusive jurisdiction of the province. This complicates the shape of financing and effectively renders municipal projects a tripartite process (federal–provincial–municipal) (Champagne 2013). High-visibility financial projects such as those related to infrastructure, especially for multi-purpose centres (Bernier and Mévellec 2016), represent the pivotal role played by municipal elected officials. In this sense, it can be likened to the French system, where municipal elected officials can play with institutional and taxation entanglements to alternately support decisions or "pass the buck" to other levels of government (Lefebvre 2010). The infrastructure program example generally illustrates the broadening of these modes of government, including traditionally vertical relationships (implicating higher levels of government) as well as horizontal partnerships (between the private sector and the community). Quebec local elected officials therefore operate in two arenas; they demonstrate their ability to access governmental budgetary resources, and they host territorial partnerships that allow them to produce state action (Jouve 2007).

As a final point to this non-exhaustive list of institutional jurisdictions where accountability should be taking place lies transparency. The Charbonneau Commission[3] unveiled a series of political and financial scandals in Quebec. This controversy has put the spotlight on decision-making processes taking place within municipalities and has contributed to making transparency an increasingly significant issue for cities. Though more detailed research remains to be done on the transparency mechanisms implemented in Quebec, the Ontario ombudsperson model, discussed in this book by Andrew Sancton (chapter 5), provides a detailed view of the interpretation of transparency in municipal council sessions. Other authors have also described a "confiscation" of democracy taking place behind closed doors on the fringes of public assembly (Desage and Guéranger 2012). Mansbridge (2009) pointed out that transparency at all costs can have perverse effects on the functioning of political deliberation by sullying the negotiation capacity of decision-makers as "they need to be able to explore avenues that, after exploration, they might repudiate. They need to able to act creatively and empathetically, without scrutinizing every word for how it will play in public" (2009, 386). According to Mansbridge, this is less about "transparency in process" but rather more about fostering a "transparency in rationale" that presents the information, facts, and reasoning that lead to decisions.

Institutional troubles have marked Quebec municipal politics since the end of the 1990s, and though we are currently moving toward an approach to municipalization that promises more clarity about municipal political actions, we are still in a transition phase in which political actors and citizens need to adjust their practices and expertise of the system in order to be part of this development. The complexity of municipal public policy is an additional challenge for the average citizen seeking to understand their immediate political environment. In this context of reduced clarity, elected officials are not inactive; instead, they are developing strategies to create visible ties between their presence and their concrete accomplishments.

TWO VERSIONS OF ACCOUNTABILITY
FOR QUEBEC LOCAL ELECTED OFFICIALS

In a study I conducted with Manon Tremblay on local elected officials (Mévellec and Tremblay 2016), which included individual testimonials, the municipal level emerged as a locus where government officials are hit with all types of demands, including those that go beyond the skill set normally expected of them. In this sense, they stand out from their colleagues in France. Geographical proximity between the citizens and city councillors is a measure of "how close they are to the people." The jurisdictions that are tied to daily life perfectly illustrate this aspect. Trimble (1995, 104) noted that there is a "private" character to municipal responsibilities that is closely tied to daily life, including housing and urban travel. More generally, elected officials are quick to point out that their political level is the closest to the public: the most accessible, the most attentive, the one most likely to understand individual problems – in other words, the most "responsive."

This generic discourse masks a certain number of subtleties that were brought to light by the Mévellec and Tremblay study. These authors identified two types of ideal profiles for city councillors. The first is "amateur and apolitical," focusing on the function of service, territorial proximity at the ward level, being the face of independent elected officials, and the continuity of commitment to the community. The other type is "professional and political" and focuses on "delivery," the city level, a close link to the municipal political parties, and a strong dissociation between politics and other social activities. Essentially, this typology puts the "service-oriented" versus "action-oriented" dichotomy already identified in other works (e.g., Klok and Denters 2013 on Europe; Koop 2015 on several large Canadian cities) at the heart of the reflection regarding relationships with citizens, territory, public servants, and political parties. These two ideal types – with the amateur type corresponding to service-oriented and the professional type to action-oriented – also allow us to ascertain the differences in the way councillors define accountability in relation to their conception of their mandate. One would qualify one as interpersonal and the other as political. In the next section, I will discuss the common ground of city councillors' commitment to responsiveness, followed by an examination of each of the two profile types (amateur and professional) and the forms of accountability to which they are drawn.

THE COMMON GROUND OF CITY COUNCILLOR RESPONSIVENESS

To begin, I again return to the 2016 study by Mévellec and Tremblay to discuss a few of the common points shared among the interviewees. In one sense, the interviews showed that the majority of elected officials (71 per cent) had significant social capital before entering municipal politics that they had generally acquired through education and community activities as well as sports and clubs (Optimists, Knights of Columbus, and Kiwanis). This finding is consistent with the study of Simard (2004). I will discuss how militant and associative capital are not mobilized by everyone in the same manner later on. Additionally, elected officials have a relatively homogeneous discourse regarding their involvement in municipal rather than provincial and federal politics. Three arguments were generally put forward. The first emphasizes that the municipal level is where the most influence is to be had (for 50 per cent of the interviewees). Not only is the municipal level the jurisdiction of day-to-day life, it is also where the concrete problems of citizens can be resolved using an equally concrete solution (in the material sense of the term) from elected officials – a decision can be made, actions can be taken, and a certain measure of accountability is assumed. A good example of this valorization of the concrete is the citizens' demand that speed reduction measures be taken, such as speed bumps; the elected official relays the request, a decision is made, and city services are dispatched to install the speed bump. The elected official then takes credit for being responsive. The second argument common to elected officials pertains to the level of proximity (for 37 per cent of elected officials) because of the small distance between the populace and government at this level and of their being involved in their communities and sharing the same living conditions as their electors. The third argument voices a type of contempt for current politics as practised at the federal and provincial levels and for a political system where party discipline is paramount. City councillors compare their autonomous decision-making to partisan constraints and to the unenviable status of backbenchers.

This brief detour into the common reasons that lead people to choose municipal over federal or provincial politics teaches us about how the concept of accountability is introduced into their arguments. The personalization of municipal politics is made possible thanks to borough elections, a traditionally non-partisan structure, and the "practical" nature of the jurisdictions, providing a "responsive" concept of accountability. In other words, city councillors feel that they are judged according to their capacity to take action. These actions are, however, variable in nature depending on their profile as an "amateur" or "professional" type of elected official.

ENTRY INTO POLITICS: SOCIAL AND POLITICAL DISTANCE

Works dealing with accountability target elections as the moment when electors confer a candidate with their mandate, who is then committed to putting it into action. Though municipal elections gladly accommodate single-issue candidates, they are rarely elected (Mévellec and Tremblay 2016; Siegel, Kushner, and Stanwick 2001), illustrating the practical limitations of an election strategy that is too narrow. To better understand the conceptions of accountability that coexist among candidates and elected officials, we will backtrack to the point in time just before the electoral campaign. In our 2016 study of the reasons and conditions that lead municipal elected officials to enter politics, several elements stood out about the way these politicians envisioned their relationship with accountability.

One group of interviewees insisted on the continuity between their path in volunteering and their entry into politics. They felt that this was simply an additional step, which they described as a "natural" part of their social trajectory. Politics therefore is not distinct from other forms of social involvement but rather part of a complex entity of social relationships. It stands to reason that this concept of politics is firmly rooted in the service aspect, evoking the Anglo-Saxon figure of a "gifted amateur" or "layperson." It is also informed by principles of equality, representation, and inclusiveness and suggests that, "notwithstanding some formal criteria of eligibility, any fellow-citizen should be able to come forward as a candidate for political office" (Steyvers and Verhelst 2012, 4) – which supposes that the selection process is inclusive for different groups of society. The concept moreover implies that a certain degree of permeability exists in the local political scene as well as in the rest of society, allowing for fluid passages between any sphere of society and the benches of city council. The elected officials are thus defined as amateurs who see themselves as being "at the service" of the community and its citizens. Most often independents, they run for office under their own name and focus on their community service experience and their involvement in the local community. They present themselves as being "no different from anyone else." Their electoral campaigns are an occasion to develop personal and individualized relationships. Their electoral platforms are often restricted, with a focus on planning issues and the provision of infrastructure for their electoral borough. Their proposed mandates are often articulated around fairly "material" elements, allowing for a relatively clear evaluation of their results. It follows that accountability is viewed as a contract that binds the candidate to their electors. However, although the local politicians' concept of accountability includes a contractual aspect, it is also marked by a closely interpersonal dimension. Along with the rest of their participation in politics, it is based on personal characteristics and their ability to serve as an interface between citizens and the city. In other words, it corresponds more or less with a notable figure whose social characteristics prevail over their political characteristics.

However, another group of interviewees, who shared the same types of social capital, indicated breaking with prior engagements as their main motivation for their entry into politics. For them, it was less about pursuing community activity at another scale than about entering into a new realm of politics where they would be given decision-making capacity and could embark on a different course of action. This group was more likely than the first group to have political capital and be ardent followers of a political party, to aspire to eventually being a candidate at the provincial level, or to be members of school boards. Community, union, and political socialization allowed them to acquire, in addition to social capital, a militant capital that they now wished to transfer to another commitment space (Matonti and Poupeau 2004). They entered politics to decide, act, and make changes. Both social and militant, they also tend to have the dual trait of being conflictive and visionary when exercising municipal mandates. Their program is less a collected list of material projects than a set of goals. Though some of this is directed at the borough, it can also include procedural elements (e.g., providing city council with new expertise, modifying certain procedural elements). This approach to municipal political activity is very different from the vision of the amateur type, who tends to view municipal commitment as a form of community engagement. The responses of this group of interviewees calls for a more narrative form of accountability.

TERRITORY: ACCOUNTABILITY VIA ACCESSIBILITY

The relationship between the access to and exercise of municipal mandates and electoral boundaries has been abundantly discussed in the literature. Several works have set out to isolate the effect of elections by district and elections "at large" on access to mandates (Trounstine and Valdini 2008) and the manner in which elected officials view mandates (Graham, Phillips, and Maslove 1998; Koop 2015; Koop and Kraemer 2016). District boundaries are considered a factor that favours the conception of a political role centred on the functions of service. When, as in Quebec, elections are held on a neighbourhood basis, elected officials tend to represent one particular community. This proximity to the electors creates a relationship of direct accountability.

The "amateur" types of elected officials strongly value this proximity. According to them, proximity, far from reducing the value of closeness, allows them to represent community at the electoral ward level and to experience an immediacy of relationships between the populace and councillors. When describing their mandate, they consider the reference territory to be the ward and not the city. Geographical proximity is expressed in positive terms such as assurance and a certain quality of representation. This means that they consider politicians more qualified to represent a given area if they live there and are directly accessible by the population they represent. Meeting electors at the grocery store, at the park, or on the street corner becomes an invaluable yet informal mechanism of accountability. Councillors also pointed out that they get faster feedback on municipal decisions and on their actions when living and working in geographic proximity to their constituents. Indeed, citizens can ask their representatives about political or even social goings-on at all times. Thus, although councillors might view this as an invasion of their privacy at times, they generally see it as positive and as a gauge of the proper functioning of democracy.

However, the relationship with the ward can also go off on another tangent. Some of the "professional" councillors have a less local concept of political work and identify, broadly speaking, more with the city as a whole than with a ward. These types of officials focus more on their involvement in municipal commissions and committees than on working on behalf of their electors. Thus, although they recognize the need to pay attention to their constituents to secure their election, they give less value to working the field (in the sense of parliamentary constituency work) than to the legislative portion of their political mandate. Additionally, for these elected officials, constant accessibility, such as meeting with constituents in formal or non-formal settings, is not valued as highly. Instead, they tend to view it as a demand that they *have to* meet, it being expected of the mandate, and as a constraint rather than an opportunity.

WHO'S RESPONSIBLE FOR WHAT? SERVICE AND DELIVERY

The "amateur" and "professional" city councillor types detailed by Mévellec and Tremblay (2016) were identified on the basis of their responses to questions regarding their entry into politics, their relationship with their ward, and what they believe to be the essential mission of their position. When asked "What is the most important part of exercising your mandate?" amateur councillors emphasized service to the electors whereas the professionals focused on delivery.

For the group of amateur councillors, political representation was mostly seen as taking the issues to city hall on behalf of the electors and supporting individuals when dealing with the municipal administration. This is, in fact, the traditional view of representation whereby the elected official constitutes an intermediary between the legislative powers, the executive, and the people. Thus, the councillor here sees her or his role as one of mediation or intercession with ward citizens in their dealings with and demands of the city. Docherty (1996), in a context pertaining to parliamentarians, referred to this role as that of a "fixer" insofar as it is focused on solving problems. According to him, representatives place emphasis on personalized services in their riding because it is the successful delivery thereof that allows them to be recognized as someone who is effective. At the municipal scale, this role of service provider allows councillors to demonstrate their ability to resolve personal problems. Like parliamentarians who are not ministers, this role is important for councillors who are less visible in decision-making, such as those not part of executive committees.

The "professional" group of councillors focused less on their service to the electors than on actions and decisions as the central elements of their practice. This includes all of the actions performed by councillors in the process of creating public policy, such as initiatives, finding solutions, and the ability to implement policies with easily identifiable deliverables. In keeping with Scharpf (1999) and Béal and Pinson (2014), the political legitimacy of this group of councillors is derived not only from their ability to represent but also from their capacity to "deliver" solutions to problems found in the city. The term "policy-maker" aptly describes the understanding of this political role for this group of councillors. In their own discourse, these elected officials insist that the municipal political role has changed and that they cannot limit their mandate to the provision of services to the electors. This indicates that the "old" system of municipal politics, which, as described above, subscribes to constant accessibility, is coming up against a "new" system that considers service to the people as subordinate to legislative functions at the city level. The "professional" guard of politicians insists that their involvement in these aspects is what inspires them, alongside the mandate to perform arbitration and mediation work. In short, their mandate revolves around projects and demonstrating a certain capacity to deliver products.

Their diverse experience in a municipal career allows them to distinguish between the interpersonal and political aspects of accountability. Thus, while the service-oriented amateur councillors are seen to demonstrate their individual responsiveness, the so-called professional councillors are considered policy-makers who emphasize community-oriented actions.

THE PARTISAN EFFECT OF ACCOUNTABILITY

The influence of political parties has seen a marked increase in popularity in Quebec since the 2000s. The issue of political parties is too big to be cover sufficiently in this chapter. We will address this issue not so much as a means of reviewing the effects of partisan organizations in the functioning of Quebec municipalities (see Mévellec and Tremblay 2013) but rather to examine how city councillors position themselves as a reaction to this new political reality. The issue of parties offers an excellent opportunity to confirm what local elected representatives consider the individual or collective nature of their position.

Independent councillors frequently express their discontent with the presence of political parties in municipal politics, generally citing three main reasons: party discipline runs counter to the individual freedoms of city councillors; the existence of parties "parliamentarizes" the functioning of city hall and goes against negotiation and effectiveness; and finding a balance between the authority of the mayor and the city councillors is compromised when the party in power has a majority of seats. Though the arguments are not particularly original in nature, they nevertheless highlight the type of legitimacy that councillors exhort – one of authenticity and a broader sense of individuality. Free of all partisan constraints, elected officials can take the time to speak "honestly" and maintain frank and direct relationships with their colleagues, the electorate, the municipal administration, and anyone else involved in municipal politics. This concept of the attitude expected of councillors is close, though not exact, in nature to the proximity discussed above. In fact, though the argument regarding party discipline dominates the discourse of councillors, it is also because, in our opinion, it corresponds to a perceived individual legitimacy in the sense of "These people … didn't vote for a party, they voted for me." This individual legitimacy is also tied to ward elections and the types of resources that are valued for their eligibility and pursuit of power. Paradoxically, although elected officials' social and political capital is an important factor in their election, once they are in their position they present themselves in their name only and claim to act on an exclusively individual basis. The issue of the presence of municipal political parties also leads independent city councillors to address the question of decision-making processes within city council. This means that their discourse emphasizes the benefits of inter-individual negotiations, compromise, and distancing themselves from conflict. The independence of city councillors is considered an essential condition to deliberation that allows for the construction of collective interest, expressed in this instance by the idea of compromise. Additionally, the independence of councillors is conceived and expressed as a necessary counterweight to the power of the mayor.

City councillors who are members of a political party obviously hold a very different opinion. They feel that belonging to a political party entitles, or even obligates, them to transform an essentially individual experience into a collective venture, a view that manifests itself as early as during the electoral campaign. The party offers a range of resources (financial, material, cognitive, and human) as a kind of safety net to candidates entering municipal politics (Mévellec and Tremblay 2013). Additionally, these councillors consider any debates within the party that are not subject to party discipline as opportunities to bring municipal issues to the table. The deliberation that takes place before city hall allows for the preparation, far from prying eyes, of the positions of party members. The majority presence of a party at the table is seen as a measure of efficiency and effectiveness. Effectively, by presenting a formal and common vision, a team can implement and begin mandates more efficiently and thereby adopt a more narrative form of accountability.

Moreover, by choosing to align with a party, city councillors can channel or shape the way they exercise their mandates in either an individual or collective manner. To conclude this point, end-of-mandate summaries are an excellent means of illustrating the variable forms of accountability. Independent elected officials only have to offer their electorate their personal summary, whereas councillors in a party have two summaries to present: one that presents the summary of their organization and the public actions they have led collectively on behalf of the city, and one at the borough level with a self-assessment of their accomplishments.

CONCLUSION

This chapter aimed at examining the accountability of local elected officials through the practices of Quebec municipal governments – namely, by analyzing certain aspects of the institutional context of that province and by looking into the meaning that elected officials give to their role in politics.

I showed that the Quebec municipal political system presents obstacles to understanding by its citizens. The complexity of the system, as well as a blurring of responsibilities in a context of multilevel governance, allowed me to reflect on the principal capacities required to monitor the work of city councillors. Clarity alone is insufficient to ensure accountability. However, in the context of poor clarity, electors risk becoming too reliant and dependent on the self-assessed discourse of elected officials. The principal–agent relationship and accountability–sanctioning model need greater systemic transparency to sufficiently reward or punish the behaviour of agents. The elements presented in the Quebec context could lead us to think that transparency is not standard practice, especially not in urban centres.

Additionally, an analysis of the ideal types of city councillors has led me to conclude that they coexist in municipal governments with very distinct ideas of their roles. I found councillors with a strongly individual and interpersonal concept of their political mandate. Elected in their own name, they are first and foremost representatives of their neighbourhood, seeing themselves playing the role of advocate between their electors and the city, with maximum accessibility considered a token of their dedication. They are certain of their individual legitimacy and are wary of political parties. Elected at the ward level, they fully endorse a vision of themselves as ward healer. Their understanding of the municipal system is fully compatible with the traditional Quebec model of the amateur (Chiasson and Mévellec 2014). Self-assessment allows them to emphasize their personal contribution as added-value. The second conception of a political mandate is that of the policy-maker at the city level for whom decision-making, vision, and a certain form of politicization are key. This type of councillor believes in the trend of professionalizing the exercise of political mandates and supports the logic behind changing the Quebec municipal political system as advocated by the U M Q (2013). Their behaviour and the assessments they defend are marked by a more collective and political conception of municipal work.

Overall, this chapter contributed practical, institutional, and cognitive elements to this book to help establish a better understanding of the conditions under which accountability and representation occur. By taking a two-fold approach of context and by examining the conceptions that city councillors have of their roles, the chapter also offered a sense of how accountability is shaped by situations and practices that extend well beyond the traditional focus on election time.

NOTES

1 The six newly created cities in decreasing size were: Gatineau, Longueuil, Sherbrooke, Saguenay, Lévis, and Trois-Rivières.
2 Other agglomerated communities include: Sainte-Agathe-des-Monts, Mont-Tremblant, Cookshire-Eaton, Rivière-Rouge, Sainte-Marguerite-Estérel, Îles-de-la-Madeleine, and La Tuque.
3 Public commission in Quebec enacted in 2011 to inquire into potential corruption in the management of public construction contracts.

REFERENCES

Béal, Vincent, and Gilles Pinson. 2012. "When Mayors Go Global: International Strategies, Urban Governance and Leadership." *International Journal of Urban and Regional Research* 38(1): 302–17.

Bernier, André, and Anne Mévellec. 2016. "Solutions, discours et politisation des amphithéâtres multifonctionnels." Paper presented at the 53rd A S R D L F colloquium, Gatineau, Quebec, July.

Bherer, Laurence, and Sandra Breux. 2011. "Démocratie locale et élections: prémices d'une comparaison," In *Les élections municipales au Québec: enjeux et perspectives*, edited by Laurence Bherer and Sandra Breux, 1–29. Québec: Presses de l'Université Laval.

Champagne, Éric. 2013. "Les programmes d'infrastructures municipales du gouvernement fédéral: une analyse de la gouvernance multiniveaux au Canada." *Télescope: Revue d'analyse comparée en administration publique* 19(1): 43–61.

Champagne, Patrick, and Renaud Patry. 2004. "La participation électorale dans les municipalités du Québec." *Muni-Stat* 1(1): 1–4.

Chiasson, Guy, and Anne Mévellec. 2014. "The 2013 Quebec Municipal Elections: What Is Specific to Quebec?" *Canadian Journal of Urban Research* 23(2): 1–17.

Chiasson, Guy, and Martin Robitaille. 2016. "Les conférences des élus ou la démocratie revisitée." Filmed 2004. Retrieved 22 January 2016: http://www4.uqo.ca/observer/DevLocal/Gouvernance/CRE.htm.

Collin, Jean-Pierre, Jacques Léveillée, and Claire Poitras. 2002. "New Challenges and Old Solutions: Metropolitan Reorganization in Canadian and US City-Regions." *Journal of Urban Affairs* 24(3): 317–32.

Cutler, Fred. 2008. "Whodunnit? Voters and Responsibility in Canadian Federalism." *Canadian Journal of Political Science/Revue canadienne de science politique* 41(3): 627–54.

Cutler, Fred, and J. Scott Matthews. 2005. "The Challenge of Municipal Voting: Vancouver 2002." *Canadian Journal of Political Science/Revue canadienne de science politique* 38(2): 359–82.

Desage, Fabien, and David Guéranger. 2012. *La politique confisquée. Sociologie des réformes et des institutions intercommunales.* Bellecombe-en-Bauges: Éditions du croquant.

Docherty, David C. 1996. "Quel genre de représentants les Canadiens veulent-ils?" *Revue parlementaire canadienne* Spring: 8–11.

Ekström, Mats, Bengt Johansson, and Larsake Larsson. 2006. "Journalism and Local Politics. A Study of Scrutiny and Accountability in Swedish Journalism." *Journalism Studies* 7(2): 292–311.

Goodman, Nicole. 2014. "Internet Voting in a Local Election in Canada." *Studies in Public Choice* (31): 7–24.

Graham, Katherine, Susan D. Phillips, and Allan Maslove. 1998. *Urban Governance in Canada.* Toronto: Harcourt Brace.

Jouve, Bernard. 2007. "La gouvernance urbaine: vers l'émergence d'un nouvel instrument des politiques?" *Revue internationale des sciences sociales* 193–94(3): 387–402.

Klok, Pieter Jan, and Bas Denters. 2013. "The Roles Councillors Play." In *Local Councillors in Europe*, edited by Björn Egner et al., 63–83. Wiesbaden: Springer.

Koop, Royce. 2015. "Institutional- and Individual-Level Influences on Service Representation and Casework in Canadian Cities." *Urban Affairs Review.* Published electronically 13 October 2015. doi: 10.1177/1078087415608955.

Koop, Royce, and John Kraemer. 2016. "Wards, At-Large Systems and the Focus of Representation in Canadian Cities." *Canadian Journal of Political Science/Revue canadienne de science politique* 49(3): 433–48.

Kushner, Joseph, and David Siegel. 2003. "Effect of Municipal Amalgamations in Ontario on Political Representation and Accessibility." *Canadian Journal of Political Science/Revue canadienne de science politique* 36(5): 1035–51.

Le Bart, Christian. 1992. *La rhétorique du maire entrepreneur: critique de la communication municipale.* Paris: Pedone.

Le Bart, Christian, and Rémi Lefebvre. 2005. *La proximité en politique. Usages, rhétoriques, pratiques.* Rennes: Presses Universitaires de Rennes.

Lefebvre, Rémi. 2010. "L'impensé démocratique de la réforme territoriale." *La vie des idées* 9 March. http://www.laviedesidees.fr/L-impense-democratique-de-la.html#nb13.

Mansbridge, Jane. 2009. "A 'Selection Model' of Political Representation." *Journal of Political Philosophy* 17(4): 369–98.

Matonti, Frédérique, and Franck Poupeau. 2004. "Le capital militant: essai de définition." *Actes de la recherche en sciences sociales* 5(155): 4–11.

Mévellec, Anne, and Étienne Audet. 2014. "Municipal Auditor General in Quebec Cities: How Much Autonomy for What Role?" Paper presented at the International Research Society for Public Management Conference, Ottawa, Carleton University, April.

Mévellec, Anne, Guy Chiasson, and Yann Fournis. 2017. "De 'créature du gouvernement' à 'gouvernement de proximité': la trajectoire sinueuse des municipalités québécois." *Revue français d'administration publique* 62: 339–52.

Mévellec, Anne, and Manon Tremblay. 2013. "Les partis politiques municipaux: la 'Westminsterisation' des villes du Québec?" *Recherches sociographiques* 54(2): 325–47.

– 2016. *Genre et professionnalisation de la politique municipale.* Quebec: Presses de l'Université du Québec.

Pinson, Gilles. 2010. "France." In *Changing Government Relations in Europe: From Localism to Intergovernmentalism*, edited by Michael Goldsmith and Edward Page, 68–87. London: Routledge.

Pitkin, Hanna Fenichel. 1967. *The Concept of Representation.* Berkeley: University of California Press.

Sancton, Andrew. 1999. "Differing Approaches to Municipal Restructuring in Montreal and Toronto: From the Pichette Report to the Greater Toronto Services Board." *Canadian Journal of Regional Science/Revue canadienne des sciences régionales* 22(1–2): 187–99.

Sancton, Andrew, and Robert Young, eds. 2009. *Foundations of Governance. Municipal Government in Canada's Provinces.* Toronto: University of Toronto Press.

Scharpf, Fritz. 1999. *Governing in Europe: Effective and Democratic?* Oxford: Oxford University Press.

Siegel, David, Joseph Kushner, and Hannah Stanwick. 2001. "Canadian Mayors: A Profile and Determinants of Electoral Success." *Canadian Journal of Urban Research/Revue canadienne de recherche urbaine* 10(1): 5–22.

Simard, Carolle. 2004. "Qui nous gouverne au municipal: reproduction ou renouvellement?" *Politique et sociétés* 23(2–3): 135–58.

Simard, Jean-François, and Yvon Leclerc. 2008. "Les centres locaux de développement 1998–2008. Une gouvernance en mutation: entre participation citoyenne et imputabilité municipale." *Revue canadienne des sciences régionales* 31(3): 615–36.

Steyvers, Kristof, and Tom Verhelst. 2012. "Between Layman and Professional? Political Recruitment and Career Development of Local Councillors in a Comparative Perspective." *Lex Localis – Journal of Local Self-Government* 10(1): 1–17.

Taylor, Zack, and Sandra McEleney. 2015. "The Advantages of Incumbency and the Determinants of Municipal Candidate Vote Share: The 2014 City of Toronto Election." Paper presented at the Canadian Political Science Association annual meeting, Ottawa, June.

Tomàs, Mariona. 2012. *Penser métropolitain? La bataille politique du Grand Montréal.* Sainte-Foy: Presses de l'Université du Québec.

Tremblay, Manon, and Anne Mévellec. 2013. "City Hall: Truly More Accessible to Women than the Legislature?" In *Continuing Presence: Women, Elections, and Political Representation in Canada*, edited by Jane Arscott, Linda Trimble, and Manon Tremblay, 19–35. Vancouver: UBC Press.

Trimble, Linda. 1995. "Politics Where We Live: Women and Cities." In *Canadian Metropolitics: Governing Our Cities*, edited by James Lightbody, 92–114. Toronto: Copp Clark.

Trounstine, Jessica, and Melody Valdini. 2008. "The Context Matters: The Effects of Single-Member versus At-Large Districts on City Council Diversity." *American Journal of Political Science* 52(3): 554–69.

UMQ (Union des municipalités du Québec). 2013. *Livre blanc.* Montreal: Union des municipalités du Québec.

Vandelli, Luciano. 2000. "La cellule de base de toutes les démocraties." *Pouvoirs* 95:5–17.

PART THREE

Issues Regarding Services and Governance in Multilevel Governments

7

Accountability and Local Collaborative Governance

Joseph Lyons and Zachary Spicer

INTRODUCTION

Much of our conceptualization of local servicing in Canada involves a single municipality producing and delivering the full range of services received by local residents. The reality, however, is much more complicated. Most Canadians receive their local services from a variety of sources. Many do come from municipalities, but in some places in British Columbia, New Brunswick, Ontario, and Quebec there are at least two tiers of municipal government. Some services are also delivered in more specialized ways: by special-purpose bodies (SPBS), agreements between neighbouring jurisdictions – called inter-local agreements – or through contracts with private companies or non-profit groups. Provincial governments play a strong role in influencing and directing all of this, given the limited authority of municipalities in Canada. In short, local service production and delivery is fragmented, with a variety of actors involved in responding to the needs of residents.

This level of fragmentation raises several questions related to accountability and transparency. How involved is the public in setting the parameters of such servicing arrangements? How aware is the public about the source of servicing within their communities? How much control do municipal officials actually have over the delivery of certain vital local services? Accountability is blurred any time a single government is not entirely responsible for a specific service. Much has been written about the accountability challenges associated with intergovernmental service delivery or contracting out. However, less scholarly attention has been paid to SPBS and inter-local agreements, which often include elements of both (see Lyons 2015a; Spicer 2014). This is a blind spot in the literature in need of correcting as the use of specialized approaches to service delivery is, if anything, increasing (Spicer 2015; Slack 1997; LeSage, McMillan, and Hepburn 2008; Sancton, James, and Ramsay 2000; Horak 2012).

Using London, Ontario, as an example, we explore the accountability of SPBS and inter-local agreements and provide new methods for measuring local accountability relationships in the Canadian context. London has been referred to as an "ordinary city" in the past, generally used by marketers for product-testing but also a frequent site for inquiry in local politics, given that the city is mid-sized in population, has a diversified economy, and is generally devoid of the "high buzz" of big cities or the "quaint identity" of smaller communities (see Bradford and Nelles 2014; Bradford 2016). Such places are left with their own "hum," as Paul Chatterton (2000) describes – "the everyday, the mundane, the ordinary, and the drabness which makes up life or urban dwellers." As such, we believe London is the ideal city to use as a case study for our examination, providing for a measure of generalizability onto other jurisdictions because of London's community characteristics.[1] Ultimately, we argue that compared to inter-local agreements, SPBS offer a superior vehicle for enhancing servicing accountability. Thus, we believe that SPBS are a better alternative than inter-local agreements for delivering higher-order and critical services.

SPECIAL-PURPOSE BODIES, INTER-LOCAL COOPERATION, AND LOCAL SERVICING

Any type of local service has two main aspects. The first is provision, which refers to the authority over the service, such as the ability to set service levels, service costs, and any sort of user fees. The second is production, which involves the ability to meet service levels and produce a particular service in accordance with community need. As mentioned above, local governments fulfill these dimensions in a variety of ways, such as internal production and delivery, contracting (either publicly or privately), or cooperatively sharing the burden of servicing with another jurisdiction. Determining the best route for delivering specific services requires weighing the relevant benefits and costs of each. Sometimes this is done locally, but in other instances it is done by higher-level governments, usually provincial ones.

One such option is special-purpose bodies (SPBs), which can be defined as autonomous local governments that provide a single or limited number of functions (see Siegel 1994a; Sancton 2015). Factors that might be considered in determining whether or not a service should be delivered by SPBs include the need for a multi-jurisdictional service area, intergovernmental coordination, organizational flexibility, and arm's-length decision-making (Siegel 1994b). Indeed, many SPBs meet one or more of these design rationales. Examples include police services boards, public health units, conservation authorities, and public transit commissions, among others. Because there is no census of governments in Canada, it is difficult to precisely determine how many SPBs exist and the full range of services they provide. However, it is safe to assume that SPBs greatly outnumber municipalities and deliver many important local services (Tindal and Tindal 2004).

Apart from their more specialized orientation, SPBs are like municipalities in many ways: they are independently governed, they have access to public money through grants, taxes, or user fees, and they have decision-making authority within their defined territorial and functional jurisdictions. The main difference, however, is that the boards of most SPBs are appointed rather than elected (see Lyons 2015a; 2015b), many provinces' school boards being important exceptions. Even when municipal politicians serve on the boards of SPBs, as they often do, they are one step removed from the electoral process. This has obvious implications for accountability, especially when it comes to political accountability.

Indeed, critics of specialization frame their arguments around some of these accountability shortcomings. They argue that SPBs confuse citizens and are insulated from public control, making them less accountable than municipal governments. Accountability is further eroded because this confusion affords politicians more opportunities for blame-shifting when things go wrong and credit-claiming when they go right (Lowery 2001). Blame-shifting aside, critics maintain that appointed board members usually defer to the professional advice of staff and actually have only limited influence over the decision-making process (Leach 1996; O'Brien 1993). Combined, these characteristics limit the opportunities for citizen oversight of or involvement with specialized governments. On the other hand, proponents of specialization argue that increasing the number of local governments within a geographic area – be they municipal governments or SPBs – has a positive effect on the behaviour of public officials and on rates of citizen participation, thereby improving accountability (Ostrom 1972; Bish 2001).

Another such option is inter-local cooperation whereby one municipality may contract another to produce or deliver a service. Two municipalities may also deliver a service jointly. Inter-local cooperation has a number of benefits, including the ability to contain policy and service problems that may spill over local boundaries. Such arrangements may also be able to lower the costs of servicing and ensure policy and service continuity throughout a region (Dollery et al. 2004; Chen and Thurmaier 208; Lackey, Freshwater, and Rupasingha 2002). Most municipalities engage in some form of inter-municipal cooperation. The most basic form is information-sharing (such as Municipal Benchmarking Network Canada). Such cooperative relationships can extend into complex, integrated joint management projects, such as a common water system or police service (Spicer 2015). In any case, municipalities have increasingly used inter-local arrangements to deliver a wide range of services, including vital services such as the delivery of water and emergency protection (Gainsborough 2001; Feiock 2013; Dollery, Grant, and Kortt 2012). These arrangements are usually the result of formal, legal contracts outlining the responsibility and financial obligation of each partner (Andrew 2008; 2009).

The practice of inter-local cooperation raises several questions about local accountability and transparency. Such arrangements shift traditional lines of accountability within municipal servicing, reducing fiscal and servicing transparency and ultimately leaving residents without adequate information to evaluate the performance of such arrangements (O'Brien 1993). Slack (1993; 1997) argues that inter-local servicing also makes it difficult for consumers and taxpayers to know whom to hold accountable for service provision because it is not always clear which government is providing the service. If a service user or taxpayer wishes to complain or gain more information about a particular service that is jointly funded or delivered, it is often not clear which government is actually responsible, even though both may be responsible for funding (Kitchen and Slack 2003).

Many trying to assess inter-local relationships within an academic context have encountered serious challenges related to limited documentation and knowledge of the agreements (Sancton, James, and Ramsay 2000). Generally, only a few people within the organization have any knowledge of the arrangement (ibid.). Additionally, very little formal documentation of any agreements exists, and where it does, such documentation is difficult to access (ibid.). Many of these are real, practical concerns residents have in accessing information about shared services. When it comes to both special-purpose jurisdictions and inter-local cooperative arrangements, residents and municipal politicians require information and the threat of sanctions to hold local actors to account. We elaborate on this below.

ACCOUNTABILITY AND TRANSPARENCY IN THEORY AND PRACTICE

While largely considered a multifaceted term (Brandsma and Schillemans 2012; Behn 2001; Mulgan 2003; Koppell 2005; Alcantara, Spicer, and Leone 2012), it is generally accepted that accountability is one of the hallmarks of representative democracy, requiring those exercising public authority to be subjected to scrutiny and evaluation (Aucoin and Jarvis 2005; Grant and Keohane 2005). Implying a relationship between elected officials and members of the electorate in its most basic form (Moncrieffe 1998), accountability is meant to promote democratic control, compliance, and continuous improvement in the use of public authority and resources (Aucoin and Heintzman 2000).

Accountability is conceived of as a type of agency relationship in which one party is understood to be an "agent" who makes some choices on behalf of the "principal" who then has the power to sanction or reward the agent (Fearon 1999). However, these principal–agent relationships come in many forms. According to Bovens (2007), there are five different kinds of accountability: political accountability (elected representatives, political parties, voters, media), legal accountability (courts), administrative accountability (auditors, inspectors, controllers), professional accountability (professional peers), and social accountability (interest groups, charities, other stakeholders). Each presents a very different principal–agent relationship, since any given group will tend to hold a different actor to account (Brandsma and Schillemans 2012; Bundt 2000; Romzek and Dubnick 1998).

These principal–agent models commonly view delegation in hierarchical terms between institutions and individuals (Brandsma and Schillemans 2012). As such, organizations are seen as relationships between those who delegate (i.e., principals) and those who are delegated to (i.e., agents) (Brandsma and Schillemans 2012). Voters may also be seen as principals who delegate power to their representatives, who act as agents. This chain of delegation continues to individual civil servants, who can also be considered as agents serving the public (principals) (Størm 2000).

No matter the accountability relationship or the actors involved, they all include three steps: information, discussion, and consequences/sanctions. The process begins in the information phase, where an agent provides an account of his or her conduct, then proceeds through a discussion phase, where the principal assesses this account, to finally conclude in a consequences phase, where an agent may or may not be punished and, therefore, held to account (Brandsma and Schillemans 2012). Such sanctions may be formal or informal and can be positive or negative (Elster 1999; Behn 2001). Throughout this iterative process, agents are made aware of the expectations for their conduct and responsibility toward the principal, creating norms and standards within the principal–agent relationship (Sinclair 1995; Pollitt 2003; Kim 2005).

As this host of literature implies, contemporary public agents usually face numerous, sometimes interconnected, accountability forums. Accountability relationships may be highly complex, especially when there is a layering of accountability or if a particular organization is accountable or perceived to be accountable to numerous sources. Koppell (2005, 94) characterizes these situations as "multiple accountabilities disorder," which occur when "conflicting expectations borne of disparate conceptions of accountability" undermine an organization's goals or effectiveness. This situation is evident in many intergovernmental relationships in Canada, as evidenced by relationships between First Nations and the Crown (Alcantara, Spicer, and Leone 2012; Imai 2007) or between the federal and provincial governments (Graefe, Simmons, and White 2013).

When the complexity of the institutional environment or relationship increases, the traditional principal–agent relationship can become blurred (Moe 2005). The problem with accountability within such arrangements is that there is not a single lead actor (or principal) who sets goals and then employs agents to accomplish them (Ebraheim and Weisband 2007, 4; Brown 1983). These types of problems have been shown to occur within federal systems, which "provide for two loci of authority" (Brown 1983, 634). As such, neither is able to authoritatively coerce the other (Graefe, Simmons, and White 2013). A similar relationship is found within inter-local relationships, since bilateral relationships between local governments also lack the same "locus of authority" identified by Brown (1983). Things can become even more problematic when it comes to SPBS, since many of them operate at a local or regional scale and have municipal representation but owe their existence to federal or provincial legislation. These relationships, then, can be best conceptualized as a collective action problem.

Accountability can be a challenging concept to measure, especially when compared across jurisdictions, scales, and functions. A number of studies have attempted to map networks of accountability relationships (Considine 2002; O'Connell, Yusuf, and Hackbart 2009; Brandsma and Schillemans 2012), while others have measured accountability expectations (Ashworth 2000; Wang 2002), individual actor accountability (Dunne and Legge 2001; Dicke 2002), and the use of sanctions to enforce accountability standards (Hanretty and Koop 2011; Lamothe and Lamothe 2009). Such studies have been helpful in trying to construct our own index to evaluate accountability in local service sharing.

Particularly helpful is the work of Skelcher, Mathur, and Smith (2005), who developed the Governance Assessment Tool (GAT) to measure the democratic performance of partnership governance in the United Kingdom. These local partnerships are often comprised of a range of actors, including governmental, private, voluntary, and community-sector actors, who commit to delivering a range of publicly available services (Sullivan and Skelcher 2002). While the deliverable product is generally a publicly available resource, such organizations differ in their democratic commitment to the public. In this paper, we examine inter-local agreements and SPBS. Because of their governmental character, they should be expected to have a high level of democratic commitment to the publics they serve. Accordingly, they should be expected to stand up well against the criteria addressed in the GAT.

The GAT includes criteria for public access, internal governance, member conduct, and external accountability – basic conceptualizations of accountability relationships that local governance arrangements could be expected to meet. The GAT incorporates measures regarding transparency, accountability, and answerability. With the information included in the GAT framework, community members are able to hold actors to account and enforce sanctions through a number of venues, mainly elections. The criteria included in Skelcher, Mathur, and Smith's (2005) work is listed in Box 7.1.

Box 7.1 Governance Assessment Criteria

A. PUBLIC ACCESS

1 Are board meetings publicly announced?

2 Are board meetings open to the press and public?

3 Is the public entitled to see reports under consideration by the board?

4 Are the reports that the board will consider available for the public to consult prior to the meeting?

5 Is the public entitled to see the minutes of board meetings?

6 Is there an annual general meeting that the public can attend?

B. INTERNAL GOVERNANCE

1 Does the partnership have a memorandum of association or another document defining its role and powers?

2 Does the partnership have a written constitution or a set of standing orders defining how it will conduct its meetings?

3 Is membership for a limited period of time only?

4 Does a quorum apply at board meetings?

5 Are board meetings protocoled with minutes?

6 Are there allowances or other payments for members?

C. MEMBER CONDUCT

1 Is there a code of conduct to regulate the behaviour of members at board meetings?

2 If there is a code, are board members required to agree to be bound by it?

3 Is there a register in which board members can express their financial and other interests?

4 Is there a system for declaring conflicts of interest at meetings?

5 Is there a procedure for ensuring that members declaring conflicts of interest take no part in the decision?

D. ACCOUNTABILITY

1 Does the partnership have to prepare an annual report?

2 Does the partnership have to prepare an annual budget?

3 Does the partnership have to prepare annual accounts?

4 Is the partnership subject to external audit?

5 Is the partnership subject to external inspection?

6 Is there a complaints process available to citizens or service users?

7 Is the partnership under the jurisdiction of an ombudsman or inspectorate?

8 Is the partnership required to meet goals together with any external third parties?

9 Does the partnership have to submit a formal report to any other bodies?

10 Can members be recalled by their nominating bodies?

Below we briefly examine London, Ontario, and discuss how some of the criteria laid out by Skelcher, Mathur, and Smith (2005) address accountability in the local collaborative governance of this city. It would be beyond the scope of this chapter to see whether each and all of London's SPBS and inter-local agreements meet the GAT criteria. Our approach, then, is to talk in general terms about the accountability of these two service delivery options.

LOCAL ACCOUNTABILITY AND TRANSPARENCY IN PRACTICE

As mentioned earlier, London has often been described as a prototypical "ordinary city," lending itself well to our task of highlighting accountability in collaborative governance. Located in southwestern Ontario, it is approximately halfway between Toronto and Detroit and is the region's administrative and commercial centre. London was incorporated as a city and separated from Middlesex County in 1855 (Spicer 2016). Since then, its boundaries have been expanded through a series of annexations. The city was exempt from the two most recent waves of municipal restructuring in Ontario, mainly because it had already annexed large swaths of adjacent territory. Indeed, during the push for the formation of two-tier regional governments in the 1960s and 1970s, London was already a de facto single-tier regional government, since it had recently annexed portions of the neighbouring townships of London and Westminster (Sancton 1998).

Similarly, a large annexation in 1993, which nearly tripled London's geographical area, spared London from an even more aggressive push for amalgamations in the 1990s (Sancton, James, and Ramsay 2000, 55). Nonetheless, the city remains linked to the county both geographically and functionally through inter-municipal agreements and regional SPBS.

Table 7.1 outlines the local government services that are delivered to residents of the City of London primarily through SPBS. Many of them are important local services, and most of the SPBS listed receive a significant proportion of their funding from the City. Because of London's relative size within the region, this applies to the regional and mega-regional SPBS as well. In fact, the existence of most of the regional SPBS can be attributed to London's status as a separate city. Elsewhere, such as in amalgamated cities and regional governments, these services are delivered municipally. A number of SPBS in London operate within the city limits, however. Residents could be forgiven for not knowing that their municipal government has only limited control over the city's police force, public libraries, and transit system. SPBS are clearly less visible than municipal governments; however, is this due more to poorly structured accountability relationships or more to their limited functionality? The GAT criteria can help us explore this question further.

Based on a review of London's SPBS, it is clear that some meet the GAT criteria whereas others do not. Because of this chapter's limited scope, websites were used as the main source of information. In addition, since websites, being on the Internet, are the only source of information that is equally available to residents, they give us a better sense of what would be accessible to members of the community.[2] Moreover, relying on information that is easily accessible also gives us some indication about how forthcoming SPBS might be in handling information that, at least according to the GAT, belongs in the public domain.

Beginning with the public access criteria, most SPBS, including the school boards, land ambulance services, police services board, health unit, transit commission, conservation authorities, and water supply boards have meetings that are announced and open to the public and the media, and the public has access to agendas, meeting minutes, and reports. Other SPBS, however, are less open to the public, such as London Hydro, Tourism London, the airport authority, and the London Economic Development Corporation. The latter two are the

Table 7.1
London, Ontario, special-purpose bodies[1]

Function	Special-Purpose Body	Geographic Scale
Affordable housing development	Housing Development Corporation	Municipal
Airport	London International Airport Authority	Sub-municipal
Economic development	London Economic Development Corporation	Municipal
Education	London District Catholic School Board/Thames Valley District School Board	Mega-regional/ mega-regional
Hydro distribution	London Hydro	Municipal
Land ambulance	Middlesex-London Emergency Medical Services	Regional
Policing	London Police Services	Municipal
Public health	Middlesex-London Health Unit	Regional
Public libraries	London Public Library	Municipal
Public transit	London Transit Commission	Municipal
Subsidized housing	London and Middlesex Housing Corporation	Regional
Tourism promotion	Tourism London	Municipal
Watershed management	Kettle Creek Conservation Authority/Lower Thames River Conservation Authority/Upper Thames River Conservation Authority	Regional/mega-regional/ mega-regional
Water production, treatment, and storage	The Elgin Area Water Supply System/The Lake Huron Water Supply System	Mega-regional/ mega-regional

[1] The classification scheme in this column is borrowed from Lucas 2016. The Housing Development Corporation was incorporated in 2016 and is in the process of transitioning to a public board. As such, it was excluded from the analysis.

least open; for example, they list the names of their board members on their websites but provide no information about the meetings. London Hydro and Tourism London do give some indication of when board meetings are held but no indication of the location, nor do they post agendas or minutes on their websites.

In that context, obtaining a complete picture of the internal governance and member conduct criteria for all of London's SPBS would require making direct inquiries with those agencies that are less open.

Nevertheless, most of the SPBS that score well on the public access criteria also provide upfront information about how board business is conducted. Those that do not score as well on the public access criteria are less likely to have this information on their websites, London Hydro being the only exception. The two school boards, whose members are directly elected, and the Upper Thames River Conservation Authority provide the most information on internal governance and member conduct. All three of these agencies have board-approved by-laws or handbooks that meet most of these criteria.

If anything, it can be said that each of London's SPBS meet at least one of the GAT's accountability criteria. At minimum, each SPB that receives funding from the City of London has to provide some account of how it spends its money. This can be done in the form of business plans that are presented to city council when drafting their budget. Each business plan is supposed to include a set of key performance indicators used to evaluate service quality. Many of the more transparent agencies go further than this, though. For example, the school boards, London Hydro, the health unit, the library, the transit commission, the London and Middlesex Housing Corporation, and all three conservation authorities provide access to at least one of the following through their websites: annual reports, annual budgets, and audited financial statements.

The GAT's accountability criteria also account for the consequences/sanctions step of the accountability relationship. The ability of citizens to apply sanctions to SPBS is limited; however, it is not completely absent. Much like the partnerships and networks that the GAT was originally designed to evaluate, elected politicians are involved in designing and establishing SPBS, and they participate in their governance. Thus, politicians can act on behalf of citizens to democratically sanction SPBS. Moreover, by providing a lot of information about their activities and holding open meetings, the more transparent SPBS create space for the public to debate and scrutinize their decisions (Sørenson and Torfing 2005). While it is certainly a burden for individual citizens to keep track of all these SPBS, if they wanted to, they could show up at meetings, ask questions, and voice opposition. Greater transparency and access also facilitates the other types of accountability relationships mentioned earlier, especially administrative, professional, and social accountability.

In sum, the results are mixed. Many of London's SPBS do have well-structured accountability relationships. The more secretive ones aside, the relative lack of visibility of SPBS seems to have more to do with their limited functionality. Apart from the airport authority, the London Economic Development Corporation, and the tourism agency, the public and municipal politicians have enough information to make informed assessments of London's SPBS. Critics of SPBS may still decry their relative lack of visibility, fulfillment of GAT criteria notwithstanding. But as our overview demonstrates, most SPBS in London provide a public account of their activities, allow for an assessment of these activities in a public forum, and are subject to the scrutiny and sanction of elected politicians and citizens.

As mentioned before, however, SPBS are not the only vehicle for collaborative governance at the local level – inter-local agreements are an option too. Table 7.2, below, lists every inter-local agreement signed between the City of London and other local governments between 1995 and 2013. This duration is long enough to account for provincial changes, such as service downloading, but short enough to ensure the likelihood that agreements are still in force and accessible for municipal clerks to retrieve. We had to contact the City directly for these agreements, since they are not available on its website – which does not say much for the accountability of inter-local agreements. It also means that we were not able to use the same basic source of information as we did in our examination of the SPBS.

From table 7.2, we can see that London has not engaged extensively in inter-local cooperative agreements with its neighbouring municipalities. Such a result is unsurprising, given that Canadian municipalities have been seen to generally use inter-local cooperative agreements at a significantly lower rate than municipalities elsewhere, especially those in the United States (Spicer 2015). With that said, London does appear to be sharing a variety of local services, some even vital, including social services. Many of the agreements concern the CMSM (Consolidated Municipal Service Manager System), which essentially consists of downloading social services policies from the provincial government, as per the Local Services Realignment Act of 1998. Because London is a separate city, it was forced to reach agreement with the county to share these services. The agreements listed in table 7.2 are a result of this provincial edict. One such agreement stemming from the CMSM even resulted in the formation of an SPB, the Middlesex-London Emergency Medical Services Board.

Other agreements of note include wastewater agreements with the neighbouring municipality of Middlesex Centre, which were designed

Table 7.2
London, Ontario, inter-local agreements

Municipalities involved	Purpose	Date
London and Middlesex County	CMSM – OW, Childcare and Social Housing	19 February 2002
London and Middlesex County	CMSM – Land Ambulance	1 January 2006
London and Middlesex County	Road Maintenance Agreement for Winter Maintenance Services	1 June 2009
London and Middlesex County	CMSM – Extension of Social Housing Agreement	1 January 2005
London and Middlesex County	Disaster and Emergency Coordination	10 May 2005
London and Middlesex County	Social Housing	1 January 2005
London and Middlesex County	Geography Mapping	11 January 2005
London and Middlesex County	Mutual Aid – Fire Protection	11 December 2007
London and Middlesex Centre	Provision of Wastewater Services to Arva	3 April 2000
London and Middlesex County	Land Ambulance	1 January 1999
London and Delaware	Water Services	1 January 1999
London and Middlesex County	Provision of CERB	1 January 1997
London and Middlesex Centre	Provision of Wastewater Services to Arva (Amendment)	21 June 2000
London, Middlesex County, Adelaide-Metcalfe, Lucan Biddulph, Middlesex Centre, North Middlesex, Southwest Middlesex, Strathroy-Caradoc, Thames Centre, Newbury	Provincial Offences	7 January 2001
London, Middlesex Centre, Lake Huron Primary Water Supply Joint Board of Management	Water Supply to Delaware	July 4, 2003
London and Thames Centre	Winter Road Maintenance	26 October 2009
London and Thames Centre	Fire Protection – Mutual Aid	23 May 2002
London and Thames County	Fire Protection – Mutual Aid	1 March 2011
London and Middlesex County	Fire Protection – Mutual Aid	28 November 2001
London and Middlesex County	Fire Protection – Mutual Aid	21 February 2000
London and Middlesex County	Waste	1 July 2010
London and the London Cross-Cultural Learner Centre	Immigration Settlement and Training	14 March 2007

to provide a limited supply of servicing to this growing area outside of the city's borders to avoid contamination of the nearby Medway Creek. The agreements were designed to avoid harm to the watershed while ensuring that Middlesex County was not given the capacity to grow beyond the city's borders.[3] Aside from this wastewater agreement and the CMSM services, there are a number of other agreements that include priority service areas, such as waste and road maintenance. The mutual aid agreements are fairly standard arrangements between municipalities that allow a fire service from another community to respond to emergencies outside of its borders.

As for the accountability measures included in these agreements, we see low levels of accountability and transparency, especially when compared against the criteria set out in works such as Skelcher, Mathur, and Smith (2005). First, none of the agreements have high levels of public access. Despite being public documents, none of the agreements are publicly available. Each of the agreements listed in this chapter was obtained only upon request. As a result, it would be difficult for any member of the public to know which services are shared and which government is actually delivering them – a key failing of local collaborative arrangements, according to many experts (Slack 1993; 1997). Overall, inter-local agreements do not require the contractual partners to prepare a report to be shown to members of the public, nor is there any type of scheduled meeting when officials could be questioned about the performance of the agreements.

Second, none of the inter-local agreements have any provisions regarding member conduct. In other words, they generally have no code of conduct, nor do they provide a list of the names of individuals (or the positions) within any organization who are responsible for governing the agreements. Third, the agreements have no provisions regarding the declaration of a conflict of interest. The list of inadequacies goes on with: low accountability given a general lack of provisions for external audit or inspection; the lack of requirements for annual reports or a performance-reporting mechanism; the lack of a complaints process; the lack of stipulations or contact information for reporting complaints about service cost or quality; and the lack of a requirement for a formal evaluation of procedures or processes.

Where we do see some strength in inter-local agreements is when it comes to internal governance. The agreements themselves do a good job at spelling out the responsibilities and payment schedules (if any) of each partner. In this sense, the agreements themselves are legally enforceable contracts, so this may be expected to protect each partner and mitigate risk. However, the agreements in London largely fail in the other categories addressed by Skelcher, Mathur, and Smith (2005) – namely, member conduct, public access, and accountability. As a whole, the governments do not allow the public to gain enough information about their contents and performance, which is a key component of local accountability relationships. Thus, residents in London, Ontario, are likely left in the dark about many aspects of the shared services and contractual arrangements the city has with many of its neighbours. The problems associated with lack of information ultimately create challenges relating to enforceability. Residents have a venue to sanction actors, but without enough information they cannot accurately hold them to account for failings in their inter-local relationships.

DISCUSSION AND CONCLUSION

While Canadian cities provide a host of services on their own, the use of local collaborative instruments, such as inter-municipal agreements and SPBs, are becoming increasingly popular methods for providing service and policy continuity throughout a region. In all likelihood, we ought to see the use of such mechanisms continue to increase well into the future. However, SPBs and inter-municipal collaboration raise important questions about accountability and transparency. When the traditional lines of servicing accountability are blurred, how involved is the public in creating and monitoring these arrangements? How well informed are citizens about the types of services they receive when they are not delivered solely by one municipality? In such scenarios, do citizens and municipal politicians have the tools they require to properly hold local actors to account for and monitor the effectiveness of such servicing relationships?

Our brief examination of London's SPBs and inter-municipal agreements reveal that neither do an excellent job of ensuring accountability and transparency in local servicing. However, SPBs perform much better than inter-local agreements, and some SPBs perform much better than others. The more transparent SPBs generally provide high levels of access to residents, produce high volumes of information about the service in question, allow for much more scrutiny of their activities, and generally allow for local actors to be held to account.

All inter-municipal agreements studied, on the other hand, lack many of the most basic accountability and transparency tools, ultimately blurring the lines of local servicing accountability and leaving local residents with insufficient information about the services they are being provided with.

While both SPBS and inter-municipal agreements are often used as a means of producing and delivering local services, we feel that higher or critical local services should be incorporated into a joint-management board or a special-purpose jurisdiction rather than an inter-municipal agreement. We believe that in contrast to inter-municipal agreements, SPBS provide a more effective means of holding local actors to account.

APPENDIX

Table 7.3
Website URLS of London's special-purpose bodies

Special-Purpose Body	Website URL
Housing Development Corporation	https://www.london.ca/residents/Housing/Housing-Programs/Pages/ProposedHousingDevelopmentCorporationInitiative.aspx
London International Airport Authority	http://flylondon.ca/about-us
London Economic Development Corporation	http://www.ledc.com/about
London District Catholic School Board	http://www.ldcsb.ca/about/bot/Pages/default.aspx
Thames Valley District School Board	http://www.tvdsb.ca/board.cfm?subpage=79700
London Hydro	https://www.londonhydro.com/site/#!/about_us/content?page=corporate-structure
Middlesex-London Emergency Medical Services	https://www.mlems.ca/about-us; https://www.middlesex.ca/local-government/meeting-dates-and-agendas
London Police Services	http://www.londonpolice.ca/en/about/Police-Services-Board.aspx
Middlesex-London Health Unit	https://www.healthunit.com/board-of-health
London Public Library	http://www.londonpubliclibrary.ca/about-my-library/board-and-administration
London Transit Commission	http://www.ltconline.ca/AboutLTC.htm

Table 7.3
Website URLs of London's special-purpose bodies (*continued*)

Special-Purpose Body	Website URL
London and Middlesex Housing Corporation	http://lmhc.ca/board-of-directors.php
Tourism London	http://www.londontourism.ca/Members/Board-of-Directors
Kettle Creek Conservation Authority	http://www.kettlecreekconservation.on.ca/about-us/board-of-director
Lower Thames River Conservation Authority	http://www.lowerthames-conservation.on.ca/about-us
Upper Thames River Conservation Authority	http://thamesriver.on.ca/about-us/boardofdirectors/
The Elgin Area Water Supply System	http://www.watersupply.london.ca/Board_Meetings.html
The Lake Huron Water Supply System	http://www.watersupply.london.ca/Board_Meetings.html

[1] All websites were accessed in August 2016. The URLs link to the pages with the most pertinent board information. Interested readers can also explore other pages on these sites for more details and data.

NOTES

1 It should be noted as well that some of the deficiencies we find in the inter-local agreements are also present in other Canadian cities. As such, we believe that our case utilized for this study is generalizable. For more information, see Spicer (2017).

2 See appendix for the website URLs.

3 For more information on the relationship surrounding growth between London and Middlesex County, see Spicer (2016).

REFERENCES

Alcantara, Christopher, Roberto Leone, and Zachary Spicer. 2012. "Responding to Policy Change from Above: Municipal Accountability and Transparency Regimes in Ontario." *Journal of Canadian Studies* 46: 112–37.

Andrew, Simon A. 2008. *Governance by Agreements: Why Do Local Governments Enter into Multilateral Agreements*. Detroit, MI: Working Group on Interlocal Services Cooperation, Wayne State University.

– 2009. "Recent Developments in the Study of Interjurisdictional Agreements: An Overview and Assessment." *State and Local Government Review* 41: 143–52.

Ashworth, Rachel E. 2000. "Party Manifestos and Local Accountability: A Content Analysis of Local Election Pledges in Wales." *Local Government Studies* 26: 11–30.

Aucoin, Peter, and Ralph Heintzman. 2000. "The Dialectics of Accountability for Performance in Public Management Reform." *International Review of Administrative Sciences* 66: 45–56.

Aucoin, Peter, and Mark D. Jarvis. 2005. *Modernizing Government Accountability: A Framework for Reform*. Ottawa: Canada School of Public Service.

Behn, Robert. 2001. *Rethinking Democratic Accountability*. Washington: Brookings Institution.

Bish, Robert. 2001. *Local Government Amalgamations: Discredited Nineteenth-Century Ideals Alive in the Twenty-First*. C.D. Howe Institute Commentary (150).

Bovens, Mark. 2007. "Analysing and Assessing Accountability: A Conceptual Framework." *European Law Journal* 13: 447–68.

Bradford, Neil. 2016. "Ordinary City at the Crossroads: London, Ontario." In *Growing Urban Economies*, edited by D. Wolfe and M. Gertler, 239–63. Toronto: University of Toronto Press.

Bradford, Neil, and Jennifer Nelles. 2014. "Innovation in an Ordinary City; Knowledge Flows in London, Ontario." In *Innovating in Urban Economies*, edited by D. Wolfe and M. Gertler, 175–96. Toronto: University of Toronto Press.

Brandsma, Gijs Jan, and Thomas Schillemans. 2012. "The Accountability Cube: Measuring Accountability." *Journal of Public Administration Research and Theory* 23: 953–75.

Brown, M. Paul. 1983. "Responsiveness versus Accountability in Collaborative Federalism: The Canadian Experience." *Canadian Public Administration* 26(3): 629–39.

Bundt, Julie. 2000. "Strategic Stewards: Managing Accountability, Building Trust." *Journal of Public Administration Research and Theory* 10: 757–78.

Chatterton, P. 2000. "Will the Real Creative City Please Stand Up?" *City* 4(3): 391–7.

Chen, Yu-Che, and Kurt Thurmaier. 2008. "Interlocal Agreements as Collaborations: An Empirical Investigation of Impetuses, Norms and Success." *American Review of Public Administration* 39: 471–89.

Considine, Mark. 2002. "The End of the Line? Accountable Governance in the Age of Networks, Partnerships and Joined-up Services." *Governance* 15: 21–40.

Dicke, Lisa A. 2002. "Ensuring Accountability in Human Services Contracting: Can Stewardship Theory Fill the Bill?" *American Review of Public Administration* 32: 455–70.

Dollery, Brian, Bligh Grant, and Michael Kortt. 2012. *Councils in Cooperation: Shared Services and Australian Local Government.* Sydney: The Federated Press.

Dollery, Brian, Neil Marshall, Andrew Sancton, and Angus Witherby. 2004. *Regional Capacity Building: How Effective Is REROC?* Wagga Wagga: Riverina Eastern Regional Organisation of Councils.

Dunne, Delmer, and Jerome Legge. 2001. "US Local Government Managers and the Complexity of Responsibility and Accountability in Democratic Governance." *Journal of Public Administration Research and Theory* 11: 73–88.

Ebrahim, Alnoor, and Edward Weisband, eds. 2007. *Global Accountabilities: Participation, Pluralism and Public Ethics.* New York: Cambridge University Press.

Elster, John. 1999. "Accountability in Athenian Politics." In *Democracy, Accountability and Representation*, edited by Adam Przeworski, Susan Stokes, and Bernard Manin, 253–78. Cambridge: Cambridge University Press.

Fearon, James D. 1999. "Electoral Accountability and the Control of Politicians: Selecting Good Types versus Sanctioning Poor Types." In *Democracy, Accountability and Responsibility*, edited by Adam Przeworski, Susan Stokes, and Bernard Manin, 55–98. Cambridge: Cambridge University Press.

Feiock, Richard C. 2013. "The Institutional Collective Action Framework." *Policy Studies Journal* 41: 397–425.

Gainsborough, Juliette. 2001. "Bridging the City–Suburb Divide: States and the Politics of Regional Cooperation." *Journal of Urban Affairs* 23(5): 497–512.

Graefe, Peter, Julie M. Simmons, and Linda A. White. 2013. "Introduction: Accountability and Governance." In *Overpromising and Underperforming? Understanding and Evaluating New Intergovernmental Accountability Regimes*, edited by Peter Graefe, Julie M. Simmons, and Linda A. White, 3–30. Toronto: University of Toronto Press.

Grant, Ruth W., and Robert O. Keohane. 2005. "Accountability and Abuses of Power in World Politics." *American Political Science Review* 99(10): 29–43.

Hanretty, Chris, and Christel Koop. 2011. "Measuring the Formal
Independence of Regulatory Agencies." *Journal of European Public
Policy* 19: 198–216.

Horak, Martin. 2012. "Multilevel Governance in Toronto: Overcoming
Coordination Challenges in the 'Megacity.'" In *Sites of Governance:
Multilevel Governance and Policy Making in Canada's Big Cities*,
edited by Robert Young and Martin Horak, 228–62. Montreal:
McGill-Queen's University Press.

Imai, Shin. 2007. "The Structure of the Indian Act: Accountability and
Governance." Research Paper for the National Centre for First Nations
Governance. Ottawa: National Centre for First Nations Governance.

Kim, Seok-Eun. 2005. "Balancing Competing Accountability
Requirements: Challenges in Performance Improvement of the
Nonprofit Human Service Agency." *Public Performance and
Management Review* 29: 147–65.

Kitchen, Harry M., and Enid Slack. 2003. "Special Study: New Finance
Options for Municipal Governments." *Canadian Tax Journal* 51:
2216–72.

Koppell, Jonathan. 2005. "Pathologies of Accountability: ICANN and the
Challenge of Multiple Accountabilities Disorder." *Public Administration
Review* 65: 94–109.

Lackey, Steven B., David Freshwater, and Anil Rupasingha. 2002. "Factors
Influencing Local Government Cooperation in Rural Areas: Evidence
from the Tennessee Valley." *Economic Development Quarterly* 16(2):
138–54.

Lamothe, Meeyoung, and Scott Lamothe. 2009. "Beyond the Search for
Competition in Social Service Contracting: Procurement, Consolidation
and Accountability." *American Review of Public Administration* 39:
164–88.

Leach, Steve. 1996. "The Indirectly Elected World of Local Government."
In *Quangos and Local Government: A Changing World*, edited by
Howard Davis, 64–76. London: Frank Cass.

LeSage, Edward, Jr, Melville L. McMillan, and Neil Hepburn. 2008.
"Municipal Shared Service Collaboration in the Alberta Capital Region:
The Case of Recreation." *Canadian Public Administration* 51: 455–73.

Lowery, David. 2001. "Metropolitan Governance from a Neoprogressive
Perspective." *Swiss Political Science Review* 7(3): 11–16.

Lucas, Jack. 2016. "Patterns of Urban Governance: A Sequence Analysis
of Long-Term Institutional Change in Six Canadian Cities." *Journal of
Urban Affairs* 39(1): 68–90.

Lyons, Joseph. 2015a. "Conservation Authority Board Composition and Watershed Management in Ontario." *Canadian Public Administration* 58: 315–32.

– 2015b. "Local Government Structure and the Co-ordination of Economic Development Policy." *Canadian Journal of Political Science* 48: 173–93.

Moe, Terry M. 2005. "Power and Political Institutions." *Perspectives on Politics* 3(2): 215–33.

Moncrieffe, Joy Marie. 1998. "Reconceptualizing Political Accountability." *International Political Science Review* 19(40): 387–406.

Mulgan, Richard. 2003. *Holding Power to Account: Accountability in Modern Democracies*. London: Palgrave Macmillan.

O'Brien, Allan. 1993. *Municipal Consolidation in Canada and Its Alternatives*. Toronto: Intergovernmental Committee on Urban and Regional Research Press.

O'Connell, Lenahan, Juita-Elena Yusuf, and Merl Hackbart. 2009. "Transportation Commissions as Accountability Structures: A Review of Their Statutory Roles and Other Attributes." *American Review of Public Administration* 39: 409–24.

Ostrom, Elinor. 1972. "Metropolitan Reform: Propositions Derived from Two Traditions." *Social Science Quarterly* 53(3): 474–93.

Pollitt, Christopher. 2003. *The Essential Public Manager*. London: Open University Press/McGraw-Hill.

Romzek, Barbara, and Melvin Dubnick. 1998. "Accountability." In *International Encyclopedia of Public Policy and Administration*, vol. 1: A–C, edited by J.M. Shafritz, 6–11. Boulder, CO: Westview Press.

Sancton, Andrew. 1998. "Negotiating, Arbitrating, Legislating: Where Was the Public in London's Boundary Adjustment?" In *Citizen Engagement: Lessons in Participation from Local Government*, edited by Katerine A. Graham and Susan D. Phillips, 163–87. Toronto: The Institute of Public Administration of Canada.

– 2015. *Canadian Local Government: An Urban Perspective*. 2nd ed. Toronto: Oxford University Press.

Sancton, Andrew, Rebecca James, and Rick Ramsay. 2000. *Amalgamation vs. Inter-Municipal Cooperation: Financing Local and Infrastructure Services*. Toronto: Intergovernmental Committee on Urban and Regional Research Press.

Siegel, David. 1994a. "The ABCs of Local Government: An Overview." In *Agencies, Boards, and Commissions in Canadian Local Government*, edited by Dale Richmond and David Siegel, 1–20. Toronto: The Institute of Public Administration Canada.

– 1994b. "The Appropriate Use of Agencies, Boards, and Commissions." In *Agencies, Boards, and Commissions in Canadian Local Government*, edited by Dale Richmond and David Siegel, 83–110. Toronto: The Institute of Public Administration Canada.

Sinclair, Amanda. 1995. "The Chameleon of Accountability: Forms and Discourses." *Accounting, Organizations and Society* 20: 219–37.

Skelcher, Chris, Navdeep Mathur, and Mike Smith. 2005. "The Public Governance of Collaborative Spaces: Discourse, Design and Democracy." *Public Administration* 83: 573–96.

Slack, Enid. 1993. "Comments on Efficiency of Delivering Local Government Services under Alternative Organizational Modes." In *Competitiveness and Delivery of Public Services*, edited by Ronald Crowley, 119–25. Kingston: Government and Competitiveness Project, School of Policy Studies, Queen's University.

– 1997. *Inter-Municipal Cooperation: Sharing of Expenditures and Revenues*. Toronto: Intergovernmental Committee on Urban and Regional Research Press.

Sørenson, Eva, and Jacob Torfing. 2005. "The Democratic Anchorage of Governance Networks." *Scandinavian Political Studies* 28: 195–218.

Spicer, Zachary. 2014. "Linking Regions, Linking Functions: Inter-Municipal Agreements in Ontario." In *IMFG Perspectives 10*. Toronto: Institute on Municipal Finance and Governance.

– 2015 ."Regionalism, Municipal Organization and Inter-Local Cooperation in Canada." *Canadian Public Policy* 41: 137–50.

– 2016. *The Boundary Bargain: Growth, Development and the Future of City–County Separation*. Montreal: McGill-Queen's University Press.

– 2017. "Bridging the Accountability and Transparency Gap in Inter-Local Collaboration." *Local Government Studies* 43(3): 388–407.

Størm, Kaare. 1997. "Democracy, Accountability and Coalition Bargaining." *European Journal of Political Research* 31: 47–62.

Sullivan, Helen, and Chris Skelcher. 2002. *Working across Boundaries: Collaboration in Public Services*. Basingstoke: Palgrave Macmillan.

Tindal, Richard C., and Susan Nobes Tindal. 2004. *Local Government in Canada*. 6th ed. Toronto: Thomson Nelson.

Wang, Xiaohu. 2002 "Assessing Administrative Accountability: Results from a National Survey." *American Review of Public Administration* 32: 350–70.

8

The Responsiveness Issue and the Blurry Lines of Accountability in Regional Transportation Planning, Governance, and Finance: The Case of Metrolinx

Fanny R. Tremblay-Racicot

INTRODUCTION

The planning, funding, construction, and maintenance/operation of regional transportation infrastructures, both roads and transit, have traditionally been under the purview of provincial highway departments and transit authorities, respectively, and subject to little public scrutiny. However, with the emergence of a new transportation paradigm that puts regional, integrated planning strategies on the political agenda, regional planning organizations, municipal governments, and citizens are now solicited to contribute to regional transportation strategies – which may or may not correspond to local interests and missions. In addition, the power and control exercised by transportation project sponsors (most often the provincial government) can overrule regional consensuses. The new paradigm also calls for transportation departments at all levels of government (i.e., federal, provincial, and municipal) to consider each transportation option on an equal footing and to dissolve any silo mentalities in road, transit, and land-use planning. These departments also become subject to greater public scrutiny, which represents a major change in the institutional and professional cultures. The issue of accountability, for example, becomes more complex and challenging when transportation projects are built and managed through public–private partnerships – namely, because financial information can then be subject to non-disclosure agreements.

Because planning for smart growth requires concentrating investments in certain areas and favouring certain modes of transportation over others (designated urban growth centres, transit, and bike/pedestrian facilities versus suburban sprawling development and highways), being responsive to local preferences might not lead to the most sustainable policy and investment choices for the region. This is particularly true in less fragmented regions, where suburbanites have the greater weight in mayoral election outcomes. In all cases, the institutional design at the regional level, comprised of the mandate, the resources, and the representational structure of the organization, helps us to explain and understand the extent of the responsiveness to local preferences (aggregated at the regional level) and the lines of accountability between the citizen, transit agencies, local governments, and the provincial government.

This chapter builds on evidence collected during a longitudinal comparative case study conducted on the 2005–06 reforms of Toronto's and Chicago's regional planning institutions and the impacts of these reforms on the planning process, transportation investments, and land-use decisions. Using semi-structured interviews and planning documents as well as transportation spending and land-use decisions, the case study compared the effects of the centralized, regulatory framework implemented in Toronto with the creation of Metrolinx and the enactment of a growth management strategy (Growth Plan for the Greater Golden Horseshoe) to the collaborative governance framework adopted in Chicago with the integration of regional transportation and land-use planning functions with the creation of Chicago Metropolitan Agency for Planning (CMAP). The research presented here primarily examines the trade-offs between the principles of accountability, democracy, and effectiveness associated with the creation of Metrolinx. Observations are drawn from the general perceptions of key informants, independent assessments, and selected policy or investment decisions, particularly concerning the Scarborough Rapid Transit (RT) replacement and extension, the Eglinton Crosstown light rail transit (LRT), the Union Pearson Express (UPX), the Toronto-York Spadina Subway Extension (TYSSE), and the Downtown Relief Line (DRL). These investment choices (or non-decisions, in the case of the DRL) illustrate the challenges that regional transportation represents for governments seeking to demonstrate accountability and responsiveness to citizens' preferences.

The chapter is organized as follows. Section 2 briefly introduces Metrolinx and the context surrounding its creation in 2006. Section 3 presents the research methods. Section 4 explains the political dynamics and institutional environment prevailing in Toronto over the past few decades. Section 5 discusses the implications of the creation of Metrolinx for local governments. Sections 6 and 7 trace the lines of accountability with regard to the board of directors of Metrolinx and analyze the implications of this new agency in terms of transportation planning, effectiveness, and investment choices. Finally, the last section provides concluding remarks regarding the impact of institutional design on accountability, democracy, and effectiveness.

THE CREATION OF METROLINX

Toronto's adoption of the Greenbelt Act in 2005 and the Growth Plan for the Greater Golden Horseshoe in 2006 was followed by the creation of the Greater Toronto Transportation Authority in 2006 (rebranded Metrolinx in 2007), which represents the third and final segment of Premier Dalton McGuinty's growth management strategy. Metrolinx was created to: 1) provide leadership in the coordination, planning, financing, and development of an integrated, multi-modal transportation network that conforms to transportation polices of the Growth Plan; and 2) act as the central agency for the procurement of local transit system vehicles, equipment, technologies, and facilities on behalf of Ontario municipalities (Government of Ontario 2006).

Metrolinx's first task was to develop a regional transportation plan – the Big Move – a \$50 billion capital plan adopted in 2008, and to plan, coordinate and set priorities for its implementation. In doing so, the agency manages the funds for integrated transportation across the region, including highway and transit infrastructure, and promotes coordinated decision-making and investment among the municipalities in the region. The mandate of Metrolinx grew in 2009 when it merged with GO Transit, the commuter bus and rail transit provider. Two other operating divisions were subsequently added: the UPX in 2010 and the Presto electronic fare card in 2011.

Metrolinx is a Crown agency under the purview of Ontario's Ministry of Transportation. At the time of its inception, the majority of the board members were local government representatives, either elected officials or civil servants. However, after the adoption of the Big Move, the board composition was modified by Premier McGuinty in 2009 such that municipal representatives and elected officials were excluded from the board and replaced by non-elected, provincial appointees.

Prior to the creation of Metrolinx, transportation infrastructure decisions were made by the Toronto Transit Commission (TTC), the City of Toronto, and the Ontario Ministry of Transportation as well as the Government of Canada, which had begun subsidizing subway capital-cost funding in 2007. Decisions surrounding subway construction, more specifically, were "highly contentious and influenced as much by ideology and self-interest as by rational calculation" (MacDonald, Sams, and Ganjavie 2013, 2), a process described as "incoherent" (Boudreau, Keil, and Young 2009, 177). Toronto transit decision-making was then labelled as disjointed and anarchic, piecemeal and political (Boudreau, Keil, and Young 2009). There was no regional planning body after the amalgamation of the six cities that once formed Metro Toronto in 1998 and the dismantlement of the Greater Toronto Services Board in 2001.

Did the creation of Metrolinx improve Toronto's regional transportation planning and decision-making processes? Does it require any trade-offs between the principles of accountability (responsibility and public scrutiny through transparency), democracy (representativeness, public debate, and deliberation), and effectiveness (cost-effectiveness and local and regional changes promoting sustainability)?

A LONGITUDINAL CASE STUDY

This study is based on semi-structured interviews, policy documents, and published and unpublished literature as well as spending and planning decisions. The aim of the research is to assess the impacts of the new institutions on the planning processes and decision outcomes and the implications of those institutions in terms of accountability, democracy, and effectiveness. In the interviews, respondents were asked about their general perception of the changes in the decision-making process brought about by the new institutional framework, as well as of transportation spending and land-use planning decisions before and after the creation of Metrolinx.

In total, fifteen respondents were recruited, all from Toronto, whose institutional affiliations represented all levels of government (federal, provincial, municipal) and types of institutions (metropolitan authorities, transit operators, non-profit organizations). Respondents were administrative personnel or executives participating in the selection of transportation investments, land-use development, or regional planning. They were involved in (or knowledgeable about) regional transportation and land-use planning decision-making processes both before and after the institutional reform.

Respondents were interviewed only once during the months of June and July 2014. These semi-structured interviews were recorded, transcribed, and analyzed using the qualitative data analysis software QDA Miner. Policy documents (regional transportation and land-use plans, plan evaluation, program evaluation, etc.), spending and planning decisions, research reports, and academic literature on the specific cases were also used to fill gaps and validate information given by respondents. The analysis focused on the process of institutional transformation, the assessment of the impacts of institutional change on sustainability outcomes, and its implications or trade-offs in terms of accountability, democracy, and effectiveness. The results are thus based on a triangulation of the respondents' perception of change, the published and unpublished literature, and the evolution of the planning processes, transportation investments, and land-use decisions before, during, and after the implementation of the reform.

THE POLITICAL AND INSTITUTIONAL CONTEXT

Prior to the 2005–06 reform, there was no institutional structure or mechanism in place at the level of the Greater Toronto and Hamilton Area to manage the growth and transportation in the region, and the latest attempt to achieve regional cooperation had been unsuccessful. This recent phase in history goes back to 1996 when the report of the Greater Toronto Area (GTA) Task Force (alias the Golden Report), set up by the provincial government of Bob Rae in 1995 to look at the economic competitiveness of the region, recommended replacing Metropolitan Toronto and the four regional municipalities with a single Greater Toronto Council having the authority to develop and implement regional policies (GTA Task Force 1996). However, because the new super-region would become a direct competitor of the province and because of a change in provincial leadership, the new government of Mike Harris pushed for the megacity of Toronto as we know it today, kept the four surrounding regions, and created the Greater Toronto Services Board (GTSB) in 1999 – rather than implementing the task force proposal of creating a super-region with extensive powers over planning and the provision of regional services (Hodge and Robinson 2001, 354–5).

The GTSB, comprised of all mayors and regional chairs, was set up to coordinate transportation and rural planning in the GTA. Constitutionally weak, underfunded, and lacking direct elections, a clear mandate, or powers of taxation, the GTSB was disbanded on the last day of 2001 (and thus lasted for only about two years) (Hodge and Robinson 2001; Keil and Boudreau 2005; Keil and Young 2008). In addition to being powerless and "cumbersome," the GTSB was also undermined by its regional board members, who somewhat "sabotaged" the organization because of fears that it would eventually become a regional government, notably by lobbying the provincial government for its dismantlement, according to some respondents. In fact, although the provincial government did not consider the GTSB as a level of government, the minister of municipal affairs did indicate, at the time of its announcement, that it could evolve into a regional government over the course of its first decade (Hodge and Robinson 2001, 354). Although the exact reasons why the provincial government shut down the GTSB remain unclear (White 2007, 40), the following quotations describe the lack of cooperation among board members and the complexities of inter-regional competition that contributed to the abolition of the GTSB:

> The regional municipalities politically felt threatened that the Greater Toronto Services Board was being set up as a regional government in waiting to replace them. So, I think, politically, that made things very, very difficult to get cooperation because they felt a competition. Whereas [Metrolinx's] mandate is solely transportation, and so, you know, there's no suggestion that Metrolinx would get into any other service areas that the municipalities are involved in. (Interview 5)

> There was a fight between [the mayor of Mississauga] and the regional governments, and it was a fight for control of regional planning, and [the mayor of Mississauga] saw the regional governments as interfering too much in local matters. So what

happened was Mississauga and Toronto got together, because [they] thought philosophically, that you couldn't plan transportation without planning and growth, they had to come together. So [they] got through the Greater Toronto Services Board to give it the power of regional planning for the region. The regional chairs voted against that and lobbied the province and that caused the end of the Greater Toronto Services Board. So it was really a fight over who decides planning issues ... I guess [the suburban mayors] saw [the GTSB] as a way to weaken the regions, because there was a historic fight between the region of Peel and Mississauga, and that kind of thing ... I think the second reason probably was regarding the point where we were going to make recommendations to the province that they needed to invest very significant money, and they didn't want to. (Interview 9)

Toronto's amalgamation, while strengthening the city, also hampered regional cooperation because its size and power added to suburban suspicions of the emergence of the so-called megacity and its attendant motives (Frisken 2001, 535; Hodge and Robinson 2001, 354). As a result, the regions and municipalities were found to be largely caught in the "local trap," incapable of cooperating under the auspices of the GTSB, although they were apparently making decisions and making progress on some policy issues (Purcell 2005). Given these intra-regional tensions, the province eventually abandoned the idea of regional cooperation, took over the mandate of developing a regional growth management strategy, and created an arm's-length transportation agency.

Without any supra-regional planning organization since the dismantlement of the GTSB in 2001, and facing continuous growth, sprawling urban development, and a need for reinvestments in transportation infrastructures, the new provincial government of Dalton McGuinty, elected in 2003, re-evaluated the options for regional governance early in its mandate. It should also be added that while the regions and municipalities were feeling threatened by the GTSB back in 1998–2001, the provincial government was also feeling threatened by the idea of a regional government:

[B]ut the growth ultimately became bigger than the regions, so the regional governments were not adequately sized to deal with growth pressures. So the province, in thinking about what it might do, I think looked at a number of solutions, I think the obvious, the most elegant simplest solution to dealing with this would have been to set up a super region, in other words amalgamate all of the regions in the Greater Toronto Hamilton Area, and continue to have a two-tier system … but I think that politically, the province looked at that and realized that in many respects, this would be a level of government almost as big as the province. They would have created an instant rival that would have been very difficult to contend with politically. (Interview 13)

This fear of the provincial government that the province could be run by a too-powerful Toronto super-region is nothing new to the provincial–regional dynamic (Pearson 1975).[1] Faced with the risk of seeing the province led by a regional government and the failure of the GTSB to achieve regional cooperation, the provincial government then became the substitute for a regional governance structure. The provincial (Liberal) government of Premier Dalton McGuinty, who was also "enamored" of the Liberal government in British Columbia, which created Translink,[2] thus opted for a legislative growth management strategy (the Greenbelt Plan and the Growth Plan) and a regional transportation agency under its purview (Metrolinx) when looking at governance options for managing the region.

IMPLICATIONS FOR LOCAL GOVERNMENTS

The creation of Metrolinx and the development of the Big Move had important implications for the local governments in the region and for Toronto in particular. Metrolinx is responsible for region-wide transportation planning and has the capacity to finance projects through the province. However, it does not own the streets and does not have a say in land use. By contrast, municipalities are responsible for local transportation planning, own the local roads, and control land uses but have nowhere near the fiscal capacity of the province. This new set-up of mandate and capacity directly affects the municipalities and transit operators in a number of different but interrelated ways.

First, the fact that regional transit projects are a Metrolinx responsibility while local transit projects are a municipal responsibility raises an issue about the integration of local transit with regional transit needs. Although regional projects might serve a regional purpose and be linked to a regional system, they also have to serve local needs and riders who make shorter trips. This tension between the regional role and the local role of transit is observable in the project design and construction phase, as in the case of the Eglinton Crosstown LRT and the Scarborough RT replacement and extension. In the same vein, the creation of Metrolinx also means that municipalities have to defend their own transit priorities against the region's transit agenda. Moreover, the municipalities view Metrolinx as yet another actor, in addition to the province and the federal government, whom they have to influence in order to pursue their transportation agenda. However, although Metrolinx constitutes another level to lobby, some respondents reported that its staff is more accessible and closer to the local level than the Ontario minister of transportation or the minister of finance.

Second, what the creation of Metrolinx has fundamentally changed is that transit funds are not transferred to a municipality or a transit agency anymore but rather stay under the purview of the province by way of Metrolinx. So again, creating Metrolinx has given the province a direct oversight of transit money and construction projects. Municipalities being the owner of the local roads, Metrolinx must obtain their permission and full collaboration before it can undertake transit development projects on local roads. Thus, from a local government standpoint, municipalities now have to collaborate and coordinate with Metrolinx for the design, construction, and implementation of transit projects, in addition to dealing with their existing (sometimes conflictual) relationship with their own transit agency and roads department.

Third, the Big Move or, more particularly, the funding priorities within the projects identified in the Big Move have created more tensions among the provincial government, municipalities, and transit authorities as well as a shift in the regional system, since the funding that was predominantly allocated to Toronto was, thereafter, partly used for the regional transit systems.

Lastly, those transit operators who are under the purview of a local council or regional municipality now also have to cooperate with a new coordinating agency that has the mandate of providing a more seamless travel experience across transit systems. For example, they have to collaborate in working toward a universal electronic payment system, the Presto fare card, as well as fare and service integration.

Given the financial cost that this effort entails, some transit authorities are less inclined to cooperate.

Overall, Toronto's 2005–06 reform of regional planning institutions implies that the municipalities follow new land-use requirements and impose a new way of working regionally in terms of transit development and operations. However, the true impacts of the reform can only be assessed by looking at the planning processes, transportation investment choices, and land-use decision outcomes.

TRACING ACCOUNTABILITY:
METROLINX BOARD COMPOSITION

The creation of Metrolinx fundamentally changed the regional transportation regime in Toronto because there was no organization responsible for regional transportation prior to the adoption of the Metrolinx Act in 2006. Since the adoption of the Greenbelt Act and the Places to Grow Act and the creation of Metrolinx in 2005–06, local governments' official plans have to conform to the province's policy requirements. In short, the "rationalization" has taken the form of centralization: regional transportation planning is under the responsibility of a provincial agency, and regional land-use planning is overseen by a cascading system of conformity.

However, the implementation of the Big Move is uncertain because the province has not adopted a transportation planning policy statement (TPPS), as enabled by the legislation, which would compel municipalities to bring their transportation master plans in conformity with the Big Move. In the absence of this legislative requirement, the implementation of the Big Move is even more subject to political interference. It is the province, especially the premier, the minister of transportation, and the cabinet, who are the decision-makers in terms of transportation funding and decision-making (namely, through MoveOntario 2020, a $17.5 billion investment plan), with Metrolinx playing a planning and advisory role (MacDonald, Sams, and Ganjavie 2013).

The trade-offs in terms of accountability, democracy, and effectiveness associated with the new transportation planning regime are associated with Metrolinx's mandate, resources, and representational structure. The latter was unilaterally changed by the provincial government in 2009, three years after the creation of the organization and after the Big Move was adopted.

At the time of its inception, Metrolinx's board of directors was comprised of eleven members: two appointees from the provincial government, four appointees from the City of Toronto, one appointee from Hamilton, and one appointee from each of the regional municipalities of Durham, Halton, Peel, and York (Government of Ontario 2006). The board composition and appointment rules were then amended in 2009 to exclude elected members and local representatives from the board and replace them with eleven non-elected members appointed by the minister of transportation (Government of Ontario 2009). Whereas the first board was controlled by local elected officials of the region, the second one is controlled by the minister of transportation.

The province justified this change in the board of directors as necessary, claiming the delivery of the Big Move required that the people involved in the prioritization process not be in conflict between their local and regional interests. However, some respondents mentioned that the "true" motive of the province for changing the board composition and appointment rules was to regain some control over regional transit and Metrolinx in general because the board was becoming too powerful and critical of the provincial government. Regardless of the province's motive, the fact that local elected representatives were entirely excluded from the Metrolinx decision-making structure was condemned by all respondents, experts, and even Metrolinx itself (Golden 2014; Munro 2013; Transit Investment Strategy Advisory Panel 2013; Metrolinx 2013).

By excluding local elected members from the board, the province went from one end of the spectrum (all elected) to the other (all non-elected). Some respondents also maintained that the change in the appointment rules, replacing local representatives with provincial appointees, was even more detrimental than the change in the board composition. Indeed, the change in appointment rules has important implications in terms of accountability and democracy because there is no longer a link between Metrolinx and the community it serves and no engagement of the locally elected representatives in the development and approval of Metrolinx's policies and strategies (Golden 2014, 15).

The board composition and appointment rules are not trivial, random decisions. On the contrary, they are quite fundamental and even the subject of political negotiations leading to the creation (and sometimes abolishment) of regional organizations. Indeed, many respondents hold that whereas the first iteration of Metrolinx improved regional transportation planning, the second iteration of the board is impeding it.

The fact that the board is now comprised of unelected provincial appointees makes the agency and its regional plan vulnerable to political interference, compromising not only its accountability but also its agency to fulfill its non-partisan, non-political mandate of making evidence-based planning recommendations and investment decisions (Golden 2014, 16). The following quotations describe the political dynamic of Metrolinx's non-elected board. The first quotation is a respondent's general account of the consequence of moving from an all-elected to an all non-elected board, whereas the second quotation is Toronto transit expert Steve Munro's recount of the provincially appointed board modus operandi, based specifically on the board's decision regarding the extension of the Scarborough subway and more broadly on his observations from having attended the public part of the board meetings starting with the agency's inception in 2006–07:

> Metrolinx is not really independent. It is on paper, but its sole shareholder is the province. And my personal opinion is that Metrolinx wouldn't do anything unless the province agrees. [Metrolinx] would never go against a minister or a position in the province. [Confidential] did as a member. [Confidential] said no, that doesn't make any sense, that's stupid [Metrolinx] shouldn't do that. [Confidential] was the only one voting that. It's politics. Here's the irony. When the premier created the board of just all citizens, the rationale was that then it would be independent and removed from politics. It was worse than ever. Because that removed the accountability of the elected members that used to be on the board that pushed back. Whereas all those people on the citizen board didn't and so the province really controls Metrolinx, that's my personal opinion. (Interview 6)

> Metrolinx board meetings are inevitably sleepy events, with lots of good news and almost no controversy. Directors ask soft questions, almost embarrassed that they might put management to some trouble. Almost always, the answers confirm that life is good, the passengers are happy, and everyone can be confident that the GTA's transit matters are in expert, dependable hands.

The board meeting held Tuesday was a bit different: it was filled
with throngs of reporters, there seeking Metrolinx's response to
transportation minister Glen Murray's two-stop Scarborough
subway announcement. Was this on Metrolinx's agenda? No.
Metrolinx doesn't do controversy, especially when the minister's
involved … Metrolinx is an agency at which the puppet-master's
hands and wires are all too obvious. Glen Murray has wounded
its credibility as an honest, unbiased provider of advice to the
province and to the public at large, and the relevance of its board
is evaporating. (Munro 2013)

Because they were part of the initial consensus leading to its adoption, local representatives on Metrolinx's board were also acting as
"champions" of the Big Move, a level of responsibility that disap-
peared once they were replaced by provincially appointed members.
As another respondent puts it, local representation on Metrolinx's
board of directors "makes it more difficult for transportation ministers and premiers to change their minds every six months about
what is politically better rather than what is transportation better"
(Interview 4).

In addition to this shortfall in terms of responsibility to the local
community, the new board appointment rules affect the transparency
of the planning and the decision-making processes in the sense that
they enable the province to interfere politically. Because the province's
transportation investment decisions are made disregarding and
muzzling the agency's professional recommendations, and following
whichever (political) criteria, the public is "very confused" about
regional transit projects, according to some respondents. An example
of this lack of transparency are the refusals of the provincial government to release information about three major transit infrastructure
projects, the Scarborough RT replacement and extension, the Eglinton
Crosstown LRT, and the UPX air–rail link. As mentioned by John
Lorinc in his "Spacing Investigation" about the Scarborough subway:

[Metrolinx's document about the true costs of the Scarborough
subway decision] are not the only documents about the Liberals'
transit plans that remain under lock and key, and therefore
beyond the reach of public scrutiny. The Liberal government …
filibustered three requests for information moved by NDP transportation critic … These are:

- a request for all documents that pertain to the plan to use subway "technology" in the Scarborough RT corridor;
- "all documents related to the operation of the Eglinton Crosstown";
- "any market studies related to ridership projections for the air–rail link."

(Lorinc 2014)

The political nature of the board (in terms of both its composition and its appointment rules) is not the only dimension of the regional institutional design that contributes to its lack of transparency. The fact that part of the board meetings occur privately was also mentioned by the respondents as a lack of transparency. As for the public part of the board meetings, one respondent mentioned that the elements discussed in those were "meaningless stuff" (Interview 6). Despite this call for transparency through public as well as media access to the board meetings, one respondent considers that making board meetings public could lead to sensationalism, saying: "I'm in favour of real accountability, documentation about how the money is spent, the process about how decisions were taken, open and honest communication. To me open and honest communication is not the same as letting a camera in. Sometimes it works the opposite. People don't say what they really mean, and as candidly because all the cameras are there you're not going to say what you really mean. So it's actually worse" (Interview 7).

The self-censorship argument aside, the evidence in this study shows that access to documentation about how money was spent is not granted and that the way in which investment decisions were made remains obscure. In addition, the board composition has another type of impact on Metrolinx's transparency (or lack thereof) in the sense that local elected officials, and elected representatives in general, are used to being in the public eye and to doing public debates in a public session. By contrast, private-sector members are not used to having highly spirited debates in public.

Aside from these implications in terms of accountability, another respondent observed that transparency could compromise budgetary efficiency insofar as if Metrolinx is transparent about planning a route or identifying a proposed new facility, speculators will start buying properties around it, thereby forcing Metrolinx to pay more for the project if it needs to secure those properties for a route or station.[3]

Another inherent trade-off, or incompatibility, between transparency, democracy, and effectiveness is that compliance with accountability and transparency guidelines (e.g., record-keeping, protocol, documentation) consumes time and money resources from infrastructure projects, yet these projects are generally under pressure to advance promptly and to minimize expenses. Transportation agencies and governments then have to find the right balance between moving a project forward in good time and maintaining the necessary level of coordination and public involvement.

THE IMPLICATIONS OF LOCAL REPRESENTATION (OR LACK THEREOF)

The general consensus among respondents is that the absence of local elected officials and/or local appointees on the Metrolinx board of directors undermines its representativeness, even though major investment decisions are not made by the board but by the provincial government, which is supposed to be representative of the population. Moreover, some respondents also find that people representing areas outside of the Greater Toronto and Hamilton Area should not have an equal say on which projects are to be constructed in Toronto, even if they should have some say about investment choices, given that some of the money is provincial, and even if Toronto is the capital of the province of Ontario. In addition to this lack of representativeness, another dimension of democracy – namely, that of "public debate and deliberation" – is not well served by the agency. Although Metrolinx has improved outreach and collaboration with stakeholders and staff from different levels of government since its inception, public debate and deliberation remains a challenge in the transportation industry that has traditionally operated behind closed doors.

The absence of local representation on the Metrolinx decision-making committee not only undermines its democratic character but also contributes to an already tense relationship with the TTC, which has resulted in unproductive delays in the implementation of the Presto fare card and the construction of Eglinton LRT (Golden 2014, 16). The following quotation describes this complex dynamic between the human resources and technical capacities of Metrolinx, the competition between Metrolinx and the TTC, and the local representation on the board of directors:

[The fact that you had the regional chairs and the mayor of Toronto on the board of directors] overcame another weakness of Metrolinx in particular, not necessarily the regional structure, which is the staff are … tell you the truth they're incompetent. They're not knowledgeable enough and they couldn't be because the only organization in this province that has the technical expertise necessary is the TTC. And it's not about having one or two people from the TTC … it's about the institutional competence and knowledge. So the TTC for example that plans an LRT line, is relying on its own history of how it analyzes its ridership and ridership projections and how you nail that into the official plan of Toronto that is protecting development ahead of time, and it knows how it relies on this data, it knows where the stop needs to be in terms of distance and all of that. Metrolinx essentially had to hire people who are really planning consultants or engineering consultants … They get bright young people, but there's no institutional history or depth, and there can't be. So while you had the regional chairs and the Mayor of Toronto on [the board], you got a whole work against that institutional structural lack of knowledge which I call incompetence. Once [they were] gone and you had citizens who didn't have that knowledge, and staff are essentially consultants, you did create a problem leading to some paralysis and lots of mistakes. There just isn't the depth of history and expertise. And that can be developed over time, but one of the lessons I take from this that you wanna do things quickly, create a new structure like this, you gotta be exceptionally careful about. Because, maybe fifteen years from now they'll have all of the institutional expertise, but they sure didn't have it the first five years, it's not possible, it's not that they're bad people, it's just not possible. The planning of the Eglinton LRT in particular, and the Finch LRT as well were delayed, probably a year, and it was because every time [the TTC] made a decision, the TTC about where, how difficult problems should be resolved, like an intersection or complicated or where a stop should be, Metrolinx would say "no, that's wrong," and then [the TTC] would have to fight [Metrolinx] on it, and brief them, and eventually, they would come to say you know what, we've thought about it, you're right, but it would take two to three months, and this happened again and again and again, and again, and again. Because of what I call this is structural incompetence. And it's one of the reasons [we] saw the TTC walked away that [said] "we're not gonna be juniors, you guys drive this project." It was for that reason, the TTC didn't respect judgement calls of Metrolinx. (Interview 9)

Another respondent does mention that Metrolinx, especially without the municipalities, is not competent or capable of effectively renewing the Big Move. To the extent that the initial board was compensating for the agency's lack of expertise in transit planning, operation, and construction, the lack of local representation on the current board is undermining its effectiveness in carrying out its mandate.

The change in Metrolinx's board composition and appointment rules that replaced local elected members with provincially appointed, non-elected members has allowed the province to bypass Metrolinx recommendations when funding transit infrastructure projects. As a result of this change in its representation structure, the transportation agency is not accountable to, or representative of, local communities anymore. Moreover, possibly as a result of the high politicization of the transit infrastructure funding issue, it has made investment choices that are questionable in terms of efficiency, notably because the province's lack of transparency makes independent assessments more difficult.

EFFECTIVENESS

In terms of the implications of Metrolinx for the principle of effectiveness, we must keep in mind that government agencies do not necessarily have the same goals as the private sector in the sense that the former has the mission of protecting the public good and providing public services rather than operating at a profit (which is more associated with the notion of efficiency). This means that respondents view Metrolinx's effectiveness less in terms of cost-efficiency and more in terms of its ability to accomplish its mandate and its focus on regional activities revolving around integration and coordination, which might result in more efficiency.

It is part of Metrolinx's mandate to create a regional transportation system integrating different modes of transportation and infrastructures and to manage procurement initiatives with smaller transit operators (Golden 2014, 19). One respondent found that this regional focus did indeed lead to greater efficiency, at some level, because instead of each municipality doing its own transit planning, proposals, and justifications – with no accountability to the region and bloated budgets because the province pays anyway – there is now a regional process looking at the associated costs and benefits of each project. However, the absence of local representation in Metrolinx decision-making also resulted in, as mentioned, unproductive delays in the implementation of the Presto fare card and the construction of the Eglinton LRT.

In addition, Metrolinx has more clout in the regional planning and operational processes than it has in the provincial decision-making process. Because municipalities are not compelled to conform to the Big Move, Metrolinx relies essentially on provincial infrastructure funding to implement the plan. The fact that Metrolinx has no independent revenue sources compromises its ability to implement the Big Move and to prioritize projects for which there is a regional consensus and that represent the best value for money. As a result, the transit projects that are moving forward are not the most cost-effective ones in terms of the expenses incurred for every new rider. The Scarborough RT replacement and extension, the TYSSE up to Vaughan Corporate Centre, the UPX, and the independent evaluation of the Big Move conducted by Michael Schabas indicate that the investment choices made do not have the best ridership potential.

Metrolinx's lack of funding autonomy and sufficiency is closely tied to the agency's independence and accountability in the sense that Metrolinx would be less prone to political influence in choosing and prioritizing the projects that represent the best value for money if it had its own independent revenue source. This absence of funding autonomy and authority to raise revenues through taxation are acknowledged and documented in the *Metrolinx Investment Strategy* (Metrolinx 2013) as well as in the final report of the Transit Investment Strategy Advisory Panel (2013).

CONCLUSION

The change in Metrolinx's board composition and appointment rules, which replaced local elected members with provincially appointed, non-elected members, has allowed the province of Ontario to bypass Metrolinx recommendations when funding transit infrastructure projects. As a result of this change in its structure of representation, the transportation agency is no longer accountable to or representative of local communities. In addition, the high politicization of the transit infrastructure funding issue has led to investment choices that are questionable in terms of efficiency, notably because the province's lack of transparency makes independent assessments more difficult. Finally, the fact that Metrolinx has no independent revenue sources compromises its ability to implement the Big Move by prioritizing projects for which there is a regional consensus and that represent the best value for money in terms of ridership potential.

What can we conclude from the Toronto reform in terms of accountability, democracy, and efficiency/effectiveness? Aside from the implications or characteristics of Metrolinx regarding accountability, democracy, and effectiveness, the empirical evidence shows that some dimensions of the regional institutional design seem to act as "guardians" of certain principles. Table 8.1 presents a summary of Metrolinx's characteristics in terms of accountability, democracy, and effectiveness and the link of these characteristics with the mandate, resources, representational structure of the agency, and impact on the planning and decision-making processes.

First of all, the principle of accountability, particularly regarding its "responsibility" dimension, and the principle of democracy with regard to its "representativeness" dimension are both maintained by the representative structure of the regional agency. In fact, the presence of local elected officials and local appointees on Metrolinx's board ensured that the local interests were represented at the regional level. In addition, the local representatives acted as the champions of the Big Move. In fact, the "political hijacking" of Metrolinx's planning and transportation decisions in Ontario were attributed to the replacement of elected local appointees with non-elected provincial appointees on the agency's board of directors. Certain dimensions of the principles of accountability and democracy are thus safeguarded when local elected officials are represented on the agency's board of directors.

Although the provincial government still controls transportation investments, the representational structure of the regional agency determines whether or not there is regional/local resistance to the provincial initiatives that are going against the regional plan. Overall, the evidence shows that local elected representatives are an essential component of a regional planning agency's board of directors – namely, because they are the watchdogs of local and regional interests and because they act as champions of the regional plan. In the same

Table 8.1
Impact of institutional design on accountability, democracy, and effectiveness

Region/ Principle	Accountability	Democracy	Effectiveness
Toronto	Metrolinx accountable to the province. No local accountability *Impact:* Transparency challenge. Metrolinx advice easily dismissed by the province	No local representation *Impact:* Public debates and regional consensus ignored by the province. Not the best use of transit funds	Metrolinx's mandate is to plan and manage transportation investments. No funding autonomy in that investment choices are provincial. *Impact:* Reinvestment in infrastructures, but not the best projects are selected.

vein, board members who are appointed by the province tend to align with the agenda pushed by the province, including by abstaining from voicing their professional opinion publicly. In addition, local representatives are connected to local administrations, transit operators, and local constituents, which offer a certain guarantee that projects materialize at the local and community levels.

Second, there is some tension between dimensions of democracy (representativeness, public debate, deliberation) and efficiency/ effectiveness. In Toronto, the political flip-flopping, the disrespect of regional consensus and democratic principles, and the lack of transparency (a dimension of accountability) were associated with transportation investment decisions that did not represent the best value for money in terms of ridership potential. In addition, although some respondents pointed out that transportation engineers dislike the public scrutiny and the consultation that comes with the regional planning processes and that time-consuming planning activities are not efficient, other respondents pointed out that consultation and outreach is an intrinsic part of the planning role of a regional agency and that it also helps in educating the public and elected officials and in achieving local buy-in for developing and implementing projects that communities want. Although the disrespect of democratic principles is associated with transportation investment choices that are not the most desirable from a sustainability standpoint, the consensual approach prevents the adoption of the most progressive or coercive policy and investment choices. Overall, in spite of the fact that the projects selected do not represent the best value for money, the reinvestment in transit infrastructures is an improvement over the financial situation prevailing before Metrolinx was created and a more sustainable investment choice than building suburban highways.

Finally, Metrolinx's ability to implement the policies and the projects identified in the Big Move is limited by its lack of independent revenue sources, which ties the principle of effectiveness to the issue of resources. In fact, the respondents identified possible independent revenue sources that would enable Metrolinx to effectively carry out its mandate without always needing provincial approval. However, the province is reluctant to give the agency more autonomy – a fairly constant and common issue of debate in regional planning politics.

To conclude, transportation infrastructure projects are frequently at the centre stage of electoral campaigns, and both local and provincial governments are highly responsive to citizens' preferences. However, this responsiveness becomes an issue when solving regional transportation issues calls for unpopular measures, such as HOV lanes, toll roads, and costly transit infrastructures that can disrupt car traffic during the construction phase (and even after). For this reason, incumbents are incentivized to adopt short-term fixes such as adding lanes and building roads, which exacerbate urban transportation problems because of induced demand. In terms of accountability, the evidence shows how power and control exercised by transportation project sponsors (most often the province) can circumvent the regional consensus. Although the establishment of Metrolinx gave the provincial government the impetus for reinvesting massively in transit, recent investment decisions in Toronto and elsewhere in Canada show that, in terms of transportation, the regional interest is better served by regional planning agencies, transit operators, and local governments than by provincial governments.

NOTES

1 There has even been a proposal to make the Toronto city-region a separate province. The idea dates back to 1948 and resurfaces every decade or so (Hodge and Robinson 2001, 355).

2 Translink is responsible for regional transportation in Greater Vancouver. Founded in 1999, it has authority over the planning and design of transportation, including roads, as well as operating and financing transit services. It is perhaps the closest to the Transportation for London (TfL) model in North America (Neptis Foundation 2014).

3 A land value capture strategy could help solve this issue (as suggested by Metrolinx and the Transit Investment Strategy Advisory Panel), but the City of Toronto does not support land value capture as a revenue tool for transit projects (Metrolinx 2014, 4).

REFERENCES

Boudreau, Julie-Anne, Roger Keil, and Douglas Young. 2009. *Changing Toronto: Governing Urban Neoliberalism*. Toronto: University of Toronto Press.

Frisken, Frances. 2001. "The Toronto Story: Sober Reflections on Fifty Years of Experiments with Regional Governance." *Journal of Urban Affairs* 23(5): 513–41.

Golden, Anne. 2014. *Governance of Regional Transit Systems: Observations on Washington, New York, and Toronto*. Washington: Wilson Center, 28 July. http://www.wilsoncenter.org/publication/governance-regional-transit-systems.

Government of Ontario. 2006. *Greater Toronto Transportation Authority Act*. 22 June. http://www.e-laws.gov.on.ca/html/source/statutes/english/2006/elaws_src_so6o16_e.htm.

– 2009. *Greater Toronto and Hamilton Area Transit Implementation Act, 2009*. 14 May. http://www.e-laws.gov.on.ca/html/source/statutes/english/2009/elaws_src_so9o14_e.htm.

GTA Task Force. 1996. *Greater Toronto: Report of the GTA Task Force*. Toronto: Queen's Printer for Ontario.

Hodge, Gerald, and Ira M. Robinson. 2001. *Planning Canadian Regions*. Vancouver: UBC Press.

Keil, Roger, and Julie-Anne Boudreau. 2005. "Is There Regionalism after Municipal Amalgamation in Toronto?" *City* 9(1): 9–22.

Keil, Roger, and Douglas Young. 2008. "Transportation: The Bottleneck of Regional Competitiveness in Toronto." *Environment and Planning C: Government and Policy* 26(4): 728–51.

Lorinc, John. 2014. "Spacing Investigation, Part 1: The Political Movements behind the Scarborough Subway." Spacing Toronto. 28 May. http://spacing.ca/toronto/2014/05/28/spacing-investigation-part-1-political-movements-behind-scarborough-subway.

MacDonald, Donald M., Scott Sams, and Amir Ganjavie. 2013. "Why Did Toronto Stop Building Subways? Understanding Multi-Level Governance in the City of Toronto." Unpublished paper.

Metrolinx. 2013. *Metrolinx Investment Strategy*. 27 May. http://wwxxcw. metrolinx.com/en/regionalplanning/funding/IS_Full_Report_EN.pdf.

– 2014. "Regional Transportation Plan Legislated Review – Introduction." Staff Report to the Board of Directors, 14 February. http://www. metrolinx.com/en/docs/pdf/ board_agenda/20140214/20140214_BoardMtg_Regional_ Transportation_Plan_Legislated_Review-Introduction_EN.pdf.

Munro, Steve. 2013. "Metrolinx Spins the Scarborough Subway." *Torontoist*, 11 September. http://torontoist.com/2013/09/metrolinx-spins-the-scarborough-subway.

Neptis Foundation. 2014. "Governance: The Third Rail That Powers Integrated Regional Transit." Policy Brief, June. http://www.neptis.org/ publications/governance-third-rail-powers-integrated-regional-transit.

Pearson, Norman. 1975. "Regional Government and Development." In *Government and Politics of Ontario*, edited by Donald C. Macdonald, 171–93. Toronto: Macmillan.

Purcell, Mark. 2005. "Scale, Urban Democracy and the Right to the City." Paper presented at the Conference on the Political Economy of Scale, York University, Toronto, 4 February.

Transit Investment Strategy Advisory Panel. 2013. *Making the Move: Choices and Consequences*. December. http://www.toronto.ca/legdocs/ mmis/2014/ex/bgrd/backgroundfile-67455.pdf.

White, Richard. 2007. *The Growth Plan for the Greater Golden Horseshoe in Historical Perspective*. Neptis Paper on Growth in the Toronto Metropolitan Region. Paper 4. December. http://www.neptis. org/sites/default/files/historical_commentary/historicalcomm_ web_200711291.pdf

Mirror Image:
The Fight against Homelessness
in Calgary and Montreal

Alison Smith

Many activists heralded the election of the federal Liberal government in 2015 as a positive step in the fight against homelessness in Canada. For decades, these activists had bemoaned the weak federal involvement in fighting homelessness and argued that ending, or even reducing, homelessness would require a much more serious federal engagement than what was seen in the 1990s and early 2000s. Since returning to power in 2015, the Liberal government has taken a number of steps to commit to reducing homelessness, including doubling funding to programs that fight homelessness and increased spending in the construction of new affordable housing.

In this chapter, I ask what this increased federal involvement in homelessness means for the responsiveness of existing efforts to reduce or end homelessness. Specifically, I look at Montreal and Calgary, where local groups have long been engaged in efforts to reduce homelessness. Further, their respective provinces (Quebec and Alberta) have also been strongly engaged in efforts to reduce homelessness, albeit in very different ways. In both these cases, the federal government was, until recently, the missing multilevel governance link.

On the one hand, we know from the literature that responsive multilevel governance is closely linked to the local level and the involvement of civil society in the policy process. Local groups (municipal governments, the third sector, or the private sector) best know their needs and their strengths. Of all the actors involved in multilevel governance, the federal government is the farthest from local. In a sense, then, the federal government's renewed interest in this area should make little difference to the responsiveness of existing efforts in Calgary and Montreal. Yet the lack of resources that has plagued this policy area means that actors at the local level have been severely limited in what they can do in the fight against homelessness. Federal funding, set to flow to the local level, should empower those actors to a certain extent. In this sense, the federal government's return is an important step toward responsive multilevel governance. Specifically, I argue that the governance model in Montreal is most likely to benefit from this increased funding, at least with respect to responsiveness. Calgary's governance model, which is very different from Montreal's, is more likely to benefit from this increased funding in terms of effectiveness (the two, of course, do not always go hand in hand).

The remainder of this chapter is divided into three parts. I first review the literature regarding responsive policy-making in Canada. I then review briefly the state of homelessness in Canada, including important recent developments at the federal level, before applying Horak's framework to the two cases at hand.

PART 1: LITERATURE REVIEW

The local level has become a powerful actor and a more important producer of social security in part because of changes to the welfare state enacted by provinces and the federal government in the 1980s, 1990s, and early 2000s. Following the Second World War and until the 1990s, the federal government, along with provincial partners, was producing up to 25,000 units of social housing per year (Shapcott 2007). Federal disinterest in housing policy began in the 1980s when investments in new housing developments decreased and existing and new housing units became more limited and targeted (toward seniors and people with disabilities, for example). In the 1990s, after transferring the responsibility for administering housing to the provinces, the federal government made the decision to stop funding new housing developments. Provinces had previously cost-shared with the federal government; with the exceptions of Quebec and British Columbia, the provinces followed suit and also made cuts to housing. This period through the 1980s and 1990s saw not just cuts to housing but to other areas of social policy as well, notably social assistance rates.

Following these decisions to cut social spending, as well as government inaction in the face of new social risks, Rice and Prince write that Canada's social safety net has become "badly frayed and close to the ground" (2013, 137). Indeed, chronic homelessness rose dramatically in the 1990s and 2000s, and experts have linked this directly to social spending cuts (Gaetz 2010; Hulchanski 2009; Layton 2008). These changes to welfare spending put great burdens on city governments: "economic restructuring and downloading of responsibilities from federal and provincial governments have a direct impact on urban governments. It is municipal governments that eventually must fill many of these program and financial gaps or bear the social costs of poverty" (Graham, Phillips, and Maslove 1998, 1).

Homelessness continued to rise through the 1990s and 2000s, but little was being done at the federal and provincial levels. In many cities, local-level actors organized and developed their own responses to homelessness. But of course city governments lack the resources to fight homelessness on their own; even when working with the private sector and the third sector, the local level is simply unable to comprehensively tackle such a complex and costly problem. Resources are severely limited, but responsibility over important policy areas such as housing, health, and justice are spread among different actors, notably with provincial and federal governments. Given the distribution of responsibilities and the high costs, tackling homelessness requires a multilevel governance approach.

In order to acknowledge a reality in which local governments are increasingly important in the governance of Canadians, Leo has developed a particular approach to multilevel governance. He asks, "how can we have policies that are truly national and yet fully take into account the very significant differences among regions and communities?" (2006, 485). His answer is deep federalism, which sees federalism not just through a legal or constitutional lens but rather as a process comprised of "voluntary arrangements short of constitutional change" (2006, 487). Deep federalism allows for flexibility and compromise among different actors, even in areas where the constitution does not afford the local level any role or responsibility.

Along with numerous collaborators, Leo has conducted multiple studies of deep federalism and multilevel governance in Canada, highlighting when deep federalism works and when it doesn't. Looking back on these case studies, Leo and August are reluctant to identify a governance model that is the most desirable either in terms of effectiveness or responsiveness. Rather, they write, "no two communities and no two policy programs are exactly alike" (2009, 506). In the case of welfare to work programs, for example, Leo and Andres find that "the municipal government offers the best vehicle for the achievement of deep federalism in the administration of welfare to work programmes" (2008, 114). In a later piece by Leo and Enns, the authors find that immigration settlement in Winnipeg has been achieved successfully "while entirely bypassing municipal government" (2009, 96). Reviewing thirteen case studies of deep federalism, Leo and August conclude that "anyone who believes that a theory of governance can be applied, like a recipe for goulash, to the production of a predictable and satisfying outcome in every individual circumstance greatly underestimates the subtlety and complexity [of] policy making and implementation" (2009, 57).

Horak similarly finds that there is no single model of multilevel governance that produces responsive or effective public policy all the time. Rather, he notes that multilevel governance arrangements are shaped by a "multiplicity of causal forces – ranging from the distribution of authority and resources to the ideology and strategic leadership skills of politicians, the institutional structure of relevant administrative bodies, and the degree of organization of social forces, among others" (2012, 349). Looking at effectiveness and responsiveness of multilevel governance, Horak does, however, identify some best practices. Notably, he writes, "local responsiveness usually (though not always) requires that local agents be actively involved in multilevel policy development, as opposed to just advocacy or implementation" (2012, 364). He argues that the private sector tends to be more involved in all stages of the policy process than the third sector and suggests that increased third-sector involvement throughout policy-making would increase responsiveness.

Responsiveness, of course, implies that there is someone, or a group of people, to whom the policy is responsive. Horak correctly recognizes that in many cases, there is no single local preference: "despite its widespread currency in the literature, the concept of 'local preferences' is, in fact, an oversimplified construct, because more often than not, local preferences in any one policy field and city are heterogeneous" (2012, 364). As I will argue below, this is particularly the case in Montreal and has the effect of lessening the benefits to responsiveness (and effectiveness) of increased federal funding in this area.

He further notes that "the distribution of resources of various kinds is key to multilevel policy influence" (2012, 364). For the latter, he acknowledges that municipalities are usually "resource-poor" in terms of revenues but frequently have "locally-grounded expertise, and this can act as a counterweight to a lack of financial resources" (2012, 365). There are a number of other factors that affect the responsiveness of multilevel policy initiatives to local preferences, but these factors all relate directly to the local government, such as formal jurisdiction over the policy area in question or the "relative economic or electoral importance of a city in intergovernmental context, which affects the inclination of provincial and federal governments to treat seriously local preferences in that city" (2012, 365). In both cases considered in this chapter, the local government is not the lead actor in the local governance network; for this reason, the analysis below considers the involvement of local-level actors in policy-making and the balance of power between two civil society groups: the private sector and the third sector.

PART 2: THE STATE OF HOMELESSNESS

Homelessness has not always existed in Canada.[1] There have long been people who were unhoused, such as those who sought temporary shelter in Montreal's Old Brewery Mission (the city's oldest homeless shelter) over the past 125 years. But as homelessness expert David Hulchanski has argued in an influential piece, we have not always had the set of problems that we today associate with the word *homelessness* (Hulchanski 2009). He writes, "[homelessness] is a catch-all term for a host of serious social and economic policy failures – more serious than in the past. Its widespread usage reflects what has happened to Canadian society – the way we organize who gets what, and our failure to have in place systems for meeting the basic human needs in a universal, inclusive fashion" (2009, 6).

Today, the *State of Homelessness in Canada* report (Gaetz, Gulliver, and Richter 2015) estimates that 235,000 Canadians experience homelessness every year. On any given night, an estimated 35,000 people are homeless. A relatively small number of people – 5,000 – are considered chronically homeless, meaning that they have been homeless for one year or more or have experienced four or more episodes of homelessness within one year. For the majority of the homeless population in Canada, homelessness is a brief, one-time experience and tends to be closely linked to poverty and a lack of affordable housing.

The Homeless Hub estimates that "ending" homelessness in Canada would cost $44 billion over ten years. "This seems like a lot," writes Gulliver-Garcia, "but it's not actually that much." She continues, "Our plan works out to about $106/Canadian annually, $2.04 weekly, just 88 cents a week more than current spending" (Gulliver-Garcia 2014). The *State of Homelessness in Canada* report further notes that this figure is only about $1.7 billion per year more than what the federal government already spends. To counter the rise of homelessness and the broader problem of housing affordability, the authors of the report recommend a total of nearly $44 billion over the course of ten years to end homelessness and ease the housing affordability crisis. They note that this is approximately $21 billion more than what was projected to be spent in 2016, which equals $50 per Canadian per year; "for less than an additional $1 per week per Canadian, we can prevent and end homelessness in Canada" (Gaetz et al. 2016, 58).

The Liberal government's first budget, released in early 2016, made a number of two-year commitments in the area of housing and homelessness, including $2.3 billion over two years for affordable housing and homelessness. This figure includes funding for the construction of new affordable housing units and the maintenance and repair of existing units, nearly $90 million for shelters for people fleeing violence, $732 million over two years for housing in First Nations communities, and $11.8 million for the Homelessness Partnering Strategy (HPS).

In its budget response, the Canadian Housing and Renewal Association (CHRA) applauded what it called a "down payment" on affordable housing, saying that CHRA members were pleased with the short-term announcements made by the government and emphasized the importance of the longer-term national housing strategy. The National Housing Strategy (NHS) at time of writing has not been released in detail, but the federal government's 2017 budget announced resources that would be allocated to it: $11.2 billion over eleven years (Press 2017). This funding includes long-term funding for the HPS, affordable housing construction and renovations, rent supplements (a voucher-type system that allows people to live in private-market housing with the help of a monthly government supplement), and investments in housing for Indigenous people.

This figure is substantially less than what experts argued for in the *State of Homelessness in Canada* report, but the Canadian Observatory on Homelessness (coh, the collective that produces the States of Homelessness report every year) welcomed the investments nevertheless. In its budget response, the coh said, "the 11-year investment in a National Housing Strategy is significant. Not only does it signal the federal government is 'back at the table,' the length of the investment means this is now a permanent program. The investment also highlights the government's commitment to flexibility and new ways of working" (Canadian Observatory on Homelessness 2017).

The funding announced in the nhs will roll out slowly, with most of the funding not being spent until 2022. Some advocates have criticized this, saying communities need the investments now. The coh takes a slightly different interpretation, saying that this delay allows for time to make sure programs are thoughtfully and carefully planned. The details of the nhs, of course, have at time of writing not been announced. Even the structure of the hps has not been released; the government has promised to have the strategy ready by the fall of 2017.

The remainder of this chapter compares the governance models that have developed around the fight against homelessness in two very different cities: Calgary and Montreal. In contrasting ways, these two cities, and their respective provinces as well, have been very active in the fight against homelessness. I first outline a brief history of the fight against homelessness and then map out the local governance model. I then compare the two local governance models and illustrate how these models are likely to engage with federal policy-making and how the federal increases in funding will likely affect the responsiveness of their efforts.

CALGARY

Calgary was the first major Canadian city to commit to ending homelessness, a promise that was made by the non-profit Calgary Homeless Foundation (chf). The chf has existed since the 1990s, but its role in the fight against homelessness grew considerably in the early 2000s when it went from a small organization of five people to a large and powerful one with a staff of more than forty. Today, the chf has an annual budget of tens of millions of dollars, including funding from all three levels of government and private-sector donors. Its plan to end homelessness was developed in the mid-2000s by a small group of people, many of whom had strong ties to the oil and gas sector (Miller and Smart 2012; Scott 2012; Smith 2016). The Calgary Committee to End Homelessness (CCEH) was created in early 2007 and was tasked with creating the ten-year plan to end homelessness. The CCEH comprised a variety of actors, including representatives from three levels of government and community groups, but its leadership team (which oversaw the development of the plan) exclusively comprised people from the business community (mostly oil and gas; see Calgary Homeless Foundation 2008, appendix 2). As the CHF chair's opening remarks on the plan note, "this is not a plan that expects government to shoulder the full burden" (Calgary Homeless Foundation 2008, 2). The CHF did, of course, note that the government plays an important part in the fight against homelessness but as a partner and not necessarily the leader, and the plan stressed that the involvement of the private sector would be "maximized" (2008, 9).

The CCEH involved community groups as well, though their influence in the development of the plan and the governance of the CHF was limited. To be sure, the original 2008 plan was written with input from these community groups; "the CCEH conducted eight public consultations on different homeless populations" in addition to a community summit that was attended by more than 300 people (2008, 44). But people from community groups were intentionally relegated to less important positions within the foundation. An actor involved in the development of the ten-year plan said, "we said ok, we'll get input from community groups, but not on the leadership team. So they were on the subcommittees" (quoted in Smith 2016).

The first plan was introduced in 2008 and ambitiously promised to end homelessness by 2018, meaning 80 per cent of the city's shelter beds would be shut down and no one would be homeless for more than one week. The plan contained a number of shorter-term "milestones," such as eliminating family homelessness in two years and closing 50 per cent of the city's emergency shelter beds within five years. Stating that there would be a considerable return on investment in the form of reduced spending on emergency services for the homeless (such as emergency rooms, police contact, and other health-related costs), the plan estimated that the total cost of implementation would be $3.2 billion, "including a total public sector contribution of approximately $1.8 billion" (Calgary Homeless Foundation 2008, 42). The operating cost projection was a further $1.2 billion. Without a plan to end homelessness, the authors of Calgary's plan estimated that the costs of homelessness could rise to more than $9 billion. This plan, and the numbers regarding the costs of homelessness and potential savings associated with ending it, were largely informed by the American experience (see Scott 2012; Smith 2016). The research and expertise that was originally developed in Calgary was largely with respect to what worked south of the border.

Three years following the introduction of the plan, it was significantly rewritten. The overall principles and values remained the same. However, "the original [2008] Plan included a number of assumptions and reflected a different landscape in Calgary ... This update describes what has been learned and achieved to date, and what needs to be done over the next seven years" (Calgary Homeless Foundation 2011, 2). The second plan maintained the commitment to end homelessness by 2018, but it noted the importance of developing specific approaches for the unique needs of certain populations (such as youth and Aboriginal people) and an increased attention to prevention. To some, this was seen as an acknowledgment that community groups were not consulted enough the first time around.

The third plan, released in 2015, is even more modest than the 2011 update. The milestones (the short-term goals), having not been accomplished within the CHF's originally stated timeline, were completely erased from this third version of the plan. The 2015 version acknowledges some failings of the past. "Most noteworthy," it says, "was our failure to recognize the essential role of emergency shelters in our homeless-serving system. We now know that about 2% of shelter stayers take up a considerable amount of shelter space, though the vast majority (84%) stay for two weeks or less" (Calgary Homeless Foundation 2015, 83). Emphasizing that certain "conditions" are required to end homelessness, the third plan appears to signal that the CHF will not in fact end homelessness by 2018 but that the organization is not wholly to blame for this. These "conditions" largely relate to government policy and investment, an apparent shift from the first plan in which the government was seen as only a small part of the solution. Over the course of these various revisions, as well as annual reports, the CHF has come to engage community partners much more extensively than it did in the development of the plan, though its leadership remains dominated by private-sector actors.

The CHF set itself up for an impossible task back in 2008. It was naive or arrogant (or both) to make that promise in the first place, though the actors involved in Calgary's efforts must be praised for their ambition and willingness to take on an impossible task. There have been notable successes in their efforts, such as stopping the rise of homelessness that was occurring in the mid-2000s. The CHF also implemented a centralized intake system and coordinated its use across the "homeless serving system" in Calgary, which refers to all agencies and groups providing services to the homeless. This system (described more fully in Dressler 2016; Milaney 2016; Nichols and Doberstein 2016) is designed to identify which homeless people have the highest needs so that they can be prioritized for services and matched with the appropriate ones. The aim is to first serve people with the "highest needs" or the most chronically homeless, those who use a disproportionate amount of services. This "systems approach" also prevents an overlap in service provision; some homeless people can get lost in the system, and as a result their needs are never fully met. This centralized system allows for services to effectively follow a person through the system, to fully know their needs, and to in effect have a person or organization responsible for that person. From a governance perspective, the successful implementation of this system has led to a very coordinated system in which actors are all working together, which is a remarkable achievement in an area of public policy as complex as homelessness. It is also a system in which the CHF has a tremendous amount of concentrated power.

This systems-based approach is a good idea and is in many ways very similar to what Scandinavian countries do, where a wide-ranging amount of information about homeless people (including mental and physical health) is shared with various services (including the police and municipally run shelters). There are some problems with the approach in Calgary, however. Importantly, there are simply not sufficient resources in Calgary to provide services for the most needy people. In other words, the coordinated intake system in Calgary is very good at identifying the people with the highest needs, but the system more broadly is not able to provide the type of housing or medical or social support needed to actually help that person. It is perhaps for this reason that the CHF is beginning to point its finger at the provincial and federal governments, correctly stating that these actors and these actors alone have sufficient resources to fully meet the needs of this population.

The province of Alberta also has a ten-year plan to end homelessness, which was introduced in 2008. The plan was created by the

Alberta Secretariat on Homelessness (an agency of the Alberta government) and promises to end homelessness by 2019. Steve Synder, who chaired the leadership committee of the CCEH, chaired the Alberta Secretariat as well. The language of the provincial plan, which emphasizes the economic cost of homelessness and the savings associated with ending it, is very similar to that of the CHF. The Alberta plan is also similar to the CHF's plan in its commitment to the Housing First approach to homelessness.

The provincial plan promised to contribute to affordable housing as an important part of the solution to homelessness. A close look at documents from the province's own housing ministry reveal that while an impressive number of homeless Albertans had been housed, the province had not contributed as much to the affordable housing stock as it had promised (see Smith 2016). An Alberta Interagency Council on Homelessness (AIC) report in 2014 emphasized that the lack of affordable housing in the province was one of the most important "risks to the Plan's success." The AIC concluded with advice for the future of the provincial ten-year plan: "at the very centre of the Council's advice is that ending homelessness and having an adequate supply of affordable housing are inseparable tasks" (Alberta Interagency Council on Homelessness 2014).

The governance of homelessness in Calgary is, as the above has shown, very coordinated between the provincial and local levels. More important for this chapter, it is highly coordinated at the local level, where power is concentrated in the CHF, which has a considerable amount of power and financial resources. The first version of the plan was driven by the private sector, and while community groups have become increasingly involved in revisions of the plan, the leadership still gives significant power to the private sector. The investments that have been made in Calgary have not been nearly enough to make good on the promise to end homelessness, however, and as the deadlines of the CHF and the Alberta government get closer and closer, they seem to be preparing themselves for failure.

MONTREAL

The governance of homelessness in Montreal is very different. The Quebec provincial government is much more interventionist than its Albertan counterpart and has a long-standing commitment to issues like the fight against poverty and social exclusion, social housing, and, more recently, homelessness. A large and influential social movement in the early 2000s led the provincial government to introduce its first action plan on poverty and social exclusion, and while the plan was not as far-reaching as advocates and activists wanted (Noël 2005), the government has continually renewed its commitment to fighting poverty ever since.

Further, Quebec is the only province in the federation to have funded the construction of social and affordable housing ever since the federal government stopped its funding in the 1990s.[2] The province introduced the AccèsLogis program in 1997, which promised to build 1,820 units of housing per year (influential housing advocacy groups had demanded 8,000 units per year at the time). The majority of these units (1,200) were for low-income people; 500 were for seniors, and the remaining 120 were for people with special needs, including the homeless, people with disabilities, and women fleeing violence (Société d'habitation du Québec 1997, 22). An estimated 25,330 units of social housing have been built by the province alone since the 1990s, and the number jumps to 37,296 when we include units that were either under development or promised as of 2014 (Société d'habitation du Québec 2014). Again, however, only a small portion is dedicated to housing the homeless, with the rest intended for low-income people.

The provincial government therefore occupies a much larger space in the world of social policy in Quebec than it does in Alberta. Even before developing its own policy and plan on homelessness, the province played a significant role in the fight against homelessness in Montreal because of the unique way the federal Homelessness Partnering Strategy (HPS) funding is implemented in Quebec. In all other provinces, this funding flows from the federal government to "community entities" that are tasked with using that funding to fight homelessness; in Calgary, this funding goes directly from the federal government to the CHF. In Quebec, however, where housing and homelessness are seen as provincial jurisdiction, and where the province jealously protects its powers, the federal funding is transferred to the provincial government. The province then distributes the funding to local-level actors.

The province of Quebec, then led by the Liberal Party, introduced a three-year plan on homelessness in 2010, which was guided by the voices of hundreds of community actors who either submitted documents to the consultations or participated directly in the process (Quebec. Ministère de l'Emploi et de la Solidarité sociale 2014). Many community groups had, however, been advocating for a policy to precede a plan. The Réseau d'aide aux personnes seules et itinérantes de Montréal (RAPSIM) noted that coordination of provincial actions was key to the logic for a provincial policy "so that the right hand and the left hand do the same thing, which is currently not the case. The best example of this is regarding public space: with the left hand, the state finances aid organizations … with the right hand, it criminalizes homeless people" (RAPSIM 2009; author's translation).

In 2012, the Parti Québécois (PQ) was elected to power. With strong ties to community groups, the PQ government made good on a campaign promise and introduced a *policy* on homelessness in 2014. The policy was the result of significant consultations and direct involvement of community groups throughout the province. Though the PQ lost the next election and was not able to develop a new plan on homelessness, the Liberals were returned to power and they did. Even the RAPSIM was impressed with the degree to which the plan followed from the policy (there were concerns that the right-of-centre Liberal party would abandon many of the values embedded in the left-of-centre PQ's policy), but the plan was criticized for its lack of funding, notably for the development of housing.

The 2010–13 plan and the 2015–20 plan are highly coordinated at the provincial level. The first plan involved nine ministries, and the 2015–20 plan includes eleven. The province is thus a very engaged and coordinated actor in the fight against homelessness. However, the local level in Montreal is also very active in developing and implementing social policy, including with respect to homelessness. The RAPSIM, as noted above, is a very influential advocacy body that has existed since the 1970s, defends the rights of people experiencing homelessness, and represents the interests of the organizations that serve the homeless population. It advocates at all levels of government (but most significantly at the provincial level) for its preferred solution to homelessness: social housing with community support. The RAPSIM's governance structure is democratic and participatory. The board comprises representatives from member organizations, all of whom are elected by the broader membership. The board is therefore comprised exclusively of service providers, and its decisions (such as its preferred solution to homelessness) reflect the perspective of the majority of its members, all of whom are service providers or researchers.

The municipal government in Montreal has recently taken an interest in homelessness and has developed an action plan on homelessness.

The plan introduced by Montreal mayor Denis Coderre in 2013 was not the first Montreal-based plan for homelessness, but it was unique in that it broke very clearly from provincial goals and priorities. Previous plans, notably Agir Ensemble, were very tied to the provincial action on homelessness. In many ways, municipal action in this area was an example of the municipality being a "taker" of public policy; the plan in 2013 resulted from the municipality becoming a "maker" of public policy. A number of the objectives in the 2013 plan – including conducting a point-in-time homeless count and creating the position of "protector" of the homeless, inspired by Vancouver advocate Judy Graves – were not priorities of the provincial government and thus represented a break from the municipality taking the lead from the province. The municipality involved a number of internal and external partners in the development of its plan. Internal partners included the police, the public transit authority, the municipal court, housing, and the social diversity division, along with a number of boroughs. External partners included provincial ministries (health and social services and immigration) as well as, among other organizations, the Mouvement pour mettre fin à l'itinérance à Montréal (MMFIM; see below) and the RAPSIM.

The MMFIM is composed of a broad range of interested actors, not just community and service organizations but also the private sector and researchers, who developed a plan to end homelessness, introduced in late 2015. The MMFIM's board involves service providers but also includes a private-sector member, an "institutional" member (from a health institution, for example), and a researcher. The plan was developed with extensive consultation with Montreal-based actors, notably the largest service providers in the city, as well as the broader MMFIM membership. It also drew on experiences in the fight against homelessness throughout the rest of Canada and Europe. The MMFIM estimates that ending homelessness in Montreal will cost $36.9 million (including $18.8 million in new funding). So far, the plan has received funding from the municipal government for implementation ($140,000 per year for five years), but the most costly parts of the plan, including specialized support teams and more affordable housing, remain unfunded.

These three local-level actors (the MMFIM, the RAPSIM, and the municipal government) do not always see eye to eye on issues relating to homelessness. Notably, the RAPSIM and the MMFIM have taken different approaches in terms of the definition of homelessness and policy solutions to it. In terms of definitions, the MMFIM uses the

Canadian definition of homelessness, developed by the Canadian Homelessness Research Network (MMFIM 2015). While this definition recognizes a broad spectrum of housing insecurity ranging from the chronically homeless to those at risk of homelessness, the RAPSIM prefers an even broader definition of homelessness that emphasizes the importance of social inclusion as well as housing. This definition favoured by the RAPSIM was introduced in the province's policy on homelessness (Gouvernement du Québec 2014).

The approaches to homelessness are also different; the RAPSIM has been very critical of Housing First, which is seen as a one-size-fits-all solution imposed by the federal government. The MMFIM, many of whose members are closely tied to the federal study that led to the adoption of Housing First (the At Home/Chez Soi study), is much less critical of Housing First. The two groups must work together, however, and are often both present on the same board or advisory council (as is the case with the development of the city's second Action Plan on Homelessness). But disagreements persist, and the fight against homelessness is highly politicized in Montreal. This is not terribly unusual, and cities like Vancouver and Toronto have seen significant clashes between advocates for the homeless over what should be done with funding dollars, for example. But much of the disagreement in this area relates to identity and how Montreal fits within Canada. In this sense, the governance model in Montreal is fragmented along old identity and to a lesser extent linguistic lines. In other words, the MMFIM sees Montreal as a Canadian city and is favourable to Canadian approaches to and definitions of homelessness, whereas the RAPSIM is more nationalist in its understanding of homelessness and its history (see Smith 2016).

The governance model in Montreal is therefore very fragmented, with powerful groups of actors taking very different approaches to the issue. In all cases, community groups are active in the leadership of these groups and have historically played an important role in social policy development at the local and provincial level. Groups have extensive expertise based on their on-the-ground experience as service providers.

DISCUSSION

Comparing these two governance models and their resulting action on homelessness shows that they have opposite strengths and weaknesses; in other words, they are mirror images. On the one hand, power is highly concentrated in Calgary, where the Calgary Homeless Foundation controls most of the funding dedicated to homelessness and has set the agenda in terms of policy development and implementation. In Montreal, power is much more diffuse, with a number of powerful actors (including the RAPSIM, the MMFIM, and the local government) putting forward their own, often contradictory approaches to homelessness. On the other hand, the balance of power among civil society actors in these two cities is very different. In Calgary, the private sector took the lead in the fight against homelessness, and while the revised versions of the plan were more inclusive of community voices, the leadership of the CHF remains dominated by the private sector. The opposite is the case in Montreal, where the private sector is a comparatively weak actor in this area and in the overall urban governance of the city (Bherer and Hamel 2012). Rather, civil society or third-sector actors are powerful and enjoy a privileged place in policy development at the provincial and local levels. These actors are involved not just in policy consultations or implementation but as full partners in policy development. A discussion of these strengths and weaknesses helps us to understand, and even begin to speculate about, how an increased federal presence at the homelessness table might affect the responsiveness of these efforts to fight homelessness.

At the local level in Calgary, the CHF has centralized power and control over homelessness, and there is very little disagreement among the local actors involved in the fight against homelessness (including the municipal government, the private sector, and the third sector). This is in large part because the private sector is so strong in the urban governance model of Calgary (Feng, Li, and Langford 2014; Miller and Smart 2012). There are, of course, disagreements, and not everyone fully agrees with the CHF's approach. This was especially the case in the early days of the ten-year plan, when large service providers (notably the Drop-In Centre) was vocally opposed to the CHF's plans (McLean 2008). Though disagreements regarding the approach to ending homelessness remain below the surface (Rassel 2014), this controversy has largely faded. At the local level therefore, there is very little power or agenda fragmentation. Further, the provincial plan on homelessness is very much in line with what the CHF has done, and the province has taken significant steps toward internal administrative alignment and coordination.

Studies of the governance of homelessness in Canada and in Europe emphasize that centralization and coordination of efforts to fight homelessness are key to effective outcomes (Boesveldt 2015; Doberstein 2016). However, while provincial and local agendas align in terms of philosophy and priorities, the investments required to fully implement those promises have not followed. This has made progress difficult, despite agreement on goals and policy instruments. Put more generously, the fact that all these very coordinated local and provincial efforts have not resulted in a significant reduction in homelessness in the province underscores how challenging homelessness is as a public policy problem. The federal infusion of funding, both for specific homelessness programs and also in the area of affordable housing, will likely help to make these local and provincial actions more effective. The federal government has not promised to end homelessness, but its emphasis on prioritizing the most chronically homeless and building more affordable housing is broadly in line with local and provincial priorities. And since the main actors are broadly in agreement about what needs to be done, this federal investment will not be divided among competing interests or priorities and should result in a reduction in homelessness in Calgary.

At the local level, Montreal is in a sense the mirror image of Calgary. There is significant power fragmentation at the local level, which is made more troublesome by significant disagreements among the powerful actors on very foundational issues such as the definition. The RAPSIM and the MMFIM are notably at odds about the solutions to homelessness, and while they both advocate for more affordable housing, there is disagreement about very fundamental questions, such as how homelessness is defined and what kind of housing (social housing or government-supplemented private rental housing) should be used in solutions to it. The city engages and supports (politically and financially) both, though it also continues to work on its own action plan on homelessness. This agenda fragmentation has made the issue of homelessness very political and risks creating important barriers in the fight against homelessness by dividing resources and possibly even having agendas that are completely at odds with one another.

The provincial government has long acted in the area of poverty, housing, and, more recently, homelessness. In developing its plan on homelessness, the province took a very coordinated and coherent approaching, bringing eleven different government departments together to make sure that the actions of one department did not contradict the actions of another. The internal cohesion at the provincial level is important from the multilevel governance perspective (see Horak 2012), but it runs into difficulty when it comes to coordinating with the deeply conflicted local level. As long as the RAPSIM and the MMFIM advocate for different solutions, effective multilevel governance of homelessness will be difficult.

One recent change that might bring some more coherence to the local level was the creation of the post of the "protector" of the homeless. This position was inspired by Vancouver advocate Judy Graves, who worked for the city but spoke with a strong, authoritative, and independent voice about homelessness. Serge Lareault, the founder of Montreal's street newspaper *l'Itinéraire*, was hired to be the city's first protector of the homeless. It is early into his mandate, but his role is to help with the implementation of policies on homelessness, to ensure that the voice of the homeless is heard at City Hall, and to develop a mayor's committee on homelessness. The former mayor, Denis Coderre, said, "he is not the mayor's protector, he is the homeless's protector … he is not here to tell me what I want to hear, he is here to speak to the reality of the street" (Corriveau 2016; my translation).

In assembling the mayor's committee on homelessness, Lareault has the difficult job of bringing together these different and disagreeing groups. His previous work as the founder of *l'Itinéraire* has given him legitimacy among community groups, since *l'Itinéraire* is a well-liked newspaper and also an important source of revenue for many low-income or homeless Montrealers. As the author of the MMFIM's plan on homelessness, however, Lareault is seen by some as partial to its approach to homelessness.

The flip side of these two governance models is the balance of power among civil society actors: in Calgary the private sector is very strong whereas in Montreal it is the third sector. When it comes to homelessness, the third sector has a closer connection to and thus a deeper knowledge of the issue than the private sector. In Montreal, even though these voices are divided, they are powerful and very organized, thanks to a policy-making tradition in Quebec and Montreal that fully involves these third-sector actors. The memberships of the RAPSIM and the MMFIM in particular are large and engaged, making them strong advocates and voices for what the populations they serve need.

An important part of the mandate given to Lareault (Montreal's homeless protector) is to represent at City Hall the voice of those people experiencing homelessness. This institutionalized form of participation of the homeless in the policy-making process should make the city's policies more responsive to local needs, especially if their feedback is brought not just to the advocacy and implementation of public policies but also to their development.

In Calgary, the private sector has taken the lead, and (as noted above) while the third sector has become more involved in the content of the plans, decision-making power rests with private-sector actors. This is, as numerous accounts have shown, the reality of urban governance in Calgary, where the private sector frequently enjoys even more power than elected officials in local decision-making (Feng, Li, and Langford 2014; Miller and Smart 2012). The private-sector actors who developed the ten-year plan took their task seriously, did extensive research on best practices, and did their best to apply the lessons from other fights against homelessness to the Calgary context. They consulted extensively with actors in other cities to learn about their successes and pitfalls, building these lessons into Calgary's plan. But this is different from knowing the day-to-day needs of the services and those who use them. Indeed, Steve Snyder, the chair of the Calgary and Alberta groups that developed plans on homelessness, told journalist Susan Scott about his initial involvement: "I'm just an observer. I don't know the facts. I'm not qualified. I'm just a business guy" (quoted in Scott 2012, 92).

Calgary and Montreal actors were involved in federal policy-making around homelessness and housing through consultations, meetings, written submissions, and lobbying efforts. Homelessness is a highly place-based phenomenon, taking different forms in urban and suburban environments, sometimes even from neighbourhood to neighbourhood (Gaetz, Gulliver, and Richter 2015). Montreal third-sector actors, given their direct link with homelessness and their deep familiarity with its different forms throughout the city, were more likely to engage in a way that would create policy that was responsive to that context.

Calgary and Montreal (and Alberta and Quebec) have in their own ways been at the forefront of the fight against homelessness. They have developed their own responses to homelessness and have built very different governance structures. Montreal's structure, with three local-level entities acting in the area of homelessness and thus high fragmentation, allows more space for debate and different opinions about what homelessness is and how it should be addressed. This fragmentation is a strength when it comes to allowing for diversity and responsiveness in the interventions with respect to homelessness. But the flip side is that this fragmentation poses barriers to effective public policy. With different actors advocating for different solutions and potentially pulling in different directions, the fight against homelessness is in many ways hindered by the fight *about* the fight against homelessness. Calgary's centralized system's main advantage is that there is a clear direction and all resources are working toward that same end. The comparatively weaker role for third-sector actors in Calgary, however, suggests that the policy may be less responsive to the needs of the services and homeless population in that city.

NOTES

1 This is a brief overview of homelessness in Canada; for a more complete version of this history, see Gaetz (2010); Gaetz, Gulliver, and Richter (2015); Hulchanski (2009); Layton (2008); RAPSIM (2003).
2 BC has also been committed to constructing affordable housing, but from 2001 to 2006 there was a freeze on new developments, whereas in Quebec this commitment has been non-stop.

REFERENCES

Alberta Interagency Council on Homelessness. 2014. *A Progress Report on Housing and Homelessness in Alberta*. Alberta.

Bherer, Laurence, and Pierre Hamel. 2012. "Overcoming Adversity, or Public Action in the Face of New Urban Problems: The Example of Montreal." In *Sites of Governance: Multilevel Governance and Policy Making in Canada's Big Cities*, edited by Martin Horak and Robert Young, 104–34. Montreal: McGill-Queen's University Press.

Boesveldt, Nienke. 2015. *Planet Homeless: Governance Arrangements in Amsterdam, Copehagen, and Glasgow*. The Hague: Eleven International Publishing.

Calgary Homeless Foundation. 2008. *Calgary's 10 Year Plan to End Homelessness, 2008–2018*. Calgary: Calgary Homeless Foundation.

– 2011. *Calgary's 10 Year Plan to End Homelessness 2008–2018, January 2011 Update*. Calgary: Calgary Homeless Foundation.

– 2015. "Home: Ending Homelessness in Calgary." Calgary: Calgary Homeless Foundation.

Canadian Observatory on Homelessness. 2017. "Canadian Observatory on Homelessness Welcomes the 2017 Federal Budget | The Homeless

Hub." Accessed 20 July 2017. http://homelesshub.ca/blog/canadian-observatory-homelessness-welcomes-2017-federal-budget.

Corriveau, Jeanne. 2016. "Serge Lareault nommé protecteur des itinérants." *Le Devoir*. Accessed 2 October 2016. http://www.ledevoir.com/politique/montreal/468483/montreal-serge-lareault-nomme-protecteur-des-itinerants.

Doberstein, Carey. 2016. *Building a Collaborative Advantage: Network Governance and Homelessness Policy-Making in Canada*. Vancouver: UBC Press.

Dressler, Jerilyn. 2016. "Coordinated Access and Assessment: Calgary, Alberta." In *Exploring Effective Systems Responses to Homelessness*, edited by Naomi Nichols and Carey Doberstein, 17–32. Toronto: The Homeless Hub Press.

Feng, Patrick, Ben Li, and Cooper Langford. 2014. "300 People Who Make a Difference: Associative Governance in Calgary." In *Governing Urban Economies: Innovation and Inclusion in Canadian City Regions*, edited by Neil Bradford and Allison Bramwell, 184–203. Toronto: University of Toronto Press.

Gaetz, Stephen. 2010. "The Struggle to End Homelessness in Canada: How We Created the Crisis, and How We Can End It." *Open Health Services and Policy Journal* 3: 21–6.

Gaetz, Stephen, Erin Dej, Tim Ritcher, and Melanie Redman. 2016. *The State of Homelessness in Canada 2016*. Toronto: Canadian Observatory on Homelessness Press.

Gaetz, Stephen, Tanya Gulliver, and Tim Richter. 2015. *The State of Homelessness in Canada 2014*. Toronto: The Homeless Hub Press.

Gouvernement du Québec. 2014. "Ensemble, pour éviter la rue et en sortir, politique nationale de lutte à l'itinérance." www.msss.gouv.qc.ca/itinerance.

Graham, Katherine A., Susan D. Phillips, and Allan M. Maslove. 1998. *Urban Governance in Canada: Representation, Resources, and Restructuring*. Toronto: Harcourt Brace Canada.

Gulliver-Garcia, Tanya. 2014. "How Much Does It Cost to End Homelessness in Canada?" Toronto: The Homeless Hub. http://homelesshub.ca/blog/ending-homelessness-cost.

Horak, Martin. 2012. "Conclusion: Understanding Multilevel Governance in Canada's Cities." In *Sites of Governance: Multilevel Governance and Policy Making in Canada's Big Cities*, edited by Martin Horak and Robert Young, 339–70. Montreal: McGill-Queen's University Press.

Hulchanski, J. David. 2009. *Homelessness in Canada: Past, Present, Future.* Canadian Policy Research Network.

Layton, Jack. 2008. *Homelessness: How to End the National Crisis.* Toronto: Penguin Books Canada.

Leo, Christopher. 2006. "Deep Federalism: Respecting Community Difference in National Policy." *Canadian Journal of Political Science/Revue canadienne de science politique* 39(03): 481–506.

Leo, Christopher, and Todd Andres. 2008. "Deep Federalism through Local Initiative: Unbundling Sovereignty in Winnipeg." *Canadian Journal of Political Science/Revue canadienne de science politique* 41(1): 93–117.

Leo, Christopher, and Martine August. 2009. "The Multilevel Governance of Immigration and Settlement: Making Deep Federalism Work." *Canadian Journal of Political Science/Revue canadienne de science politique* 42(02): 491–510.

Leo, Christopher, and Jeremy Enns. 2009. "Multi-Level Governance and Ideological Rigidity: The Failure of Deep Federalism." *Canadian Journal of Political Science/Revue canadienne de science politique* 42(1): 93–116.

McLean, Linda. 2008. *Beyond Ending Homelessness: An Alternative Perspective.* Calgary: The Drop-In and Rehab Centre.

Milaney, Katrina. 2016. "Systems Planning: A Case Study of the Calgary Homeless Foundation's System Planning Framework." In *Exploring Effective Systems Responses to Homelessness*, edited by Naomi Nichols and Carey Doberstein, 482–95. Toronto: The Homeless Hub Press.

Miller, Byron, and Alan Smart. 2012. "Ascending the Main Stage? Calgary in the Multilevel Governance Drama." In *Sites of Governance: Multilevel Governance and Policy Making in Canada's Big Cities*, edited by Martin Horak and Robert Young, 26–52. Montreal: McGill-Queen's University Press.

MMFIM (Mouvement pour mettre fin à l'itinérance à Montréal). 2015. "Mettre fin à l'itinérance: objectif 2020 – fin de l'itinérance chronique et cyclique." Montreal: MMFIM.

Nichols, Naomi, and Carey Doberstein, eds. 2016. *Exploring Effective Systems Responses to Homelessness.* Toronto: The Homeless Hub Press.

Noël, Alain. 2005. "Lutte contre la pauvreté ou lutte contre les pauvres?" In *L'annuaire du Québec 2005*, edited by Michel Venne, 504–13. Montréal: Fides.

Press, Jordan. 2017. "Federal Budget 2017: Liberals Dedicate Billions for Affordable Housing." *The Huffington Post.* Accessed 20 July 2017.

http://www.huffingtonpost.ca/2017/03/22/federal-budget-affordable-housing-liberals_n_15548174.html.

Quebec. Ministère de l'Emploi et de la Solidarité sociale. 2014. *Bilan – plan d'action interministériel en itinérance 2010–2013*. Quebec: Gouvernement du Québec.

RAPSIM (Réseau d'aide aux personnes seules et itinérantes de Montréal). 2003. *Comprendre l'itinérance*. Montréal: RAPSIM. www.rapsim.org.

– 2009. *Pour une politique plus qu'un plan d'action en itinérance*. Montréal: RAPSIM. Accessed 8 August 2016. http://www.rapsim. org/102/Politiqueeeneitinerance.montreal.

Rassel, Jason van. 2014. "Controversial Affordable Housing Project Faces New Opposition." *Calgary Herald*. Accessed 26 March 2016. http:// calgaryherald.com/news/local-news/controversial-affordable-housing-project-faces-new-opposition.

Rice, James, and Michael Prince. 2013. *Changing Politics of Canadian Social Policy*. 2nd ed. Toronto: University of Toronto Press.

Scott, Susan. 2012. *The Beginning of the End: The Story of the Calgary Homeless Foundation*. Calgary: The Calgary Homeless Foundation.

Shapcott, Michael. 2007. *Ten Things You Should Know about Housing and Homelessness*. Toronto: The Wellesley Institute.

Smith, Alison. 2016. "Filling the Gap: Cities and the Fight against Homelessness in Canada." PhD thesis, Montreal, Université de Montréal.

Société d'habitation du Québec. 1997. *L'action gouvernementale en habitation: orientation et plan d'action*. Québec: Gouvernement du Québec.

– 2014. *Suivi de la réalisation des logements AccèsLogis Québec et Logement Abordable Québec au 30 septembre 2014*. Quebec: Gouvernement du Québec.

CONCLUSIONS

Accountability and Responsiveness at the Municipal Level: Limitations and Opportunities

Ruth Dassonneville

In representative democracies, citizens delegate decision-making to a small number of representatives. The delegation of power is usually decided on by means of elections occurring at different levels of government. For this process of delegation by means of an election to function well, and for representative democracy in general to be considered legitimate, it is of foremost importance that representatives – once elected – act in the best interest of the citizens (Pitkin 1967).

Voters as well as elected representatives have a role to play and can act to strengthen the public opinion–policy nexus – that is, the link between the preferences of the citizens and the policies that representatives implement. For citizens, this means they have to go out and vote on election day and choose representatives whose opinions and policy proposals closely align with their own policy and issue preferences (Thomassen and van Ham 2014). Comparative research shows that citizens are quite capable of doing so. For example, voters are able to situate political parties on an ideological left–right axis, and the proximity rule (i.e., choosing the ideologically most proximate party) appears to explain well what parties citizens vote for on election day (Dalton, Farrell, and McAllister 2011; Thomassen and van Ham 2014). The representatives for their part, once elected, have to be responsive to public opinion. Responsiveness entails, on the one hand, acting on what was promised during the election campaign and abiding by the party platforms that representatives were elected on (Stokes 1999) while being continuously attentive and responsive to changes in public opinion during their time in office on the other (Wlezien and Soroka 2012). Moreover, the fact that elections are held recurrently ensures a feedback link. In other words, when casting a vote citizens are not only deemed to consider what candidates and parties are promising for the future but also to evaluate candidates' past performance (Downs 1957; Key 1966). In this way, citizens also use their vote to hold incumbent governments accountable, "retaining in office those incumbents who perform well and ousting from office those who do not" (Manin, Przeworski, and Stokes 1999, 10). For evaluating which incumbents have performed well, voters could evaluate whether elected politicians have fulfilled their election pledges (Thomson et al. 2017). In addition to this – rather narrow – mandate perspective on accountability, voters could conceive of representatives as "trustees," giving representatives more room for manoeuver and only evaluating in election times whether incumbents appear to have acted in the best interest of the citizens (Andeweg and Thomassen 2005; Pitkin 1967). This room for manoeuver can be important, since it allows incumbents to react to unexpected events or changed circumstances without being punished for such flexibility by the voters (Stokes 1997). In addition, a trustee perspective on accountability can help us to understand how accountability functions in the absence of clear party platforms with election pledges – as is often the case at the local level. Performance evaluations effectively appear to have an important impact on the probability of re-electing the incumbent on election day. A rich literature on economic voting, for example, shows a strong correlation between subjective evaluations of the economy as well as objective economic indicators on the one hand and the odds of voting for the incumbent on the other (Stegmaier and Lewis-Beck 2013). Perhaps even more important than the presence of such a mechanism of reward and punishment is the mere possibility of punishment. Indeed, it is argued that it is especially the fear of being voted out of office that incentivizes representatives to govern well (Maravall 1999). In summary, for elections to serve as an effective mechanism for achieving democratic representation, it is essential that citizens use their votes to signal their policy preferences, that elected representatives are responsive – in terms of what they have promised, in terms of what public opinion wants, and in terms of what is in the best interest of the citizens – and that voters are capable of voting out of office incumbents who do not deliver on their promises or who underperform in terms of policy outcomes. At the local level, and in the Canadian context, how well do the respective elements in this chain between citizens' preferences and policy outcomes function? This question is of huge importance – explaining why, in my opinion, the contribution of this book cannot be underestimated. By scrutinizing the functioning of the respective elements in this chain of representation in the local context, the nine chapters of this book together offer valuable insights into the quality of Canada's local democracy.

RESPONSIVENESS AND ACCOUNTABILITY AT THE LOCAL LEVEL

The chapters of this book each focus, in their own way, on two of the three mechanisms just introduced: responsiveness and accountability. Overall, the guiding questions of this book are whether, once elected, local incumbents are responsive to their citizens and to what extent citizens hold incumbents accountable when they are not responsive or when citizens are dissatisfied with their work.

Examining these questions with a focus on the local level is highly important for two reasons: one, the central place that local politics plays in politics and in citizens' lives, and two, the gap the book fills in the literature and the insights it provides with respect to research on other levels of governance as well as some fundamental political science theories.

It is easy to make the case for the importance of the local level of governance for democracy and for citizens in general. To begin, it is the local level that is closest to the citizens. Decisions taken at the local level have a direct impact on people's lives and are very concrete. Policy and policy change are highly visible at a local level as well. Moreover, the distance between constituents and their political representatives is smallest at the local level, meaning that citizens can here voice their opinions and have an impact on decisions more easily than at other levels of governance. It is therefore not surprising that processes of democratic innovation and efforts to strengthen democracy are to a large extent focused on the local arena (Barber 2013; Cornwall and Coelho 2007). When local democracy functions well, citizens will easily sense this. Conversely, when responsiveness and accountability are hampered at the local level, citizens will immediately see the malfunctioning of local democracy as well.

The local level is also highly important insofar as the majority of all elected officials, taken together, are representatives of this level

(Trounstine 2009). Thus, if we wish to understand the behaviour of representatives and their interaction with public opinion, it seems natural to focus on this – in terms of numbers – largest level of governance. Yet very few studies that aim to investigate the opinion–policy link place emphasis on the local level. This is not to say that the local level is never addressed in research that examines the responsiveness of representatives to public opinion or the extent to which incumbents are held accountable by voters. However, these studies usually link the local level to another, higher level of governance deemed more worthy of scholars' attention. Thus, studies focusing on a purely local opinion–policy nexus are rare. The literature on economic voting, for example, which examines whether incumbents are held accountable for the state of the economy, originally focused on the national level only, with studies investigating the link between national GDP growth rates or national-level unemployment rates and the popularity of the governing incumbent. Over time, evidence for such a national-level link (arrow 1 in figure 10.1) has been found in an increasingly large and diverse set of countries (Stegmaier and Lewis-Beck 2013), prompting scholars to begin refining the basic reward–punishment mechanism based on economic conditions. Some researchers of economic voting did this by paying closer attention to the local level, albeit while retaining the national level as the focus of this field of study. For example, a number of publications have shown that national-level conditions can affect voters' choices for a subnational or local level. That is, the local (or regional) ballot is used by voters to credit or blame the national incumbent for his or her national-level performance (arrow 2 in figure 10.1) (Auberger and Dubois 2011; Fauvelle-Aymar and Lewis-Beck 2011; Jérôme and Lewis-Beck 1999; Martins and Veiga 2013). In addition, scholars have argued that local conditions affect voting behaviour in national elections as well (arrow 3 in figure 10.1). Their studies show that variation in local economic conditions help a great deal in explaining how well the national incumbent performs in a specific region or area (Johnston and Pattie 2001; Johnston et al. 2000). Somewhat surprisingly, the local conditions– local vote link has received substantially less attention (though there are exceptions; see, e.g., Berry and Howell 2007; Dassonneville, Claes, and Lewis-Beck 2016; Boyne et al. 2009). This lack of focus on the local level in the economic voting literature is an example of what holds for research on democratic representation in general. While the

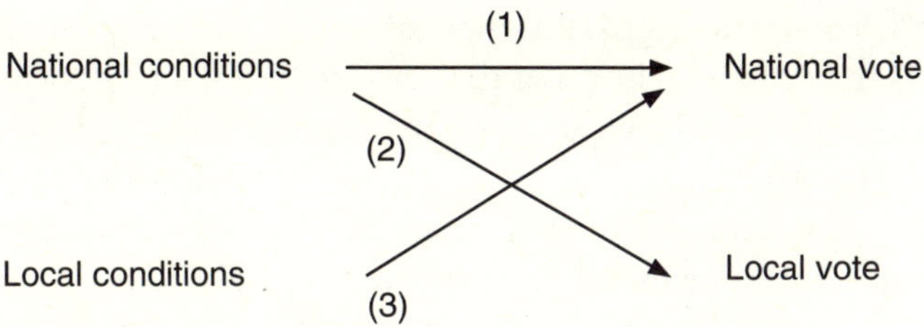

Figure 10.1 Public opinion and policy at different levels
of government

local level is the level with the most elected representatives, and also
the level of governance that is closest to the citizens, we know relatively little about the local public opinion–policy nexus. This book
exactly addresses this question and in doing so fills an important gap
in the literature. The insights it provides, furthermore, travel well
beyond the purely local level.

OPPORTUNITIES FOR LOCAL-LEVEL RESPONSIVENESS AND ACCOUNTABILITY

A number of specificities of the local context, and of the Canadian
local context in particular, make studying responsiveness and accountability at this level highly relevant for scholars of representative
democracy in general.

First, the local political arena in Canada is largely a non-partisan
context. This is relevant because ever since the publication of *The
American Voter* (Campbell et al. 1980), scholars have pointed out
that partisan affiliations function as a perceptual screen. That is, an
identification with a particular party colours citizens' perceptions of
and evaluations of political actors and political events. Consequently,
partisans are less likely to hold "their" party accountable when it does
not deliver or does not perform or in cases of misbehaviour (Achen
and Bartels 2016; Taber and Lodge 2006). By contrast, in a context
with weak or non-existent partisan attachments, citizens can hold
incumbent politicians accountable in an unbiased way. It should be
noted, however, that the Canadian context is – mostly – explicitly
non-partisan, which does not exclude the presence of implicit partisan
ties, a point to which I will return below.

Second, and relatedly, parties that run for election at the municipal level in Canada have – in general – no formal links to parties at the provincial or federal level. In this way, another source of noise that hampers accountability mechanisms is weakened in the context of Canadian local elections. Indeed, previous research has indicated that voters regularly make use of their vote in "second-order" elections to send a signal to parties that govern at another level (Reif and Schmitt 1997). If, however, there are no obvious links between the parties on the ballot in a local context to the parties at upper levels of government, it becomes difficult to see how voters could use their local ballots to punish or reward actors at another level. In summary, the absence of cross-level links between parties makes for a context in which voters can effectively judge the local level and local actors on their own merits.

Theoretically, therefore, one can expect the mechanism of accountability to be particularly strong in municipal elections in Canada. At the local level, voters' partisan bias will be limited, and there are no direct links to other levels of governance that could dominate the local context either. From a research perspective, this makes for a highly interesting context. Given claims of weakening partisan attachments across advanced democracies (Dalton 2013; Dalton and Wattenberg 2002) and given that scholars expect accountability to be strengthened in low-partisan environments (Kayser and Wlezien 2011), the topic of how democracy functions in a context with weak partisan ties becomes all the more important. One could therefore consider the local level a laboratory for investigating the functioning of democracy in a context with weak or absent partisan affiliations (see Couture, Breux, and Bherer, chapter 3 in this book). In this sense, this book speaks to a much broader audience than to scholars of local politics or Canadian politics only. Indeed, the implications of the research that is presented here are much wider.

The mechanism of accountability was addressed more directly in these chapters than was the topic of responsiveness, although the implications of accountability on the latter are evident. When voters hold incumbents to account, or are capable of doing so, incumbent politicians and parties have strong incentives to be responsive – in terms of their election promises as well as in terms of being attentive to shifts in public opinion. As a result, if accountability mechanisms are indeed particularly strong at the local level, then the same can be deemed to hold for responsiveness.

LIMITATIONS TO LOCAL-LEVEL RESPONSIVENESS
AND ACCOUNTABILITY

Despite these opportunities, the contributions in this book point out important limitations to accountability (and responsiveness) at the local level. These limitations relate to the absence of parties, citizens' limited knowledge about the local level and local actors, short-term considerations, and limited clarity of responsibility. In what follows I will address each of these limitations in turn and by doing so summarize the main arguments presented in this book.

A first and important limitation to accountability and responsiveness at the local level relates to the absence of stable political parties. As Stephenson, McGregor, and Moore claim in chapter 1, "party labels tie candidates to previous contests and governments." It is generally considered somewhat problematic for the accountability mechanism to function if an incumbent does not or cannot run for re-election, for example because of term limits (Manin 1997). However, in a context with fairly stable parties and party labels, even if an incumbent mayor does not run for re-election, her or his party can still be held accountable for the mayor's performance. In contrast, when party labels are unstable and new teams are formed in the run-up to each election, citizens are basically deprived of the possibility of holding the incumbent accountable for her or his performance. The implication would be that an incumbent who decides not to run for re-election is free to shirk accountability and has no incentive to be responsive to citizens' preferences (Manin, Przeworski, and Stokes 1999). Clearly, the absence of any possibility of holding incumbents accountable threatens the function of elections as a mechanism to realize democratic representation. It should be noted, however, that there often are implicit partisan ties between candidates and particular parties (Cutler and Matthews 2005). In addition, Stephenson, McGregor, and Moore's chapter in this volume shows that voters are inventive and can find additional cues to link a previous incumbent to the candidates running for election. In the context of the Toronto 2014 municipal election, for example, family links were used as a heuristic, and Doug Ford was held accountable for his brother's performance. It seems, then, that citizens are sufficiently inventive to find heuristics that allow them to hold someone accountable for the performance of an incumbent who does not run for re-election. However, whether these alternative cues are truly informative and whether it is "fair" to use them are questions open to debate.

Second, citizens may lack knowledge not only to evaluate all candidates running for local office but also to evaluate the performance of the local incumbent. The impact of this lack of knowledge becomes evident from Lucas and Sayers's chapter (chapter 4) in this book. The re-election rates they report for incumbents are stunningly high, indicating that these candidates have an advantage over the others that is simply based on name recognition. Strong accountability mechanisms, in contrast, seem hardly at play at the local level. Nonetheless, this book also gives indications of how this lack of knowledge and accountability might be overcome. The chapter by Sancton (chapter 5) argues that when incumbents' behaviour receives substantial media coverage and a considerable amount of attention, this incumbency advantage vanishes completely. The author's description of the case of the Greater Sudbury and London incumbent councillors even indicates that broad media coverage of incumbents' misbehaviour can translate into very strong punishments in the polling booth. The implication is that incumbents cannot hope to escape punishment for misconduct even in a low-knowledge context. The media can thus play an important role in informing citizens and allowing for accountability, and their impact is arguably so big because the local context is non-partisan. We know from previous research that even if political scandals or allegations of corruption break, they do not always affect the vote – to a large extent because partisans are "turning a blind eye" (Anduiza, Gallego, and Muñoz 2013). By contrast, without a partisan bias citizens are unbound and incumbents might end up getting severely punished. At the same time, the implication of this scenario is that the media may have too much impact. If all the information that citizens have for evaluating the incumbent's performance comes from the media, and if this information quite forcefully drives their behaviour, then journalists and other non-elected officials (e.g., the ombudsman in this case) can basically decide on the re-election of local councillors.

Third, in the second chapter of this book, about the re-election of incumbents, Couture and Breux show that in the non-partisan and non-ideological local context, short-term benefits such as tax cuts are likely to guide voters' choices. Such behaviour does signal accountability – that is, voters reward incumbents for tax cuts. Furthermore, it indicates responsiveness, since political actors and parties appear responsive to citizens' preferences for lowering taxes, at least in the election year. However, in this context it is important to point out the difference between responsive parties on the one hand and responsible parties on the other (Mair 2009). While responsive actors seek to respond to citizens' short-term interests and, by doing so, win votes, responsible parties are oriented toward governing in the best interests of citizens, albeit taking into account the long-term interests of citizens as well. The take-home message from this chapter is thus that the presence of responsiveness and accountability at the municipal level is not, in and of itself, indicative of a well-functioning democracy (see also Achen and Bartels 2016).

Fourth, a number of chapters in this collection highlight that responsibility at the local level is not well defined. That is, it is not clear who is responsible for particular services, decisions, or policies, and consequently it is not clear who should be held accountable for these services, decisions, and policies. Lyons and Spicer's chapter (chapter 7) focuses on agreements for inter-municipal cooperation and how they limit the extent to which local councillors can be held accountable. They argue that accountability is reduced in particular because of a lack of transparency on the agreements and conduct of these inter-municipal cooperations. Tremblay-Racicot, for her part, in chapter 8, attributes the complexity of accountability at the local level to decisions taken by non-elected committees. Since members of these boards are not elected and do not run for re-election, she argues, citizens have no opportunity to judge their performance in the voting booth.

Finally, in chapter 9, Smith focuses on the issue of homelessness in Calgary and Montreal. She draws attention to the role of fragmentation of jurisdiction and argues that disagreement between different actors renders policy implementation more difficult.

THE LOCAL CONTEXT: SPECIFIC OR NOT?

Given the lack of stable parties and partisan ties at the local level, the local context should make for strong accountability and hence responsiveness as well (see Couture, Breux, and Bherer in this book). Obviously, this could only be expected to hold when an incumbent runs for re-election, as Stephenson, McGregor, and Moore argue in this book. However, the contributions in this book do more to highlight elements that *limit* the attribution of accountability as well as responsiveness at the local level. This raises the question of whether these elements are really that unique to the local level. I would claim that they do not have to be considered as such and that they, by and large, exist at other levels of government as well. The findings presented in this book are therefore more generalizable to other levels of government, or to government in general, than one might expect from a book on municipal politics. In the following I summarize the three main findings.

First, while citizens' knowledge about local politics and the amount of information available for informing oneself about the local level might well be limited, we should not overestimate the extent to which citizens are informed about politics at other levels of governance. Delli Carpini and Keeter (1997) have famously questioned the extent to which electorates are knowledgeable and have the information that is necessary to make political decisions and to participate in politics. In addition, Prior (2014) has argued that in the current high-choice media environment, where information is more readily available yet not necessarily consumed any more often because of that, accountability in general depends on a small segment of citizens, such as "news junkies." Furthermore, even these "news junkies," if they get news exclusively from like-minded people on social media, cannot be trusted to hold incumbents to account (Sunstein 2001; but see Diehl, Weeks, and de Zuniga 2016). Therefore, the lack of knowledge about politics and the implications this has for accountability are not problems that are specific to the local context alone. If there is any crucial difference between the local context and other levels of government, it is, I would argue, the absence or weakness of partisan affiliations. As a result, political information can affect attitudes without the biasing and intervening role of partisan ties. When there is information – even if it is rare – it is more likely to influence and steer public opinion in a particular way. Importantly, studying the impact of information in such an apartisan context sheds light on the consequences of a more general trend toward dealignment.

Second, the voters' and actors' focus on the short term, as evident from the business-cycle effects reported in the chapter by Couture and Breux, need not be considered specific to the local level either. As the authors indicate, business-cycle effects can and have been observed in other contexts as well (Nordhaus 1975; Persson and Tabellini 1990). Importantly, scholars have argued that across advanced democracies, the gap between responsiveness on the one hand and responsibility on the other is increasing. Mair (2009), for example, has argued that the over-time weakening of linkages between parties and citizens gives less room to parties to be responsible and pushes them to be more short term–oriented and vote-seeking. Here again, the local apartisan context under examination in this book gives valuable insights into the consequences of a more widespread trend in voters' and parties' behaviour.

Third, the focus of Lyons and Spicer, Tremblay-Racicot, and Smith (chapters 7, 8, and 9) on the importance of clarity of responsibility is in alignment with the orientations of the large body of literature on the topic (see part 3 of this book). Scholars of economic voting, for example, have argued that the clarity of responsibility – and therefore also reward and punishment for economic conditions – is weakened when political power is more dispersed. To refer to just one area of research, the economic vote is argued to be weaker under coalition governments, under a minority government, in two-chamber systems, or in federal countries (Cutler 2008; Hobolt, Tilley, and Banducci 2013; León and Orriols 2016; Powell and Whitten 1993). The chapters in this book more specifically focus on the impact of inter-municipal cooperation and the role of non-elected committees on the blurring of accountability. Perhaps the most obvious parallel with what can be observed at other levels of governance is hence to be found in the trend toward economic globalization and political integration. For example, the presence of agreements for inter-municipal cooperation has some resemblance with the process of European integration. The impact of non-elected committees on policy and decision-making, furthermore, is not specific to the local level either, with, for example, the International Monetary Fund or the World Bank exercising a strong influence on countries' economic policies. Research on economic voting has indicated that processes of economic integration effectively reduce the clarity of responsibility and, consequently, mechanisms of accountability (Hellwig and Samuels 2007; Lobo and Lewis-Beck 2012). Once more, the behaviour at the local level that is studied in this book proves to be reflective of and therefore insightful for understanding trends and patterns of change at other levels of governance as well. For all these reasons, the local context is not only interesting in and of itself but can also be considered a laboratory for investigating the consequences of some widely observed processes of change in advanced democracies.

INSIGHTS ON RESPONSIVENESS AND ACCOUNTABILITY
AT THE LOCAL LEVEL AND AVENUES FOR FURTHER RESEARCH

Combined, what do the chapters in this book contribute to our knowledge of responsiveness and accountability at the municipal level and to our knowledge about the functioning of democracy at a local level and democracy more generally?

The municipal level is presented as quite particular in a number of ways, and these particularities undoubtedly affect the extent to which actors are responsive and the extent to which voters hold them accountable. Most important, the absence of stable parties and partisan identities should theoretically allow for strong accountability, since voters in this context are unfettered by partisan biases. The potential for accountability, and responsiveness, at the local level is therefore large.

Nevertheless, huge barriers remain – and it is these barriers to accountability and responsiveness at the local level that receive ample attention in this book. That is, the local context is characterized as a low-information environment where short-term considerations dominate in voters' assessment of incumbents' performance and where clarity of responsibility is low and blurred by things such as inter-municipal cooperation or the role of non-elected committees in decision-making. These barriers, as I have argued in the previous section, can be expected to reduce accountability and responsiveness. Looking to other levels of governance can be informative in this regard, since the same or similar processes have been found to reduce accountability and responsiveness in national-level elections, for example.

With a large potential for but huge barriers to accountability and responsiveness, at the local level, what evidence does this book offer for both phenomena? Despite important barriers, the contributions included in this book clearly give indications of some accountability. That is, local incumbents are punished sometimes. Re-election rates among incumbents are effectively very high, as indicated by Lucas and Sayers in this book. Yet incumbents are not free of punishment, as the chapters by Stephenson, McGregor, and Moore; Sancton; and Couture and Breux point out. Thus, while difficult, accountability is definitely not impossible at the local level.

In a sense, this book is only the beginning. The logical next step in the endeavour to assess accountability and responsiveness at the local level – and therefore the functioning of the local representative democracy – would be to thoroughly examine the uniqueness of the local level by means of an analysis that covers multiple levels of government. Doing so would allow scrutiny of the impact of lower levels of information on the local level on the one hand and of the non-partisan character of this context on the other. By looking at the local context from a comparative perspective, we hope to arrive at a well-founded judgment about the quality of local democracy, especially with regard to the other levels of government.

In addition, the findings presented here and the issues discussed in the chapters call for even more research on the local level. The insights this book provides arouse curiosity about the exact impact of each of the characteristics focused upon. A promising avenue for further research in this regard involves exploiting existing variation at the local level – variation between geographical contexts (municipalities, regions, provinces) as well as variation over time. Doing so would help to answer the question of under what conditions and what circumstances voters are holding local incumbents accountable and would allow us to identify what it might take for local incumbents to be responsive to public opinion. Such an approach is quite data-intensive, as is evident from Couture and Breux's chapter in this book. Yet in pursuing such an approach, studies on local contexts have a major advantage over the cross-national comparative studies on which most of our knowledge about accountability and responsiveness is based. That is, in a comparative analysis of different local contexts (e.g., municipalities) within a single country, a lot of confounding factors are controlled for by the fact that most institutional factors are constant across municipalities. In addition, the impact of major events and shifts in public opinion is not an issue – namely, because time, as a factor, is generally held constant in analyses of behaviour across municipalities during one specific local election (Boulding and Brown 2015). Over the past decade, the literature on party competition has turned to examining variation at the subnational level when testing general theories (Bäck 2008; Skjæveland, Serritzlew, and Blom-Hansen 2007), and there is no doubt that other areas of research will follow suit. In that context, scholars of local politics have an important role to play in effecting this turn and in sharing their findings from studying the local level within the broader field of political science in general.

This book offers extremely valuable insights into the functioning of local democracy and does so by focusing on two key mechanisms: accountability and responsiveness. These insights are of interest to a wide audience and will travel well beyond the community of scholars of local politics. As such, they can also be expected to give prominence to local politics as an object of research attention. Overall, further research should continue exploiting variation at the local level in order to develop a better understanding of important theories in the field of political science in general.

REFERENCES

Achen, Christopher H., and Larry M. Bartels. 2016. *Democracy for Realists: Why Elections Do Not Produce Responsive Government*. Princeton, NJ: Princeton University Press.

Andeweg, Rudi B., and Jacques J. Thomassen. 2005. "Modes of Political Representation: Toward a New Typology." *Legislative Studies Quarterly* 30(4): 507–28.

Anduiza, Eva, Aina Gallego, and Jordi Muñoz. 2013. "Turning a Blind Eye: Experimental Evidence of Partisan Bias in Attitudes toward Corruption." *Comparative Political Studies* 46(12): 1664–92.

Auberger, Antoine, and Eric Dubois. 2011. "The Influence of Local and National Economic Conditions on French Legislative Elections." *Public Choice* 125(3/4): 363–83.

Bäck, Hanna. 2008. "Intra-party Politics and Coalition Formation. Evidence from Swedish Local Government." *Party Politics* 14(1): 71–89.

Barber, Benjamin J. 2013. *If Mayors Ruled the World: Dysfunctional Nations, Rising Cities*. New Haven, CT: Yale University Press.

Berry, Christopher R., and William G. Howell. 2007. "Accountability and Local Elections: Rethinking Retrospective Voting." *Political Science* 69(3): 844–58.

Boulding, Carew, and David S. Brown. 2015. "Do Political Parties Matter for Turnout? Number of Parties, Electoral Rules and Local Elections in Brazil and Bolivia." *Party Politics* 21(3): 404–16.

Boyne, George A., Oliver James, Peter John, and Nicolai Petrovsky. 2009. "Democracy and Government Performance: Holding Incumbents Accountable in English Local Governments." *Journal of Politics* 71(4): 1273–84.

Campbell, Angus, Philip Converse, Warren Miller, and Donald Stokes. 1980. *The American Voter*. Unabridged edition. Chicago: University of Chicago Press.

Cornwall, Andrea, and Vera Schatten Coelho. 2007. *Spaces for Change? The Politics of Citizen Participation in New Democratic Arenas*. London: Zed Books.

Cutler, Fred. 2008. "Whodunnit? Voters and Responsibility in Canadian Federalism." *Canadian Journal of Political Science* 41(3): 627–54.

Cutler, Fred, and J. Scott Matthews. 2005. "The Challenge of Municipal Voting: Vancouver 2002." *Canadian Journal of Political Science* 38(2): 359–82.

Dalton, Russell J. 2013. *The Apartisan American: Dealignment and Changing Electoral Politics*. Thousand Oaks, CA: CQ Press.

Dalton, Russell J., David M. Farrell, and Ian McAllister. 2011. *Political Parties and Democratic Linkage. How Parties Organize Democracy*. Oxford: Oxford University Press.

Dalton, Russell J., and Martin P. Wattenberg. 2002. *Parties without Partisans: Political Change in Advanced Industrial Democracies*. Oxford: Oxford University Press.

Dassonneville, Ruth, Ellen Claes, and Michael S. Lewis-Beck. 2016. "Punishing Local Incumbents for the Local Economy: Economic Voting in the 2012 Belgian Municipal Elections." *Italian Political Science Review* 46(1): 3–22.

Delli Carpini, Michael X., and Scott Keeter. 1997. *What Americans Know about Politics and Why It Matters*. New Haven, CT: Yale University Press.

Diehl, Trevor, Brian E. Weeks, and Homero Gil de Zuniga. 2016. "Political Persuasion on Social Media: Tracing Direct and Indirect Effects of News Use and Social Interaction." *New Media & Society* 18(9): 1875–95.

Downs, Anthony. 1957. *An Economic Theory of Democracy*. New York: Harper and Row.

Fauvelle-Aymar, Christine, and Michael S. Lewis-Beck. 2011. "Second-Order Elections and Economic Voting: The French Regional Example." *Rivista Italiana di Scienza Politica* 41(3): 369–84.

Hellwig, Timothy, and David Samuels. 2007. "Voting in Open Economies. The Electoral Consequences of Globalization." *Comparative Political Studies* 40(3): 283–306.

Hobolt, Sara, James Tilley, and Susan Banducci. 2013. "Clarity of Responsibility: How Government Cohesion Conditions Performance Voting." *European Journal of Political Research* 52(2): 164–87.

Jérôme, Bruno, and Michael S. Lewis-Beck. 1999. "Is Local Politics Local? French Evidence." *European Journal of Political Research* 35(2): 181–97.

Johnston, Ron J., Daniel Dorling, Ian MacAllister, Helena Tunstall, and David Rossiter. 2000. "Local Context, Retrospective Economic Evaluations, and Voting: The 1997 General Election in England and Wales." *Political Behavior* 22(2): 121–43.

Johnston, Ron J., Daniel Dorling, Ian MacAllister, Helena Tunstall, David Rossiter, and Charles Pattie. 2001. "'It's the Economy Stupid' – But

Which Economy? Geographical Scales, Retrospective Economic
　　Evaluations and Voting in the 1997 British General Elections." *Regional
　　Studies: The Journal of the Regional Studies Association* 35(4): 309–19.
Kayser, Mark A., and Christopher Wlezien. 2011. "Performance Pressure:
　　Patterns of Partisanship and the Economic Vote." *European Journal of
　　Political Research* 50(3): 365–94.
Key, Valdimer O. 1966. *The Responsible Electorate: Rationality in Presi-
　　dential Voting 1936–1960.* Cambridge, MA: Harvard University Press.
León, Sandra, and Lluís Orriols. 2016. "Asymmetric Federalism and
　　Economic Voting." *European Journal of Political Research* 55(4):
　　847–65.
Lobo, Marina Costa, and Michael S. Lewis-Beck. 2012. "The Integration
　　Hypothesis: How the European Union Shapes Economic Voting."
　　Electoral Studies 31(3): 522–8.
Mair, Peter. 2009. *Representative vs Responsible Government.* MPIfG
　　Working Paper 09/8. Cologne: Max Planck Institute for the Study of
　　Societies.
Manin, Bernard. 1997. *The Principles of Representative Government.*
　　Cambridge: Cambridge University Press.
Manin, Bernard, Adam Przeworski, and Susan C. Stokes. 1999.
　　"Introduction." In *Democracy, Accountability and Representation,*
　　edited by Adam Przeworski, Susan C. Stokes, and Bernard Manin, 1–26.
　　Cambridge: Cambridge University Press.
Maravall, José María. 1999. "Accountability and Manipulation." In
　　Democracy, Accountability and Representation, edited by Adam
　　Przeworski, Susan C. Stokes, and Bernard Manin, 154–96. Cambridge:
　　Cambridge University Press.
Martins, Rodrigo, and Francisco J. Veiga. 2013. "Economic Voting in
　　Portuguese Municipal Elections." *Public Choice* 155(3): 317–34.
Nordhaus, William D. 1975. "The Political Business Cycle." *Review of
　　Economic Studies* 42(2): 169–90.
Persson, Thomas, and Guido Tabellini. 1990. *Macroeconomic Policy,
　　Credibility and Politics.* London: Harwood.
Pitkin, Hanna. 1967. *The Concept of Representation.* Los Angeles:
　　University of California Press.
Powell, G. Bingham, and Guy D. Whitten. 1993. "A Cross-National
　　Analysis of Economic Voting: Taking Account of the Political Context."
　　American Journal of Political Science 37(2): 391–414.
Prior, Markus. 2014. "Conditions for Political Accountability in High-
　　Choice Media Environment." In *The Oxford Handbook of Political*

Communication, edited by Kate Kenski and Kathleen Hall Jamieson. Oxford: Oxford University Press.

Reif, Karlheinz, and Hermann Schmitt. 1997. "Second-Order Elections." *European Journal of Political Research* 31(1/2): 109–24.

Skjæveland, Asbjørn, Søren Serritzlew, and Jens Blom-Hansen. 2007. "Theories of Coalition Formation: An Empirical Test Using Data from Danish Local Government." *European Journal of Political Research* 46(5): 721–45.

Stegmaier, Mary, and Michael S. Lewis-Beck. 2013. "Economic Voting." In *Oxford Bibliographies in Political Science*, edited by Richard Valelly. New York: Oxford University Press.

Stokes, Susan C. 1997. "Democratic Accountability and Policy Change: Economic Policy in Fujimori's Peru." *Comparative Politics* 29(2): 209–26.

– 1999. "What Do Policy Switches Tell Us about Democracy." In *Democracy, Accountability and Representation*, edited by Adam Przeworski, Susan C. Stokes, and Bernard Manin, 98–130. Cambridge: Cambridge University Press.

Sunstein, C. 2001. *Echo Chambers: Bush v. Gore, Impeachement, and Beyond*. Princeton, NJ: Princeton University Press.

Taber, Charles S., and Milton Lodge. 2006. "Motivated Skepticism in the Evaluation of Political Beliefs." *American Journal of Political Science* 50(3): 755–69.

Thomassen, Jacques, and Carolien van Ham. 2014. "Failing Political Representation or a Change in Kind? Models of Representation and Empirical Trends in Europe." *West European Politics* 37(2): 400–19.

Thomson, Robert, et al. 2017. "The Fulfillment of Parties' Election Pledges: A Comparative Study on the Impact of Power Sharing." *American Journal of Political Science* 61(3): 527–42.

Trounstine, Jessica. 2009. "All Politics Is Local: The Reemergence of the Study of City Politics." *Perspectives on Politics* 7(3): 611–18.

Wlezien, Christopher, and Stuart N. Soroka. 2012. "Political Institutions and the Opinion-Policy Link." *West European Politics* 35(6): 1407–32.

Do Responsiveness and Accountability Matter at the Municipal Level?

Jérôme Couture and Sandra Breux

This work aimed at finding answers to the question: Do responsiveness and accountability matter at the municipal level? The various chapters suggested possible answers to this question from three perspectives: theoretical, empirical, and normative. From a theoretical point of view, the texts addressed the issue of accountability through three lenses, allowing us to enhance our theoretical knowledge of political competition, of the careers and functions of local elected officials, and of public policies and their congruence with citizen preferences. From an empirical point of view, the authors presented new data that will – without any doubt – contribute to improving our still limited understanding of the Canadian municipal level. Finally, from a normative point of view, each text examined three distinct elements: 1) the presence of municipal political parties; 2) the role of information; and 3) the relationship between the effectiveness of a policy and its responsiveness to public preferences.

In this second and last conclusion, we first offer a summary of each chapter, followed by a presentation of the theoretical, empirical, and normative contributions of these texts. In closing, we return to the importance of the informational context that is unique to this level of government.

MUNICIPAL POLITICAL PARTIES

The first part of the book focused on the context of political competition in Canadian municipalities. In chapter 1, Stephenson, McGregor, and Moore started with the premise that a non-partisan system can be expected to lead to more responsiveness and accountability than a partisan system. Their argument: partisan ties stymie responsiveness and accountability in the sense that partisans who vote at all costs for their preferred party are less likely to be fazed by government performance. However, the authors also showed that even in an election where no candidate runs under the banner of a party, as was the case with the 2014 election in Toronto, partisan ties nonetheless have an impact on responsiveness and accountability.

In fact, the authors' regression analysis of a wide range of Toronto voters showed that the presence of a partisan gap at other levels of government influenced voters' assessment of the performance of then-mayor Rob Ford. The analysis also found that voters were prone to see ideological ties between Rob Ford and his brother Doug Ford, who replaced him as candidate for mayor, which also affected their assessment. Thus, Stephenson, McGregor, and Moore's results show that voters tend to use partisan-type heuristics to reduce the cost of voting, even in strictly non-partisan elections. Their results also highlight that voters' assessment of a candidate who has the support of an incumbent mayor – who is not running – can be affected by the opinions that those voters have of this former elected official.

In chapter 2, Couture and Breux affirmed that it is theoretically possible to conceive of responsiveness and accountability in a competition model where there are no political parties –namely, by using the citizen-candidate model. It is the nomination process rather than the presence of different options of political governance that then explains the two mechanisms. Indeed, rather than rewarding or punishing political parties, the voter her- or himself has the choice to run, or not, as a candidate. If satisfied with the policies currently in place in the municipality, the voter will not have enough incentive to present her- or himself as a candidate. This model could thus explain the high rate of acclamation in non-partisan electoral landscapes in Canada.

The authors also underlined that voters react to changes in property taxation during the election year, which they link to the presence of a political business cycle. Indeed, their regression analysis showed that the electoral results of incumbent mayors running for re-election in the Quebec municipal elections from 2009 to 2013 negatively correlated with changes in the tax rate. They also underscored the fact that voters do not respond to a changed economic situation. This means that those mayors were directly punished or rewarded for a situation that fell under their responsibility.

In addition, Couture and Breux determined that there is an interaction effect between taxation and the presence (or absence) of political parties. In municipalities where there are no political parties, voters seem more inclined to reward the incumbent mayor who reduced taxes. Conversely, in municipalities where there are political parties, voters are more likely to punish incumbent mayors for an increase in taxation. A process akin to responsiveness and accountability thus exists in the absence of political parties, although the two mechanisms operate somewhat differently in this type of environment.

In chapter 3, Couture, Breux, and Bherer conducted a systematic review of the political parties present in the 2013 and 2014 elections of the ten largest cities in Quebec and British Columbia. The latter are the only two Canadian provinces where such formations are permitted by law. The authors found that political competition is configured differently from one city to the next. In some cities there are no political parties, in others there is only one party, and in yet others there are two or more parties. However, the ability of a system of competition to promote accountability and responsiveness is directly related to the clarity of responsibility. This clarity has two dimensions: the formal dispersion of government power and the cohesion of the incumbent government. Based on these two criteria, the authors argued that accountability and responsiveness increase with the number of parties.

Based on their review, Couture, Breux, and Bherer proposed three typologies allowing for the determination of how partisan or non-partisan systems relate to responsiveness and accountability. Within systems of competition where there are parties, we find majority parties, cohabitations with independent mayors, and cohabitations with minority-party mayors. Majority governments can be expected to be more accountable and more responsive to the needs of the population. In non-partisan competition systems, by contrast, there may well be other types of modalities. They considered it unlikely that a board composed of independent representatives would *not* lead to informal coalitions between the members. The presence of such coalitions allows for more cohesion. In addition, candidates' political preferences with regard to the top level of government can influence the choice of voters.

Finally, the authors proposed a typology of municipal political parties based on two dimensions. The first one concerns the fact that the initial formation of a party is usually triggered either by candidates or by interest groups or activists. The second dimension concerns the fact that discipline within a party may be rigid or loose. The typology uses these two dimensions to distinguish between the following four types of partisan formations: governing coalitions, programmatic parties, electoral coalitions, and citizens' movements. According to the authors, governing coalitions are the most likely to be accountable and responsive.

From a theoretical point of view, part 1 provided a discussion of the relationship between a partisan or a non-partisan system and the process of responsiveness and accountability. By focusing on the voter, Stephenson, McGregor, and Moore (chapter 1) argued that non-partisan systems are more conducive to accountability and responsiveness than partisan systems. Couture and Breux (chapter 2), for their part, placing greater emphasis on the political supply, showed that both systems of competition can trigger mechanisms of responsiveness and accountability whereby the non-partisan system is deemed to present weaknesses. In the latter case, responsiveness and accountability are only possible if there is an incumbent in the running. In addition, the non-partisan system was found to promote elections by acclamation. Overall, the main theoretical contribution of this chapter is the idea of resorting to the citizen-candidate model. In chapter 3, Couture, Breux, and Bherer, focusing on partisan organizations, showed that the relationship between the system of competition and the two mechanisms under study is complex. The authors leaned in favour of the partisan system, which they consider more conducive to responsiveness and accountability. For this, they envisioned different modalities within both the partisan and non-partisan systems of competition. In addition, the authors proposed that different types of parties can, each in its own way, support (or not) the two key concepts.

From an empirical point of view, the contribution of part 1 is important. Indeed, the three chapters presented a systematic portrait of the phenomenon under study. In chapter 1, data from the Toronto Election Study served to analyze a Canadian municipal election based on individual data. Such work is very innovative in this field of study, especially as the discovered results are surprising to say the least. It also appears that voters' actions and behaviour in municipal elections is fairly similar to that in elections at the upper levels of governments, even though these latter contexts are quite different. Essentially, voters were found to use partisan-type heuristics, even in the absence political parties. In chapter 2, the authors identified a parameter for evaluating the performance of a municipal government that goes beyond the specific contexts of each municipality: the tax rate. Indeed, while the economic situation is an issue that tends to dominate most provincial or federal elections, it is the tax rate that has a broad impact on municipal elections in Quebec. Finally, chapter 3 offered a first systematic overview of the political parties present in the major cities of Quebec and British Columbia.

From a normative point of view, part 1 asks the question: Should we encourage the emergence of political parties? This question, which is not new (Peterson 1981; Williams and Adrian 1959; Alford and Lee 1968), is important because only two provinces allow the existence of local political parties. The theories and empirical results presented in this part of the book allow us to address this question with greater nuance. For example, part 1 points to evidence that suggests that the presence of political parties at the municipal level, far from being a panacea, has an impact on the functioning of democracy. The relevance of municipal political parties thus warrants more in-depth research, going beyond our current knowledge that these formations allow for a renewal of the political class, offer support to candidates, and are information vectors (Breux 2013). Together, the texts of part 1 inspire us to go further and to engage in research on the relevance of municipal political parties on the basis of their roles as informants. Their main questions are: Does the political information that political parties disseminate vary according to the form of the party? Is this information taken into account by the voter? Do voters feel that they need this information in order to make their choice?

MUNICIPAL ELECTED OFFICIALS

Part 2 of the book was concerned with municipal officials. In chapter 4, Lucas and Sayers analyzed the political career trajectories of all elected officials in Edmonton and Calgary between 1885 and 2015. They showed that during that period, the time spent on councils became longer, the turnover of municipal councils decreased, and the re-election rate of incumbents increased sharply. Moreover, many municipal officials went on to pursue a political career at the provincial level, and some even made the leap to the federal level. The authors' quantitative methodology, founded on sequence analysis, allowed them to identify three descriptive labels for career patterns among municipal officials: municipal amateurs, municipal professionals, and provincial climbers.

In their conclusion, Lucas and Sayers put forth the hypothesis that the transition from a council composed primarily of municipal amateurs to one having more municipal professionals would not be conducive to responsiveness. By contrast, they posit that the emergence of provincial climbers would be conducive to responsiveness. Finally, they consider that in a context of a high rate of re-election of incumbents, a mayor's ambition to move on to a higher level of government would likewise lead to more responsiveness to the preferences of the population. In this case, the authors emphasized that a low level of accountability and a high level of responsiveness can coexist, even if a positive relationship between these two concepts is the more common scenario.

In chapter 5, Andrew Sancton analyzed the results of the 2014 municipal elections in Greater Sudbury and London, Ontario. These elections had the peculiarity of having a low rate of re-election of incumbents, making them truly distinct from the municipal elections typically found in Canada. The common characteristic of the defeated candidates in these elections is that they were denounced by the Ontario ombudsman for having attended informal council meetings, considered illegal in Ontario.

However, the author argued that it is unclear how it would be possible for such meetings *not* to take place in a partisan context. Moreover, such meetings are quite normal and common practice at the provincial and federal levels. The conclusions of the ombudsman about these meetings were widely reported in the local media in both cities, which essentially translated into political power in favour of the ombudsman. The fact that the media was able to provide him with this power can be explained by the deficient informational context that is typical of non-partisan municipal elections in Canada. In such a context, incumbents, who are usually little accountable, can find themselves very vulnerable to negative information circulating about them.

In chapter 6, Anne Mévellec argued that the complexity of the municipal system and the confusion of responsibilities in a context of multilevel governance compromise responsiveness and accountability. Moreover, according to her the clarity of the system is not sufficient to ensure accountability. In an environment where information is insufficient or of poor quality, voters may become dependent on the self-assessments issued and disseminated by the politicians themselves. The author held that voters need more transparency in order to be able to reward or punish the behaviour of incumbents.

Following a series of interviews with municipal elected officials in Quebec, Mévellec also showed that responsiveness and accountability coexist with regard to the role of politicians at this level of government. Each of these concepts can be linked to a theoretical model of democratic representation. On the one hand, there are politicians who match the profile of the municipal amateur quite well. These see themselves above all as representatives of their borough, are sure of their legitimacy as independents, and are suspicious of political parties. This type of elected official aligns with the selection model in which the principal and the agent are seen as sharing similar objectives. The latter is, in fact, the very reason why voters vote for this type of politician. Then there are elected officials who have more of a decision-maker profile and who advocate for a professionalization of political mandates. The self-assessment of the latter type of politicians is marked by a more collective and political understanding of the elected office at the municipal level. This approach can be associated with the sanction model in which elected officials are punished collectively when they veer too much from the interests of their constituents.

From a theoretical point of view, part 2 of this book launched a discussion around a typology of the different profiles of elected officials and of the impact that each type of politician can have on responsiveness and accountability. The chapters by Lucas and Sayers (chapter 4) and by Mévellec (chapter 6), while agreeing on the concept of municipal amateurs and municipal professionals, had different explanations. For Lucas and Sayers, the transition from amateur to professional elected official is the result of the low level of accountability of local politicians in Canada. This weak accountability is likely to have an adverse effect on responsiveness. The most important theoretical contribution of their chapter is certainly the introduction of the profile of the provincial climbers, whose presence is likely to counteract the negative effect of the municipal professionals on responsiveness. Mévellec, for her part, made an important distinction. According to her, the responsiveness or accountability of municipal amateurs is an individual matter, while for municipal professionals, who are first and foremost the decision-makers, these two processes have more of a collective nature in that they are part and parcel of their mandate. In this way, professionalization can trigger the electoral sanctioning mechanism. The confrontation of the selection model and the sanction model, discussed in this chapter, is a very relevant theoretical contribution to understanding the Canadian local political scene.

From the empirical angle, the text by Andrew Sancton (chapter 5) reminded us to what extent the study of controversies allows us to bring to light dynamics that otherwise remain hidden. The empirical contribution of this chapter is quite substantial. To our knowledge, this is the first-ever study reporting the presence of informal coalitions among independent elected officials in a non-partisan context. Moreover, the results showed that voters disapproved of these coalitions, just as a political party would have been. One might add that they were not punished for poor performance but rather because negative information was circulating about them. These results show that accountability at the local level does not always have something to do with responsiveness. From another perspective, Lucas and Sayers (chapter 4) presented a study based on a gigantic collection of data, something rarely seen in analyses of the Canadian municipal scene. Their study was also based on sequence analysis, which is a promising methodological innovation for political science.

From a normative point of view, this second part of the book raised the question of the role of information in municipal democracy. The chapter by Mévellec (chapter 6) advanced the need to increase transparency in order to reduce voters' reliance on the self-assessment of elected officials. More transparency necessarily means that the production of information is performed by an entity that lies outside of the politicians' realm. The chapter by Sancton (chapter 5), for its part, showed that the information produced by one type of organization can have a determinant impact on the victory or defeat of an incumbent, even if this information has little to do with the performance of politicians.

These reflections echo part 1 of the book by stressing yet again the importance of information in the process that determines a voter's choice. Essentially, the texts examine the following three questions: 1) How does the voter get information? 2) What information is available? 3) How is the available information, regardless of its nature, likely to influence a person's vote?

MULTILEVEL GOVERNANCE

Part 3 of this book concerns multilevel governance. In chapter 7, Lyons and Spicer explained that the instruments of cooperation between municipalities, such as the inter-municipal service agreements or the creation of SPBS, are increasingly used to deliver services in Canadian cities. However, these instruments raise questions about political accountability and transparency in the management of these services. When the responsibility for a service cannot be attributed clearly, it can become difficult to involve and inform the public about it. In addition, it may become complicated for municipal officials to monitor the effectiveness of a service when the daily management is entrusted to a third party that does not fall directly under their jurisdiction.

Lyons and Spicer analyzed all instruments of cooperation in the city of London, Ontario. They showed that it is possible to ensure some accountability and some transparency for a local service that is shared among different municipalities. Based on these two criteria, they argue that SPBS outperform inter-municipal service agreements. In addition, there are organizations that do much better than others in this regard. These organizations are characterized by greater accessibility for residents and generate more information about the service. In addition, they allow more control over their activities by local elected officials.

In chapter 8, Fanny Tremblay-Racicot studied the change in the composition of the board of directors of Metrolinx, a transport agency, which had replaced locally elected members with non-elected members who were appointed by the provincial government. Her chapter demonstrates that this change allowed the province to circumvent the recommendations previously made by the board. As a result, the funding of some public transport infrastructure projects was promoted to the detriment of others.

Since this change, Metrolinx is no longer directly accountable to the community it serves. The author also pointed out that there is a tension between the dimensions of representativeness and effectiveness. She suggested that the non-respect of a regional consensus that had been reached and the lack of transparency in decision-making led to investments in transportation that do not represent the best quality–price ratio in terms of the potential client base. In addition, the capacity to implement policies and projects outlined in a regional plan was shown to be limited by the low level of own-source revenues generated by this regional body.

Tremblay-Racicot concluded the chapter by mentioning that transport infrastructure projects are often at the heart of election campaigns. This means that local and provincial governments are very sensitive to citizens' preferences. However, this responsiveness becomes a problem when it comes time to solve regional transportation problems that call for unpopular measures. For example, the interests of citizens living downtown cannot always be matched with those of the suburbs.

In chapter 9, Alison Smith compared the politics of homelessness in Montreal and Calgary. Jurisdiction over the issue of homelessness is shared between the three levels of government. The author put forth the hypothesis that the more power and resources lean in favour of local agents, the more policy will be sensitive to the preferences of local actors. She also argued that the fragmentation between the different levels of government is likely to raise barriers to implementing effective public policy. In Calgary, there is very little disagreement between the different actors involved in the fight against homelessness. In Montreal, by contrast, fragmentation is greater because the provincial government has a clear-cut policy on the subject – namely, one that clashes with the visions of some local actors.

Calgary and Montreal have thus developed distinct governance structures. The more complex structure, in Montreal, has three strictly local entities and provides more space to deliberate on best practices at the municipal level. At the same time, with actors advocating different solutions, this structure invariably results in a lack of cohesion in the city's overall plan of action. According to Smith, the main advantage of Calgary's centralized system is that the resources of all levels of government are oriented toward the same goal. However, the advantage in Montreal is that the institutionalization of the integration of the homeless in the development of policies is likely to result in policies that are better able to meet local needs.

From a theoretical point of view, the three chapters of part 3 focused on the tension existing between the multiple bodies that share the responsibility over a service. For the analysis of multilevel governance, the theoretical contribution of the chapter by Lyons and Spicer (chapter 7) is to have distinguished the function of provision from the function of production, allowing us to go beyond the simple determination of who has authority over a service. The chapter by Smith (chapter 9), for its part, is a convincing operationalization of the multilevel governance approach of Horak, who emphasizes the role of local and private stakeholders in the success of a public policy. Finally, the chapter by Racicot-Tremblay (chapter 8) defined the accountability and effectiveness of a policy in a context where decision-making can be anarchical.

From the empirical point of view, the interesting aspect of this last part of the book is its study of the concepts of accountability and responsiveness from the different angles of possible collaboration between governments. Lyons and Spicer focused on inter-municipal relations, Tremblay-Racicot on the link between the local, regional, and provincial levels, and Smith on the relationships between the local, provincial, and federal levels. Moreover, the chapter by Lyons and Spicer proposed an analytical framework for measuring the transparency and accountability of inter-municipal structures, which could very well apply to contexts other than the city of London. Finally, the chapters by Tremblay-Racicot and Smith, drawn from their doctoral dissertations, offered very detailed descriptions of the policies under consideration.

From a normative point of view, part 3 addressed a very important question in the field of public policy: Is there a conflict of values between the effectiveness of a policy and its responsiveness to the preferences of the population? The chapter by Lyons and Spicer showed that it is possible to inform and involve the public in inter-municipal services structures. However, not all organizations or all agreements achieve this in a satisfactory manner. Tremblay-Racicot clearly pointed to this conflict of values. Indeed, her assertion that the responsiveness of the provincial government can be detrimental to the effectiveness of policy is most interesting. This proposition is refreshing because we often hear, with reason, that it is above all the responsiveness of local governments that can impede the success of a regional policy. The discrepancy between the preferences of citizens from the suburbs and those from downtown can also have repercussions on the choice of policies by the upper levels of government. Finally, the chapter by Smith argued that it is fragmentation rather than responsiveness that compromises the performance of a public policy. In fact, her overall argument resembles, to some extent, that of Tremblay-Racicot. The imbalance of power in favour of the provincial government in Quebec undermines the effectiveness of the policies of the City of Montreal. Behind these different propositions lies, once again, the issue of information: what issues are highlighted by elected officials and for what reasons?

In conclusion, we return to our initial question: Do responsiveness and accountability matter at the municipal level? From the theoretical point of view, it was shown that the two mechanisms can be operationalized at the municipal level but that they have limitations. These limitations were also identified in the concluding chapter by Ruth Dassonneville. By and large, discussions addressing the theoretical point of view were equivocal, whether they concern the effect of political parties, the professionalization of political mandates, or the fragmentation of accountability. From the empirical perspective, only the chapter by Couture and Breux (chapter 2) identified a more widespread existence of these two mechanisms within municipalities. The chapter by Sancton (chapter 5), for its part, contributed perhaps the most extreme, or unexpected, finding by showing that electoral sanctioning had nothing to do with either responsiveness or accountability in the cases under consideration. Finally, with regard to the normative point of view, part 2 of the book underlined that the responsiveness mechanism does not necessarily work for issues that go beyond the local framework. In sum, responsiveness and accountability are possible at the municipal level, where the phenomenon and its theoretical and normative limits can be empirically observed.

Finally, this book implicitly emphasized the importance that information plays in the quality of representation. In the introduction, we mentioned the role of information in the accountability/responsiveness mechanisms, which Gerstlé sums up as: "Information thereby allows us to establish a link between responsiveness to the public's preferences on the one hand and accountability for results on the other. The latter is understood to, at best, reveal the social demands and, at worst, condition said demands, and the former is seen to ultimately shape and distribute the information" (2003, 884; our translation). Information thus constitutes a key parameter in political representation and as such may well play a greater role in municipal politics – characterized by the relative absence and weaker flow of information – than at the upper levels of government (Cutler and Matthews 2005). This element, however, brings us to the potential specificity of municipal politics. While municipal elections are different from national elections (Oliver, Ha, and Callen 2012), Holbrook and Weinschenk, studying the US context, make the following observation: "At the same time, we note important ways in which elections in large cities are very similar to elections at other levels of government: incumbents raise a lot more money than challengers; 'quality' challengers tend to wait for open-seat contests; and incumbents are returned to office at a rate very similar to that of U.S. senators" (2014, 45).

Based on these findings, we project two main avenues of research for advancing our understanding of municipal politics in Canada.

One concerns the role of information in the process whereby voters decide on their candidate of choice. This could include an examination of the way in which voters obtain information, the type or quantity of information available, the issues that voters are likely to pay more attention to, and the sources of the information. The second main research path would seek, by means of a more in-depth analysis of municipal politics, to verify the extent to which the specificity of this level of politics vis-à-vis other political levels is dependent on the size of the municipality (Breux, Couture, and Goodman 2016). Together, these two avenues of research thus span a wide and diverse range of topics that, we hope, will be pursued by the researchers who are currently working in this dynamic field of research.

REFERENCES

Alford, Robert R., and Eugene C. Lee. 1968. "Voting Turnout in American Cities." *The American Political Science Review* 62(3): 796–813.

Bagues, Manuel, and Berta Esteve-Volart. "Politicians 'Luck of the Draw': Evidence from the Spanish Christmas Lottery." Journal of Political Economy 124(5): 1269–94.

Breux, Sandra. 2013."À quoi servent les partis politiques municipaux." *Relations* 768(16). Accessed 28 July 2017. http://www.cjf.qc.ca/fr/relations/article.php?ida=3247.

Breux, Sandra, Jérôme Couture, and Nicole Goodman. 2016. "Fewer Voters, Higher Stakes? The Applicability of Rational Choice for Voter Turnout in Quebec Municipalities." *Environment and Planning C: Government and Policy*. Published online before print 4 November 2016. doi:10.1177/0263774X16676272.

Cutler, Fred, and J. Scott Matthews. 2005. "The Challenge of Municipal Voting: Vancouver 2002." *Canadian Journal of Political Science* 38(2): 359–82.

Gerstlé, Jacques. 2003."La réactivité aux préférences collectives et l'imputabilité de l'action publique." *Revue française de science politique* 53(6): 859–85.

Holbrook, Thomas M., and Aaron Weinschenk. 2014. "Campaigns, Mobilization and Turnout in Mayoral Elections." *Political Research Quarterly* 67(1): 42–55.

Oliver, Eric, Shang Ha, and Zachary Callen. 2012. *Local Elections and the Politics of Small Scale Democracy*. Princeton, NJ: Princeton University Press.

Peterson, Paul E. 1981. *City Limits*. Chicago, London: University of Chicago Press.
Williams, Oliver P., and Charles R. Adrian. 1959. "The Insulation of Local Politics under the Nonpartisan Ballot." *The American Political Science Review* 53(4): 1052–63.

Contributors

LAURENCE BHERER is an associate professor at the Department of Political Science at the Université de Montréal. Her research mainly deals with participatory democracy and urban policies. Her current research projects focus on the professionalization of public participation and on the structuring of municipal politics.

SANDRA BREUX is an associate professor at the Centre culture urbanisation société of the INRS (Institut national de la recherche scientifique). Over the years she has developed a research area on the Canadian municipal level. Her research interests focus on municipal representative democracy and the role of territory on individual behaviour. She is also interested in notions of urban design and housing as well as in innovative methodological approaches.

JÉRÔME COUTURE has a background in political science and is currently a postdoctoral fellow, under the supervision of Sandra Breux, at the INRS (Institut national de la recherche scientifique). His thesis is about municipal elections in Quebec. He is also a specialist in quantitative methods, which he has been teaching for four years at Laval University.

RUTH DASSONNEVILLE is an assistant professor at the Department of Political Science at the Université de Montréal where she holds the Canada research chair in electoral democracy. Her main research interests are dealignment, voting behaviour, economic voting, and election forecasting. Her work has been published in, among others, *Electoral Studies*, *European Journal of Political Research*, *Party Politics*, and *West European Politics*.

JACK LUCAS is an assistant professor of political science at the University of Calgary. Jack studies institutional and policy change in Canadian cities, with a focus on urban political authority, urban governance, and the long-term development of the Canadian state.

JOSEPH LYONS is an assistant professor in the Department of Political Science at Western University. His current research addresses the policy consequences of local structural variation.

MICHAEL MCGREGOR is assistant professor in the Department of Politics and Public Administration at Ryerson University. He holds degrees in political science and biological engineering. His research interests lie in the fields of political behaviour, Canadian politics, and municipal elections.

ANNE MÉVELLEC is an associate professor in the School of Political Studies at the University of Ottawa. Her research focuses on the sociology of territorial public action in Canada and in particular on the formation and professionalization of municipal officials. In that context, she explores the profiles, backgrounds, and practices of elected officials as well as municipal political parties, the representation of francophones outside Quebec, and the role of elected officials in forest governance.

AARON MOORE is an associate professor in the Department of Political Science at the University of Winnipeg and a fellow at the Institute on Municipal Finance and Governance, Munk School of Global Affairs, University of Toronto.

ANDREW SANCTON, a native of Montreal, received his Honours BA from Bishop's University and his doctoral degree in politics from Oxford University. Most of his academic career has been spent as a professor of political science at Western University. He was chair of his department from 2000 until 2005 and was for many years the director of its Local Government Program, which offers an MPA degree designed for local government managers. He has published widely on Canadian municipal issues. He was an expert witness in both the Toronto and Montreal court cases that unsuccessfully challenged the municipal amalgamations in those cities. His 2008 book, *The Limits of Boundaries: Why City-Regions Cannot Be*

Self-Governing, was one of five books shortlisted that year for the Donner Prize for the best Canadian book on public policy. His latest book is the second edition of *Canadian Local Government: An Urban Perspective*, published in 2015 by Oxford University Press Canada.

ANTHONY SAYERS is an associate professor in the Department of Political Science at the University of Calgary. His research deals with major political institutions, including political parties, elections, federalism, and parliaments. He is particularly interested in the organizational and campaigning aspects of political parties and the distribution of power in federal states. He also writes on Alberta provincial politics.

ALISON SMITH is an assistant professor of political science at the University of Toronto. Her research interests include welfare state change, social policy, inequality, and homelessness. She obtained her PhD from l'Université de Montréal and is currently working on a manuscript based on her PhD dissertation.

ZACHARY SPICER is a visiting researcher with the Institute on Municipal Finance and Governance and a senior associate with the Innovation Policy Lab at the Munk School of Global Affairs. He recently served as an assistant professor in the Department of Political Science at Brock University. He received his PhD in political science from Western University and completed post-doctoral fellowships with the Munk School of Global Affairs at the University of Toronto and the Laurier Institute for the Study of Public Opinion and Policy (LISPOP) at Wilfrid Laurier University. He is a member of the Laboratory on Local Elections and also serves on LISPOP's Management Board. His research has been featured in a number of academic journals, including *Canadian Journal of Political Science*, *Journal of Urban Affairs*, *Urban Affairs Review*, *Canadian Public Policy*, and *Canadian Public Administration*. His first book, *The Boundary Bargain: Growth, Development and the Future of City-County Separation*, was released by McGill-Queen's University Press in 2016.

LAURA STEPHENSON is an associate professor of political science at Western University. She specializes in political behaviour, both Canadian and comparative. Her research focuses on understanding how institutions and context influence attitudes, electoral preferences, and engagement with politics. She is the co-editor of *Voting Behaviour in Canada* (UBC Press 2010) and the co-author of *Fighting for Votes* (UBC Press 2015).

FANNY R. TREMBLAY-RACICOT holds a PhD in urban studies from Temple University (2015). She received her BA and MA from Laval University in political science (2006 and 2010). Specializing in metropolitan governance and sustainable urban development, her current postdoctoral research at the *Chaire In.SITU* (ESG-UQAM) focuses on affordable housing in transit-oriented developments in Canada.

Index

Abbotsford, 86

AccèsLogis, 234

acclamation, 51, 70, 153, 267, 269

accountability (definition), 5, 181,
249

Achen, Christopher H., 11, 253, 257

Act Respecting Elections and
Referendums in Municipalities
(1978), 50

agglomeration councils, 158

Alberta: homelessness, 229–33;
local career, 111–25

anti-median voter, 65

apolitical attitude, 50

Bartels, Larry M., 11, 78, 253, 257

British Columbia: housing policy,
224; municipal political parties,
9, 85–8, 96, 133

Burnaby, 86–7

Calgary: homelessness, 229–33;
political careers, 111–25

Calgary Committee to End
Homelessness (CCEH), 230

Calgary Homeless Foundation,
229–31

Campbell, Angus, 26, 253

Charbonneau Commission, 160

Chicago Metropolitan Agency for
Planning, 201

Chow, Olivia, 29

citizen candidate model, 53

clarity: of municipal politics, 155–
160; of responsibility, 84, 89–95,
255, 259–60, 268

Coderre, Denis, 99, 236, 240

Coquitlam, 88

Dalton, Russell J., 21, 23, 249,
254

deep federalism, 225

Delta, 88

demerged cities, 158

Downs, Anthony, 10, 26, 49, 57–9,
79, 250

dynastic politicians, 28, 29, 30, 40

economic vote/economic voting,
10, 52, 252–9

Edmonton, 111–17

effectiveness, 168–9, 182, 192,
201–4, 214–24

efficiency, 213–19

electoral punishment, 41, 57–9,
    250, 252, 256–60, 267

Ferejohn, John, 51, 55
Fiorina, Morris P., 26, 52, 83
fiscal illusion, 66
Fontana, Joe, 141
Ford, Doug, 25–41, 255, 267
Ford, Rob, 25, 28–41, 132, 267
fragmentation: of local service
    production and delivery, 177;
    of power, 239–42

Gatineau, 86
Gerstlé, Jacques, 3, 6, 49
Governance Assessment Tool (GAT),
    183
Growth Plan for the Greater
    Golden Horseshoe, 201–2

incumbency: accountability, 108;
    electoral success, 134–6; local
    careers, 110, 113–14
information deficit/low-
    information context, 12, 26–9,
    109, 156, 193
inter-local cooperation/collabora-
    tion agreement, 178–92
International City Management
    Association, 135
inter-regional competition, 205

Kelowna, 86
Key, Valdimer O., 26, 52, 78, 250

Langley, 88
Laval: charter, 157; municipal par-
    ties, 86, 91, 99
Lemieux, Vincent, 77, 78, 81
Lévis, 86, 88

Lewis-Beck, Michael S., 52, 250–1,
    259
London, Ontario: accountability,
    186–92; incumbents, 132–3;
    Ontario ombudsman, 132–47
Longueuil, 87, 158

Mansbridge, Jane, 154–5
Matichuk, Marianne, 138–40
McGuinty, Dalton, 202, 206
Metrolinx, 216–20
Michigan School, 10
Montreal: governance of homeless-
    ness, 233–7; local response to
    homelessness, 223; mayor part of
    minority municipal party, 86, 91;
    and municipal auditor general,
    157–8; Project Montréal party,
    96
Mouvement pour mettre fin à
    l'itinérance à Montréal, 236
multi-jurisdictional service area,
    179
municipal auditor general, 157
municipal mergers, 157–9
municipal political parties: absence/
    existence, 9, 50–1, 55, 63;
    Province of Quebec, 50; rele-
    vance, 7
municipalization, 159–61

nationalization of local election, 49,
    81–2
Nordhaus, William D., 52, 66, 258

Ontario: mergers, 156; municipal
    elections, 132–6; transportation,
    202–9; two-tier government, 177
Ontario ombudsman, 13, 133–4,
    136–7, 146–8

partisanship: cross-level, 24–8, 33; measures, 31–4; relationship with accountability, 10, 24, 40; municipal context, 50
personalization of power, 51, 77, 89, 163
Pitkin, Hannah, 108, 154
political career: career duration, 109, 111–12, 121–5; municipal amateur, 123–5, 163–4; professional, 123–9, 162–70; provincial climbers, 124–9; trajectory, 110, 117
principal–agent theory/perspectives, 5, 154, 170, 181
Projet Montreal party, 96, 99
proximity, 155–6, 166
public–private partnerships, 201

Quebec (province): homelessness, 233–7; institutional reform, 156–60; municipal elections, 50–3, 85–9, 134, 154; role of city councillors, 165–70; two-tier government, 177
Quebec City, 87, 91, 157–8

Réseau d'aide aux personnes seules et itinérants de Montréal (RAP-SIM), 238–41
responsiveness, 10; accountability, 10, 65; citizen-candidate model, 53, 58; definition, 5, 249; ideological ties, 77; quasi-party, 24, 25, 28, 29, 30, 41; typology, 94–7

Richmond, 86
Rodriguez, John, 138, 148

Saguenay, 88
sanctions: accountability, 181, 182–8; ombudsman, 149; sanctions model, 154–70
Sherbrooke, 87
size of municipality, 12, 82, 278
special-purpose bodies, 177–9
Sudbury, 132–3, 136–41
Surrey, 86, 88
system of municipal electoral competition, 85; multi-partisan system, 88–9; non-partisan system, 76, 84–95, 266–9; uni-partisan system, 86, 88–9

Terrebonne, 87
Toronto: Big Move, 202–17; homelessness, 237; mayoral race, 28–30; Metrolinx, 201–17
Toronto Election Study, 15, 25, 30, 40, 269
Tory, John, 23, 132
transparency: inter-local cooperation, 180–92; of the municipal system, 154–70; regional transit projects, 212–19
transportation project sponsors, 220
Trois-Rivières, 88
Trounstine, Jessica, 7–8, 51, 82, 134, 165, 252

Vancouver, 86–7